THE BEST

OF

Thoreau's Journals

Edited with an Introduction by

CARL BODE

SOUTHERN ILLINOIS UNIVERSITY PRESS
Carbondale and Edwardsville

Feffer & Simons Inc., *London and Amsterdam*

CONTENTS

FOREWORD

Diary of a Private Man

At the age of twenty Henry Thoreau came home, a Harvard graduate, to his village of Concord. And there he stayed except for some modest excursions, over the years, to other parts of the country. A slight if wiry man, with a drooping nose and an uneasy eye, he made a consistently poor impression on those in Concord who thought themselves his betters. He promptly demonstrated that he was the kind of young fellow who took the negative in any debate and felt uncomfortable if he happened to be in the majority. Because a Harvard graduate was supposed to do useful, even significant, work Thoreau started out by looking for a post as a schoolteacher. Several times he found one but then for one reason or another gave it up. For eight months he was employed as a tutor to a nephew of Ralph Waldo Emerson. He did odd jobs, some of them for Emerson himself. He went to live in the woods for two years. Gradually he settled on two occupations, neither of which Harvard had prepared him for. One was surveying; the other was helping his father to make pencils and grind graphite. He allowed these employments to take only a small part of his time. The rest he spent in walking around the outskirts of Concord, by day and night, and writing down what he saw there. At forty-four he died, a disappointment to most people who knew him.

After leaving Harvard he had taught himself to write by starting a diary. It was hard to shake off the influence of his college courses in English composition but he managed it and began to speak with his own voice. His proved to be no routine journal. He penned thousands and thousands of words and as he filled the pages of the blank books he bought, his true occupation grew clear to him. It was to be an observer of nature, first, and of man, second. It was to watch the world around Concord with unmatched intensity, to savor its beauties, and to point out the implications of

7

what he saw for the conduct of man's life. Thanks to his college reading of the classics he had aspirations to be a poet and this was his way of defining the poet's function.

He systematically set down his observations. There were few days that he skipped. At intervals, as the months and years went along, he quarried from the journal most of the material he put into the two books and the two dozen articles he published during his lackluster career as a writer. Long after he had died and even after his writing had begun to attract a measure of attention, the senior citizen of his village remarked that he could see no reason for printing the journal of Henry Thoreau.

Today we recognize him as one of the great writers of the Western world. One of his two books, *Walden,* is issued in a score of editions in this country and is read in translation in many countries besides our own. His essay on civil disobedience influenced Mahatma Gandhi at the start of the twentieth century and still influences the most ardent disciples of civil rights today. Thoreau is especially rewarding to read in our times because he shows an iron-firm grasp of principles we increasingly neglect. In particular he shows us that man was made to be free. He insists that most American living, with its meaningless round of dull work and noisy recreation, is dreadful to endure. And man free is not only happier but better. This is the essence of Thoreau's doctrine. He never preaches it heavily, however, and he often announces that he is not preaching it at all.

What he has to say he says wisely, tartly. His writing is both pure and lucid, with a kind of plain elegance to it. Among his works the journal has always been least read. It discourages the reader because it is so big—fourteen volumes in the collected *Writings.* A good deal of it seems repetitious; some of it seems routine. Yet in those manifold pages there is an ample share of the best of Thoreau.

The initial item is dated October 22, 1837, two months after he left Harvard. It runs: " 'What are you doing now?' he asked. 'Do you keep a journal?' So I make my first entry today." The man who asked was Emerson, who became as good a friend as Thoreau would ever let any man be. Yet even this early, Thoreau announced that he needed to be alone. He concentrated on himself, ignoring others. In fact he took his urge for solitude up to the edge of paradox. "I avoid myself," he asserted. Actually he did not; he put a good deal of himself into his new journal. He put many other things as well, for he soon arrived at the right use of it. It was the place for much rather than for little. It was the place for registering nearly everything. Selection and discrimination were wrong since he could never tell till later what might be "the wealth of India . . . in that confused heap." This was not the way he had been taught in Cambridge and yet his system, if it could be called that, obviously worked. Thoreau himself marveled, "Of all strange and unaccountable things this journalizing is the strangest." It became his daily letter, he said, to the gods. He tried to make it a record of the things he loved. He was human, however; as he grew older he grew harder and, especially in the last years of his life, put in his strictures too on the things he hated, above all slavery and greed.

But mainly the journal was a record of what he loved, whether transient or permanent. To make the record he found he had to live—and move. He knew there were writers who sat at their desks with nothing stirring but their pens. Not Thoreau. He felt that the "writing which consists with habitual sitting" was mechanical and dull. He found that he had to walk constantly through the fields and woods around Concord; he was glad to make that his primary business.

Though the world he traveled over around Concord seemed to him almost too broad, he felt he had to become saturated in it. He had to be thoroughly involved not only for his own sake but so that he could report on it cogently and well. He noted in the journal that "A writer who does not speak out of a full experience uses torpid words, wooden or lifeless words, such words as 'humanitary,' which have a paralysis in their tails."

The journal is the record of a man who made what he observed part of himself and in the process made himself a great writer. Thoreau's signal accomplishment is not solely a matter of passive absorption of nature. It is also an overtly intellectual activity. As the seasons go along we see Thoreau lessoning himself. He acquires a professional expertise in his descriptions of nature. He reads the writers on painting so that he can learn to paint with words. He quotes the eminent authority of his day, John Ruskin, and such others as the sensitive British artist William Gilpin. When he has reached his mid-thirties he is still learning. He writes for example in the journal for January 1854, when he is thirty-six, that "Gilpin, in his essay on the 'Art of Sketching Landscape,' says: 'When you have finished your sketch therefore with Indian ink, as far as you propose, tinge the whole over with some light horizon hue.'" Thoreau comments that he has often been attracted by this harmonious tint in Gilpin's drawings and that he himself has often observed it in nature, particularly at sunset. And he puts it into his paragraphs.

If Thoreau the artist periodically painted his landscape and limned his outer weather, he did not neglect his inner weather. In the journal we see at intervals signs of his unconscious. He paid special attention to his dreams. He noted the nights when he had them and he speculated about what they meant. He recalled the most frequent of the dreams of his childhood, the dream of Rough and Smooth. He felt that it came to symbolize his whole existence. He announced that all his waking experience could be divided into periods of rough and smooth, of insanity and sanity. In his dreams he attained a fullness of being, a measure of divine life, that was denied to him when he was awake. He proceeded easily from the belief in the power of dreams to the belief that the world of thought was more real than the world of observed objects. The reality within his mind was far stronger than the reality he saw on the outskirts of Concord. But the result was not that he ignored that vivid natural world around him. It was that he saw it, and the objects that composed it, with a kind of illumination. When he described the world of nature he made it shine with his personal light. He set forth the inwardness of what he saw.

It was in his journal that he developed the art of the emblem, which became his favorite art. He would inspect a natural scene with a close and loving eye. Then he would both describe it and suggest what it meant. He himself would be found deep in the description and all his senses would be open and involved. What he wrote was seldom perfect prose. It was too spontaneous for that and besides, as he said, he was apt to include everything. But the result is unique. For instance, on an October day in 1851 he stands watching a hillside, with its rich autumnal colors of maple and ash and the permanent green of pine. Then he says:

The witchhazel here is in full blossom on this magical hillside, while its broad yellow leaves are falling. Some bushes are completely bare of leaves, and leather-colored they strew the ground. It is an extremely interesting plant—October and November's child, and yet reminds me of the very earliest spring. Its blossoms smell like the spring, like the willow catkins; by their color as well as fragrance they belong to the saffron dawn of the year, suggesting amid all these signs of autumn, falling leaves and frost, that the life of Nature, by which she eternally flourishes, is untouched. It stands here in the shadow on the side of the hill, while the sunlight from over the top of the hill lights up its topmost sprays and yellow blossoms. Its spray, so jointed and angular, is not to be mistaken for any other. I lie on my back with joy under its boughs. While its leaves fall, its blossoms spring.

Wood and water, meadow and hill, appear again and again in the pages of the journal. But Thoreau makes no apology for repetition; nature never duplicates. No two oak leaves are alike. Nor does the man who inspects them remain the same. The result is rarely dull. "We never tire," Thoreau says, "of the drama of the sunset."

He looks at a pine cone as if he had not seen one before, and he sets down its description with as much care as if he would not see one again.

Against the changing scenery move many forms of life. Thoreau finds them all worthy of remark, from the gnats and woodlice to the turtles, muskrats, and foxes. He is always willing to "write the biography of an animal." He is willing to sit for an hour to watch a painted tortoise lay her eggs in moistened sand.

Sometimes, as Thoreau grew older, he observed too mechanically. He became in a sense scientific. He gradually learned the names for things—and used them. The names, all too often Latin, substituted for the felt reality. By the time he reached his mid-thirties he had become a botanist, an entomologist, an ecologist. At the same time he became less of a prose poet, less sentient, less—if you will—spiritual. He himself realized that he was watching too narrowly and categorically. "I fear that the character of my knowledge is from year to year becoming more distinct and scientific," he wrote in August 1851. And one day in September of the next year he scolded himself. "I must walk more with free senses. It is as bad to *study* stars and clouds as flowers and stones. I must let my senses wander as my thoughts, my eyes see without looking." He needed to look more casually, more

obliquely. He needed to remember that some of the finest
things were seen with the side of the eye. He needed to let
nature come to him instead of seeking her out.

Thoreau was at the midpoint of his career when he so ex-
horted himself. His walks and writing had always been
systematic before but now in the early 1850's they looked
paradoxically like work. The unorthodox Ellery Channing
was the closest thing to a constant companion that Thoreau
had at this time, and he has left us the best sketch of the
man and his habits we have. It occurs in the chapter
"Nature" of Channing's *Thoreau the Poet-Naturalist*. He says,
among other things, that Thoreau was accustomed to walk
about three hours each afternoon. He always carried a notebook and he often took along a spyglass, a ruler, and a sur-
veyor's tape. Into the notebook he put the jottings that he
would that evening expand in the journal. He never trusted
his memory but penciled all his data into the pages of the
notebook. His pockets were capacious and in them he stuffed
the articles he collected on his jaunts—stones, nuts, lichens,
whatever they might be. He tried to overlook nothing of interest and he tried to make his journal a comprehensive
record. Ellery Channing summed up the attitude of the mature Thoreau when he said that "the walk, with him, was for
work." On the other hand, we need to realize that Channing
himself was biased, for sustained effort to him was anathema.

The journal is chiefly a nature diary. But far from exclusively. Many a page is devoted to man, to man the individual and man in the mass; to man seen directly and man
seen with the side of the eye; to man in the state of nature
and man corrupted by society.

It was the natural man who appealed to Thoreau. Like
Thoreau he lived outdoors and lived simply. He spent much
of his time alone. When he had a relation with a fellow man
it was on a one-to-one basis. What was communicated was
largely factual. It was laconic; in Thoreau's experience the
information given and received was apt to be bits of wood-
lore. Here in point is a paragraph, dated January 30, 1855,
on a favorite of Thoreau's, George Minott:

> Minott today enumerates the red, gray, black, and
> what he calls the Sampson fox. He says, 'It's a sort
> of yaller fox, but their pelts ain't good for much.' He
> never *saw* one, but the hunters have told him of them.
> He never saw a gray nor a black one. Told how Jake

Lakin lost a dog, a very valuable one, by a fox leading him on to the ice on the Great Meadows and drowning him. Said the raccoon made a track very much like a young child's foot. He had often seen it in the mud of a ditch.

With such as Minott he was willing to pass the time of the day. But he also responded to those who never spoke to him. He once exclaimed, "How I love the simple, reserved countrymen, my neighbors, who mind their own business and let me alone."

Civilized man made Thoreau uncomfortable. Even when he was as noble and generous as Emerson, Thoreau could never establish a rapport with him. When Thoreau talks in the journal about friendship he becomes least attractive. He sets an impossible standard for his friend; indeed he demands perfection. "Fatal is the discovery that our friend is fallible, that he has prejudices. He is, then, only prejudiced in our favor. What is the value of his esteem who does not justly esteem another?" We see Thoreau complain again and again about how hard the true friend is to find. What Thoreau says he wants, but evidently does not really want, is a relationship so intimate that it dissolves all barriers. "Between two by nature alike and fitted to sympathize there is no veil and can be no obstacle." He urges his friend to throw aside the customs of civilization. He urges him to stand naked but is too reserved to do so himself. His defense is that he is temperamentally cold to other human beings. He cannot help it, he asserts, and he will not apologize for it. "I am of the nature of stone," he says piously; "It takes the summer's sun to warm it."

With the passage of the years the separation grew greater. "Farewell, my friends," he wrote in March 1856, "my path inclines to this side of the mountain, yours to that. For a long time you have appeared further and further off to me. I see that you will at length disappear altogether."

But if Thoreau's strictures on his friends strike us as being undeserved, this is by no means true either for his strictures on other men or on the mass of men. Scattered through the journal are etchings of individual fools or knaves whom he encountered. There is, for instance, the man who has Thoreau do a surveying job for him and then remarks that he cannot pay at the moment. Thoreau dryly comments that the man later sent him a quart of huckleberries, an

ominous gift since Thoreau was no special friend of his.
Thoreau adds that the fellow has yet to pay him in full.
There is the man who asks Thoreau merely to "run a line"
for him in the woods and as Thoreau interrogates him reveals that it is a complex job of professional surveying. There
is the village shoemaker who brassily sells Thoreau leaky
boots. There is the family who tear apart the huckleberry
bushes to whip the berries into their basket, and then calmly leave the carnage.

His criticisms of man in the mass are twofold. Man is interested in little more than money and man is grossly lacking
in civic virtue. The meanness for most men of making a living
is a theme throughout the journal. Getting and spending is
the essence of American life, and to Thoreau material success
is worse than failure: "It is fouler and uglier to have too
much than not to have enough." His criticism of man as a
citizen develops in the middle and late years of the journal.
It is aroused above all by Concord's—and Massachusetts'
and America's—indifference to Negro slavery. As the conflict
over slavery began to permeate American life he saw with
amazement that his townsmen were apt either to ignore the
iniquity of human bondage or else to defend it.

There were a few exceptions of course, notable antislavery
men in Massachusetts and beyond. The most notable to
Thoreau was a Kansan, John Brown; for him Thoreau acquired a reverence he would accord to no other man. Brown's
dramatic and symbolic raid on Harpers Ferry in October 1859
stirred him profoundly. It moved him to the point of war.
He wrote in the journal, "I do not wish to kill or be killed,
but I can foresee circumstances in which both of these things
would be by me unavoidable."

The pages of the journal are filled during the fall and winter of this year with his praise of Brown and his condemna-
tion of the mass of Americans for their indifference to slavery
and their resentment of Brown for battling against it.
Through word and deed Thoreau tried to rally his fellow
citizens to Brown's holy war. The journal reflects his limited
success.

But we should not want to distort the journal. The im-
passioned pages occasioned by the raid on Harpers Ferry are
not characteristic. The general tone is amiable; there is more
light than heat.

The journal houses his deepest feelings, his most private
thoughts. It offers us a clearer insight into him, in more ways

than one, than do the now famous works which he himself set before the public. And it offers us a fresh insight into life in general. With Thoreau we can look at it with the eye of innocence because we do it in a new way. Every now and then he literally looked at nature upside down. He would bend over and peer through his legs at the inverted landscape with surprise and pleasure. He looked at man the same way, though not with pleasure, at man who drudged during his days and wasted his nights. Thoreau turned the American scale of values upside down; that is perhaps his greatest service to us.

Of the various forms in which Thoreau has left his writing, the journal is one of the best. As Thoreau himself puts it: "I do not know but thoughts written down thus in a journal might be printed in the same form with greater advantage than if the related ones were brought together in separate essays. They are now allied to life, and are seen by the reader not to be far-fetched."

CARL BODE
University of Maryland

Sources

FOR THE SELECTIONS

The selections in this book come from the fourteen volumes of the printed journal, published in 1906 as part of *The Writings of Henry David Thoreau* and edited by Bradford Torrey with the help of Francis Allen. Thoreau generally drew from his journal for the initial drafts of the works he published during his lifetime, so to avoid duplication the selections given here are those generally found in the journal alone. The manuscript of the journal is in the Pierpont Morgan Library in New York City. The thirty-nine assorted notebooks that make it up are housed in a pine box that we believe Thoreau himself built. There is no individual notebook for each year in spite of the fact that this is the way journals usually run. Sometimes Thoreau filled less than one blank book during a year, sometimes more. The earliest manuscript volumes are a bit deceiving because they do not include the whole diary but only the pieces left over after he incorporated the main parts into the essays and books he hoped to publish. Significantly, at the head of the first notebook he put: "Gleanings or What Time Has Not Reaped of My Journal." But once we get through the 1840's the full journal, day by day, is spread before us. A few bits of the journal survive outside the Morgan Library, some from the period 1842–1843 in the Houghton Library of Harvard College and others from the period 1843–1844 in the Huntington Library in San Marino. Part of the Huntington fragments are published in *The First and Last Journeys of Thoreau*, which F. B. Sanborn issued in 1905, and some of those are reprinted in this book.

FROM

The Journals

1837

Born on July 12, 1817, in Concord, Massachusetts, Thoreau spent most of his boyhood there. In 1833 he entered Harvard College as a freshman. He learned more from the college library than from either his teachers or his fellow students. After making a good if not awe-inspiring record he received his diploma in 1837 and returned, readily, to Concord. He soon attracted the friendly interest of his notable neighbor Ralph Waldo Emerson. Perhaps partly because of Emerson's example he began to make himself into a writer. He started a diary shortly after coming home. Only a portion remains but we can still see that it included not only personal observations and general reflections but also many quotations from classic authors. It is in part what was then called a "commonplace book," in which favorite excerpts from one's reading were copied down. The style in the journal shows a youthful stiffness. Some of it in fact is downright dull, with only a hint of the brilliant, completely individual writing soon to come.

Oct. 22. "What are you doing now?" he asked. "Do you keep a journal?" So I make my first entry today.

SOLITUDE

To be alone I find it necessary to escape the present—I avoid myself. How could I be alone in the Roman emperor's chamber of mirrors? I seek a garret. The spiders must not be disturbed, nor the floor swept, nor the lumber arranged.

THE FOG

Oct. 27. The prospect is limited to Nobscot and Annursnack. The trees stand with boughs downcast like pilgrims beaten by a storm, and the whole landscape wears a sombre aspect.

So when thick vapors cloud the soul, it strives in vain to escape from its humble working-day valley, and pierce the dense fog which shuts out from view the blue peaks in its horizon, but must be content to scan its near and homely hills.

DUCKS AT GOOSE POND

Oct. 29. Two ducks, of the summer or wood species, which were merrily dabbling in their favorite basin, struck up a retreat on my approach, and seemed disposed to take French leave, paddling off with swan-like majesty. They are first-rate swimmers, beating me at a round pace, and—what was to me a new trait in the duck character—dove every minute or two and swam several feet under water, in order to escape our attention. Just before immersion they seemed to give each other a significant nod, and then, as if by a common understanding, 'twas heels up and head down in the shaking of a duck's wing. When they reappeared, it was amusing to observe with what a self-satisfied, darn-it-how-he-nicks-'em air they paddled off to repeat the experiment.

THE ARROWHEAD

A curious incident happened some four or six weeks ago which I think it worth the while to record. John [Thoreau's brother] and I had been searching for Indian relics, and been successful enough to find two arrowheads and a pestle, when, of a Sunday evening, with our heads full of the past and its remains, we strolled to the mouth of Swamp Bridge Brook. As we neared the brow of the hill forming the bank of the river, inspired by my theme, I broke forth into an extravagant eulogy on those savage times, using most violent gesticulations by way of illustration. "There on Nawshaw-tuct," said I, "was their lodge, the rendezvous of the tribe, and yonder, on Clamshell Hill, their feasting ground. This was, no doubt, a favorite haunt; here on this brow was an eligible lookout post. How often have they stood on this very spot, at this very hour, when the sun was sinking behind yonder woods and gilding with his last rays the waters of the Musketaquid, and pondered the day's success and the morrow's prospects, or communed with the spirit of their fathers gone before them to the land of shades!

"Here," I exclaimed, "stood Tahatawan; and there" (to complete the period) "is Tahatawan's arrowhead."

We instantly proceeded to sit down on the spot I had pointed to, and I, to carry out the joke, to lay bare an ordinary stone which my whim had selected, when lo! the first I laid hands on, the grubbing stone that was to be, proved a most perfect arrowhead, as sharp as if just from the hands of the Indian fabricator!!!

SUNRISE

Oct. 30. First we have the gray twilight of the poets, with dark and barry clouds diverging to the zenith. Then glows the intruding cloud in the east, as if it bore a precious jewel in its bosom; a deep round gulf of golden gray indenting its upper edge, while slender rules of fleecy vapor, radiating from the common centre, like light-armed troops, fall regularly into their places.

SAILING WITH AND AGAINST THE STREAM

Nov. 3. If one would reflect, let him embark on some placid stream, and float with the current. He cannot resist the Muse. As we ascend the stream, plying the paddle with might and main, snatched and impetuous thoughts course through the brain. We dream of conflict, power, and grandeur. But turn the prow down stream, and rock, tree, kine, knoll, assuming new and varying positions, as wind and water shift the scene, favor the liquid lapse of thought, far-reaching and sublime, but ever calm and gently undulating.

TRUTH

Nov. 5. Truth strikes us from behind, and in the dark, as well as from before and in broad daylight.

SUNRISE

Nov. 17. Now the king of day plays at bo-peep round the world's corner, and every cottage window smiles a golden smile—a very picture of glee. I see the water glistening in the eye. The smothered breathings of awakening day strike the ear with an undulating motion; over hill and dale, pasture and woodland, come they to me, and I am at home in the world.

ICE-HARP

Dec. 5. My friend tells me he has discovered a new note in nature, which he calls the Ice-Harp. Chancing to throw a handful of pebbles upon the pond where there was an air chamber under the ice, it discoursed a pleasant music to him.

Herein resides a tenth muse, and as he was the man to discover it probably the extra melody is in him.

FACTS

Dec. 16. . . . How indispensable to a correct study of Nature is a perception of her true meaning. The fact will one day flower out into a truth. The season will mature and fructify what the understanding had cultivated. Mere accumulators of facts—collectors of materials for the master-workmen—are like those plants growing in dark forests, which "put forth only leaves instead of blossoms."

CRYSTALS

Dec. 23. Crossed the river today on the ice. Though the weather is raw and wintry and the ground covered with snow, I noticed a solitary robin, who looked as if he needed to have his services to the Babes in the Woods speedily requited.

In the side of the high bank by the Leaning Hemlocks, there were some curious crystallizations. Wherever the water, or other causes, had formed a hole in the bank, its throat and outer edge, like the entrance to a citadel of the olden time, bristled with a glistening ice armor. In one place you might see minute ostrich feathers, which seemed the waving plumes of the warriors filing into the fortress, in another the glancing fan-shaped banners of the Lilliputian host, and in another the needle-shaped particles, collected into bundles resembling the plumes of the pine, might pass for a phalanx of spears. The whole hill was like an immense quartz rock, with minute crystals sparkling from innumerable crannies. I tried to fancy that there was a disposition in these crystallizations to take the forms of the contiguous foliage.

1838

Unshackled though he aimed to be, Thoreau felt that he ought to look for work. He tried for some months to get a permanent job as a teacher but was unsuccessful. He even went to Maine in his search. In June he opened his own small school in Concord, terms $6 per quarter. Meanwhile the call of the woodlands and streams around Concord grew insistent. He gave the first of what would be a number of public lectures at the Concord Lyceum and elsewhere. The subject was "Society"; the surviving parts of the journal include some of his notes for it. The journal also reveals the early stages of the four kinds of writing that would give it enduring distinction: the descriptions of nature, the descriptions of wild life, the reflections on man's conduct, and the sketches of characters in the human comedy. In addition there is a fair amount of his youthful poetry as well, again, as considerable quotation from classic writers.

HEAVEN ON EARTH

Jan. 6. As a child looks forward to the coming of the summer, so could we˙ contemplate with quiet joy the circle of the seasons returning without fail eternally. As the spring came round during so many years of the gods, we could go out to admire and adorn anew our Eden, and yet never tire.

SAXONS

Jan. 15. After all that has been said in praise of the Saxon race, we must allow that our blue-eyed and fair-haired ancestors were originally an ungodly and reckless crew.

27

WE MAKE OUR OWN FORTUNE

Jan. 16. Man is like a cork which no tempest can sink, but it will float securely to its haven at last. The world is never the less beautiful though viewed through a chink or knot-hole.

SOCIETY

Feb. 9. It is wholesome advice—"to be a man amongst folks." Go into society if you will, or if you are unwilling, and take a human interest in its affairs. If you mistake these Messieurs and Mesdames for so many men and women, it is but erring on the safe side—or, rather, it is their error and not yours. Armed with a manly sincerity, you shall not be trifled with, but drive this business of life. It matters not how many men are to be addressed—rebuked—provided one man rebuke them.

SMALL TALK

To manage the small talk of a party is to make an effort to do what was at first done, admirably because naturally, at your fireside.

INFLUENCE

Feb. 13. It is hard to subject ourselves to an influence. It must steal upon us when we expect it not, and its work be all done ere we are aware of it. If we make advances, it is shy; if, when we feel its presence, we presume to pry into its freemasonry, it vanishes and leaves us alone in our folly —brimful but stagnant—a full channel, it may be, but no inclination.

FEAR

All fear of the world or consequences is swallowed up in a manly anxiety to do Truth justice.

OLD BOOKS

Feb. 15. The true student will cleave ever to the good, recognizing no Past, no Present; but wherever he emerges from the bosom of time, his course is not with the sun—eastward or westward—but ever toward the seashore. Day and night pursues he his devious way, lingering by how many a Pierian spring, how many an Academus grove, how many a sculptured portico!—all which—spring, grove, and portico—lie not so wide but he may take them conveniently in his way.

GREECE

Feb. 16. In imagination I hie me to Greece as to enchanted ground. No storms vex her coasts, no clouds encircle her Helicon or Olympus, no tempests sweep the peaceful Tempe or ruffle the bosom of the placid Aegean; but always the beams of the summer's sun gleam along the entablature of the Acropolis, or are reflected through the mellow atmosphere from a thousand consecrated groves and fountains; always her seagirt isles are dallying with their zephyr guests, and the low of kine is heard along the meads, and the landscape sleeps—valley and hill and woodland—a dreamy sleep. Each of her sons created a new heaven and a new earth for Greece.

SUNDAY

Feb. 18. Rightly named Suna-day, or day of the sun. One

is satisfied in some angle by wood-house and garden fence to bask in his beams—to exist barely—the live-long day.

SPRING

I had not been out long today when it seemed that a new Spring was already born—not quite weaned, it is true, but verily entered upon existence. Nature struck up "the same old song in the grass," despite eighteen inches of snow, and I contrived to smuggle away a grin of satisfaction by a smothered "Pshaw! and is that all?"

WHAT TO DO

March 5. . . . But what does all this scribbling amount to? What is now scribbled in the heat of the moment one can contemplate with somewhat of satisfaction, but alas! tomorrow—aye, tonight—it is stale, flat, and unprofitable—in fine, is not, only its shell remains, like some red parboiled lobster-shell which, kicked aside never so often, still stares at you in the path.

March 14. . . . If thy neighbor hail thee to inquire how goes the world, feel thyself put to thy trumps to return a true and explicit answer. Plant the feet firmly, and, will he nill he, dole out to him with strict and conscientious impartiality his modicum of a response.

Let not society be the element in which you swim, or are tossed about at the mercy of the waves, but be rather a strip of firm land running out into the sea, whose base is daily washed by the tide, but whose summit only the spring tide can reach.

But after all, such a morsel of society as this will not satisfy a man. But like those women of Malamocco and Pelestrina, who when their husbands are fishing at sea, repair to the shore and sing their shrill songs at evening, till they hear the voices of their husbands in reply borne to them over the water, so go we about indefatigably, chanting our stanza of the lay, and awaiting the response of a kindred soul out of the distance.

JOURNEY TO MAINE

May 3–4. Boston to Portland.

What, indeed, is this earth to us of New England but a field for Yankee speculation? The Nantucket whaler goes a-fishing round it, and so knows it—what it is, how long, how broad, and that no tortoise sustains it. He who has visited the confines of his real estate, looking out on all sides into space, will feel a new inducement to *be* the lord of creation.

We must all pay a small tribute to Neptune; the chief engineer must once have been seasick.

Midnight—head over the boat's side—between sleeping and waking—with glimpses of one or more lights in the vicinity of Cape Ann. Bright moonlight—the effect heightened by seasickness. Beyond that light yonder have my lines hitherto been cast, but now I know that there lies not the whole world, for I can say it is there and not here.

May 4. Portland.

There is a proper and only right way to enter a city, as well as to make advances to a strange person; neither will allow of the least forwardness nor bustle. A sensitive person can hardly elbow his way boldly, laughing and talking, into a strange town, without experiencing some twinges of conscience, as when he has treated a stranger with too much familiarity.

May 5. Portland to Bath via Brunswick; Bath to Brunswick.

Each one's world is but a clearing in the forest, so much open and inclosed ground. When the mail coach rumbles into one of these, the villagers gaze after you with a compassionate look, as much as to say: "Where have you been all this time, that you make your début in the world at this late hour? Nevertheless, here we are; come and study us, that you may learn men and manners."

May 6. Brunswick to Augusta via Gardiner and Hallowell.

May 7. We occasionally meet an individual of a character and disposition so entirely the reverse of our own that we wonder if he can indeed be another man like ourselves. We doubt if we ever could draw any nearer to him, and understand him. Such was the old English gentleman whom I met with today in H. Though I peered in at his eyes I could not discern myself reflected therein. The chief wonder was how we could ever arrive at so fair-seeming an intercourse upon so small ground of sympathy. He walked and fluttered like a strange bird at my side, prying into and making a handle of the least circumstance. The bustle and rapidity of our communication were astonishing; we skated in our conversation. All at once he would stop short in the path, and, in an abstracted air, query whether the steamboat had reached Bath or Portland, addressing me from time to time as his familiar genius, who could understand what was passing in his mind without the necessity of uninterrupted oral communication.

May 8. Augusta to Bangor via China.

May 10. Bangor to Oldtown.
The railroad from Bangor to Oldtown is civilization shooting off in a tangent into the forest. I had much conversation with an old Indian at the latter place, who sat dreaming upon a scow at the waterside and striking his deerskin moccasins against the planks, while his arms hung listlessly by his side. He was the most communicative man I had met. Talked of hunting and fishing, old times and new times. Pointing up the Penobscot, he observed, "Two or three mile up the river one beautiful country!" and then, as if he would come as far to meet me as I had gone to meet him, he exclaimed, "Ugh! one very hard time!" But he had mistaken his man.

May 11. Bangor to Belfast via Saturday Cove.

May 12. Belfast.

May 13. To Castine by sailboat "Cinderilla [*sic.*]"

May 14. Castine to Belfast by packet, Captain Skinner. Found the Poems of Burns and an odd volume of the "Spectator" in the cabin.

May 15. Belfast to Bath via Thomaston.

May 16. To Portland.

May 17. To Boston and Concord.

MAY MORNING

May 21.

The schoolboy loitered on his way to school,
Scorning to live so rare a day by rule.
So mild the air a pleasure 'twas to breathe,
For what seems heaven above was earth beneath.

Soured neighbors chatted by the garden pale,
Nor quarrelled who should drive the needed nail;
The most unsocial made new friends that day,
As when the sun shines husbandmen make hay.

How long I slept I know not, but at last
I felt my consciousness returning fast,
For Zephyr rustled past with leafy tread,
And heedlessly with one heel grazed my head.

My eyelids opened on a field of blue,
For close above a nodding violet grew;
A part of heaven it seemed, which one could scent,
Its blue commingling with the firmament.

CONSCIOUSNESS

Aug. 13. If with closed ears and eyes I consult consciousness for a moment, immediately are all walls and barriers dissipated, earth rolls from under me, and I float, by the impetus derived from the earth and the system, a subjective, heavily laden thought, in the midst of an unknown and infinite sea, or else heave and swell like a vast ocean of thought, without rock or headland, where are all riddles solved, all straight lines making there their two ends to meet, eternity and space gambolling familiarly through my depths. I am from the beginning, knowing no end, no aim. No sun illumines me, for I dissolve all lesser lights in my own intenser and steadier light. I am a restful kernel in the magazine of the universe.

RESOURCE

Men are constantly dinging in my ears their fair theories and plausible solutions of the universe, but ever there is no help, and I return again to my shoreless, islandless ocean, and fathom unceasingly for a bottom that will hold an anchor, that it may not drag.

EVENING SOUNDS

Aug. 26. How strangely sounds of revelry strike the ear from over cultivated fields by the woodside, while the sun is declining in the west. It is a world we had not known before. We listen and are capable of no mean act or thought. We tread on Olympus and participate in the councils of the gods.

THE LOSS OF A TOOTH

Aug. 27. Verily I am the creature of circumstances. Here I have swallowed an indispensable tooth, and so am no whole man, but a lame and halting piece of manhood. I am conscious of no gap in my soul, but it would seem that, now the entrance to the oracle has been enlarged, the more rare and commonplace the responses that issue from it. I have felt cheap, and hardly dared hold up my head among men, ever since this accident happened. Nothing can I do as well and freely as before; nothing do I undertake but I am hindered and balked by this circumstance. What a great matter a little spark kindleth! I believe if I were called at this moment to rush into the thickest of the fight, I should halt for lack of so insignificant a piece of armor as a tooth. Virtue and Truth go undefended, and Falsehood and Affectation are thrown in my teeth—though I am toothless. One does not need that the earth quake for the sake of excitement, when so slight a crack proves such an impassable moat. But let the lame man shake his leg, and match himself with the fleetest in the race. So shall he do what is in him to do. But let him who has lost a tooth open his mouth wide and gabble, lisp, and sputter never so resolutely.

SPHERE MUSIC

Sept. 2. The cocks chant a strain of which we never tire. Some there are who find pleasure in the melody of birds and chirping of crickets—aye, even the peeping of frogs. Such faint sounds as these are for the most part heard above the weeping and wailing and gnashing of teeth which so unhallow the Sabbath among us. The moan the earth makes is after all a very faint sound, infinitely inferior in volume to its creakings of joy and gleeful murmurs; so that we may expect the next balloonist will rise above the utmost range of discordant sounds into the region of pure melody. Never so loud was the wail but it seemed to taper off into a piercing melody and note of joy, which lingered not amid the clods of the valley.

FLOW OF SPIRITS IN YOUTH

Sept. 15. How unaccountable the flow of spirits in youth. You may throw sticks and dirt into the current, and it will only rise the higher. Dam it up you may, but dry it up you may not, for you cannot reach its source. If you stop up this avenue or that, anon it will come gurgling out where you least expected and wash away all fixtures. Youth grasps at happiness as an inalienable right. The tear does no sooner gush than glisten. Who shall say when the tear that sprung of sorrow first sparkled with joy?

ALMA NATURA

Sept. 20. It is a luxury to muse by a wall-side in the sunshine of a September afternoon—to cuddle down under a gray stone, and hearken to the siren song of the cricket. Day and night seem henceforth but accidents, and the time is always a still eventide, and as the close of a happy day. Parched fields and mulleins gilded with the slanting rays are my diet. I know of no word so fit to express this disposition of Nature as Alma Natura.

BYRON

Dec. 8. Nothing in nature is sneaking or chapfallen, as somewhat maltreated and slighted, but each is satisfied with its being, and so is as lavender and balm. If skunk-cabbage is offensive to the nostrils of men, still has it not drooped in consequence, but trustfully unfolded its leaf of two hands' breadth. What was it to Lord Byron whether England owned or disowned him, whether he smelled sour and was skunk-cabbage to the English nostril or violet-like, the pride of the land and ornament of every lady's boudoir? Let not the oyster grieve that he has lost the race; he has gained as an oyster.

1839

Thoreau fell in love. The girl was Ellen Sewall, a charming seventeen-year-old from Scituate, Massachusetts, who was making a summer visit to Concord. He wrote in the journal, "There is no remedy for love but to love more." This same summer he and his brother John made a boat trip on the Concord and Merrimack rivers, camping and exploring along the way. It was a delightful experience which would lead to the first of the two books Thoreau published during his lifetime. The journal we have left for this year is marked by an unusually large amount of youthful philosophizing. There are, for example, paragraphs headed "Disappointment," "The Poet," "Friendship," and "Growth."

THE POET

March 3. He must be something more than natural—even supernatural. Nature will not speak through but along with him. His voice will not proceed from her midst, but, breathing on her, will make her the expression of his thought. He then poetizes when he takes a fact out of nature into spirit. He speaks without reference to time or place. His thought is one world, hers another. He is another Nature—Nature's brother. Kindly offices do they perform for one another. Each publishes the other's truth.

MORNING

April 4. The atmosphere of morning gives a healthy hue to our prospects. Disease is a sluggard that overtakes, never encounters, us. We have the start each day, and may fairly distance him before the dew is off; but if we recline in the bowers of noon, he will come up with us after all. The morning dew breeds no cold. We enjoy a diurnal reprieve in the beginning of each day's creation. In the morning we do not believe in expediency; we will start afresh, and have no patching, no temporary fixtures. The afternoon man has an interest in the past; his eye is divided, and he sees indifferently well either way.

DRIFTING

Drifting in a sultry day on the sluggish waters of the pond, I almost cease to live and begin to be. A boatman stretched on the deck of his craft and dallying with the noon would be as apt an emblem of eternity for me as the serpent with his tail in his mouth. I am never so prone to lose my identity. I am dissolved in the haze.

DISAPPOINTMENT

April 7. Sunday. The tediousness and detail of execution never occur to the genius projecting; it always antedates the completion of its work. It condescends to give time a few hours to do its bidding in.

RESOLVE

Most have sufficient contempt for what is mean to resolve that they will abstain from it, and a few virtue enough to abide by their resolution, but not often does one attain to such lofty contempt as to require no resolution to be made.

SOCIETY

April 14. There is a *terra firma* in society as well as in geography, some whose ports you may make by dead reckoning in all weather. All the rest are but floating and fabulous Atlantides which sometimes skirt the western horizon of our intercourse. They impose only on seasick mariners who have put into some Canary Island on the frontiers of society.

CIRCUMSTANCES

April 24. Why should we concern ourselves with what has happened to us, and the unaccountable fickleness of events, and not rather [with] how we have happened to the universe, and it has demeaned itself in consequence? Let us record in each case the judgment we have awarded to circumstances.

ACQUAINTANCE

Cheap persons will stand upon ceremony, because there is no other ground; but to the great of the earth we need no introduction, nor do they need any to us.

THE KINGDOMS OF THE EARTH

April 25. If we see the reality in things, of what moment is the superficial and apparent? Take the earth and all the interests it has known—what are they beside one deep surmise that pierces and scatters them? The independent beggar disposes of all with one hearty, significant curse by the roadside. 'Tis true they are not worth a "tinker's damn."

PICTURE

April 30. Of some illuminated pictures which I saw last evening, one representing the plain of Babylon, with only a heap of brick-dust in the centre, and an uninterrupted horizon bounding the desert, struck me most. I would see painted a boundless expanse of desert, prairie, or sea, without other object than the horizon. The heavens and the earth—the first and last painting—where is the artist who shall undertake it?

May 11. The farmer keeps pace with his crops and the revolutions of the seasons, but the merchant with the fluctuations of trade. Observe how differently they walk in the streets.

VICE AND VIRTUE

May 16. Virtue is the very heart and lungs of vice: it cannot stand up but it lean on virtue.

Who has not admired the twelve labors? And yet nobody thinks if Hercules had sufficient motive for racking his bones to that degree. Men are not so much virtuous as patrons of virtue, and every one knows that it is easier to deal with the real possessor of a thing than the temporary guardian of it.

MY ATTIC

June 4. I sit here this fourth of June, looking out on men and nature from this that I call my perspective window, through which all things are seen in their true relations. This is my upper empire, bounded by four walls, viz., three of boards yellow-washed, facing the north, west, and south, respectively, and the fourth of plaster, likewise yellow-washed, fronting the sunrise—to say nothing of the purlieus and outlying provinces, unexplored as yet but by rats.

The words of some men are thrown forcibly against you and adhere like burs.

RENCOUNTER

June 22. Saturday. I have within the last few days come into contact with a pure, uncompromising spirit, that is somewhere wandering in the atmosphere, but settles not positively anywhere. Some persons carry about them the air and conviction of virtue, though they themselves are unconscious of it, and are even backward to appreciate it in others. Such it is impossible not to love; still is their loveliness, as it were, independent of them, so that you seem not to lose it when they are absent, for when they are near it is like an invisible presence which attends you.

That virtue we appreciate is as much ours as another's. We see so much only as we possess.

July 25. There is no remedy for love but to love more.

Aug. 31. . . . . While I write here, I hear the foxes trotting about me over the dead leaves, and now gently over the grass, as if not to disturb the dew which is falling. Why should we not cultivate neighborly relations with the foxes? As if to improve upon our seeming advances, comes one to greet us nosewise under our tent-curtain. Nor do we rudely repulse him. Is man powder and the fox flint and steel? Has not the time come when men and foxes shall lie down together?

Hist! there, the musquash by the boat is taking toll of potatoes and melons. Is not this the age of a community of goods? His presumption kindles in me a brotherly feeling. Nevertheless, I get up to reconnoitre, and tread stealthily along the shore to make acquaintance with him. But on the riverside I can see only the stars reflected in the water, and now, by some ripple ruffling the disk of a star, I discover him.

THE WISE REST

Sept. 17. Nature never makes haste; her systems revolve at an even pace. The bud swells imperceptibly, without hurry or confusion, as though the short spring days were an eternity. All her operations seem separately, for the time, the single object for which all things tarry. Why, then, should man hasten as if anything less than eternity were allotted for the least deed? Let him consume never so many eons, so that he go about the meanest task well, though it be but the paring of his nails. If the setting sun seems to hurry him to improve the day while it lasts, the chant of the crickets fails not to reassure him, even-measured as of old, teaching him to take his own time henceforth forever. The wise man is restful, never restless or impatient. He each moment abides there where he is, as some walkers actually rest the whole body at each step, while others never relax the muscles of the leg till the accumulated fatigue obliges them to stop short.

As the wise is not anxious that time wait for him, neither does he wait for it.

AESCHYLUS

Nov. 5. There was one man lived his own healthy Attic life in those days. The words that have come down to us evidence that their speaker was a seer in his day and generation. At this day they owe nothing to their dramatic form, nothing to stage machinery, and the fact that they were spoken under these or those circumstances. All display of art for the gratification of a factitious taste is silently passed by to come at the least particle of absolute and genuine thought they contain. The reader will be disappointed, however, who looks for traits of a rare wisdom or eloquence, and will have to solace himself, for the most part, with the poet's humanity and what it was in him to say. He will discover that, like every genius, he was a solitary liver and worker in his day.

We are accustomed to say that the common sense of this age belonged to the seer of the last—as if time gave him any vantage ground. But not so: I see not but Genius must ever take an equal start, and all the generations of men are virtually at a standstill for it to come and consider of them. Common sense is not so familiar with any truth but Genius will represent it in a strange light to it. Let the seer bring down his broad eye to the most stale and trivial fact, and he will make you believe it a new planet in the sky.

As to criticism, man has never to make allowance to man; there is naught to excuse, naught to bear in mind.

All the past is here present to be tried; let it approve itself if it can.

GROWTH

We are not apt to remember that we grow. It is curious to reflect how the maiden waiteth patiently, confiding as the unripe houstonia of the meadow, for the slow moving years to work their will with her—perfect and ripen her—like it to be fanned by the wind, watered by the rain, and receive her education at the hands of nature.

These young buds of manhood in the streets are like buttercups in the meadows—surrendered to nature as they.

Nov. 7. I was not aware till today of a rising and risen generation. Children appear to me as raw as the fresh fungi on a fence rail. By what degrees of consanguinity is this succulent and rank-growing slip of manhood related to me? What is it but another herb, ranging all the kingdoms of nature, drawing in sustenance by a thousand roots and fibres from all soils.

REGRET

Nov. 13. Make the most of your regrets; never smother your sorrow, but tend and cherish it till it come to have a separate and integral interest. To regret deeply is to live afresh. By so doing you will be astonished to find yourself restored once more to all your emoluments.

DESPONDENCY

Nov. 14. There is nowhere any apology for despondency. Always there is life which, rightly lived, implies a divine satisfaction. I am soothed by the raindrops on the door-sill; every globule that pitches thus confidently from the eaves to the ground is my life insurance. Disease and a raindrop cannot coexist. The east wind is not itself consumptive, but has enjoyed a rare health from of old. If a fork or brand stand erect, *good* is portended by it. They are the warrant of universal innocence.

FAREWELL

Nov. 19.

> Light-hearted, thoughtless, shall I take my way,
> When I to thee this being have resigned,
> Well knowing where, upon a future day,
> With us'rer's craft more than myself to find.

Nov. 29. Many brave men have there been, thank Fortune, but I shall never grow brave by comparison. When I remember myself I shall forget them.

BRAVERY

Dec. 2. A rare landscape immediately suggests a suitable inhabitant, whose breath shall be its wind, whose moods its seasons, and to whom it will always be fair. To be chafed and worried, and not as serene as Nature, does not become one whose nature is as steadfast as she. We do all stand in the front ranks of the battle every moment of our lives; where there is a brave man there is the thickest of the fight, there the post of honor. Not he who procures a substitute to go to Florida is exempt from service; he gathers his laurels in another field. Waterloo is not the only battle-ground: as many and fatal guns are pointed at my breast now as are contained in the English arsenals.

1840

Thoreau made his first faint mark as a writer. In the new Transcendentalist magazine the Dial *he published his first poem, a lyric on Ellen Sewall's little brother, and his first prose piece, a brief essay on a Roman poet. In summer his love for Ellen ripened and she certainly became more deeply interested in him. In November her father decreed against the marriage and Thoreau would never, in the traditional sense of the term, fall in love again. At midyear he ended his first journal, which had run to 546 pages, and began his second one. The philosophizing continues to be prominent; the descriptions of nature become more detailed and deft.*

Jan. 19.

> By a strong liking we prevail
> Against the stoutest fort;
> At length the fiercest heart will quail,
> And our alliance court.

FRIENDS

Jan. 26. They are like air bubbles on water, hastening to flow together.

History tells of Orestes and Pylades, Damon and Pythias, but why should not we put to shame those old reserved worthies by a community of such?

Constantly, as it were through a remote skylight, I have glimpses of a serene friendship-land, and know the better why brooks murmur and violets grow.

This conjunction of souls, like waves which meet and break, subsides also backward over things, and gives all a fresh aspect.

I would live henceforth with some gentle soul such a life as may be conceived, double for variety, single for harmony —two, only that we might admire at our oneness—one, because indivisible. Such community to be a pledge of holy living. How could aught unworthy be admitted into our society? To listen with one ear to each summer sound, to behold with one eye each summer scene, our visual rays so to meet and mingle with the object as to be one bent and doubled; with two tongues to be wearied, and thought to spring ceaselessly from a double fountain.

Feb. 16. Divination is prospective memory.

There is a kindred principle at the bottom of all affinities. The magnet cultivates a steady friendship with the pole, all bodies with all others. The friendliness of nature is that goddess Ceres who presides over every sowing and harvest, and we bless the same in sun and rain. The seed in the ground tarries for a season with its genial friends there; all the earths and grasses and minerals are its hosts, who entertain it hospitably, and plenteous crops and teeming wagons are the result.

Feb. 18. All romance is grounded on friendship. What is this rural, this pastoral, this poetical life but its invention? Does not the moon shine for Endymion? Smooth pastures and mild airs are for some Corydon and Phyllis. Paradise belongs to Adam and Eve. Plato's republic is governed by Platonic love.

Feb. 20. The coward's hope is suspicion, the hero's doubt a sort of hope. The gods neither hope nor doubt.

March 2. Love is the burden of all Nature's odes. The song of the birds is an epithalamium, a hymeneal. The marriage of the flowers spots the meadows and fringes the hedges with pearls and diamonds. In the deep water, in the high air, in woods and pastures, and the bowels of the earth, this is the employment and condition of all things.

March 16. The cabins of the settlers are the points whence radiate these rays of green and yellow and russet over the landscape; out of these go the axes and spades with which the landscape is painted. How much is the Indian summer and the budding of spring related to the cottage? Have not the flight of the crow and the gyrations of the hawk a reference to that roof?

The ducks alight at this season on the windward side of the river, in the smooth water, and swim about by twos and threes, pluming themselves and diving to peck at the root of the lily and the cranberries which the frost has not loosened. It is impossible to approach them within gunshot when they are accompanied by the gull, which rises sooner and makes them restless. They fly to windward first, in order to get under weigh, and are more easily reached by the shot if approached on that side. When preparing to fly, they swim about with their heads erect, and then, gliding along a few feet with their bodies just touching the surface, rise heavily with much splashing and fly low at first, if not suddenly aroused, but otherwise rise directly to survey the danger. The cunning sportsman is not in haste to desert his position, but waits to ascertain if, having got themselves into flying trim, they will not return over the ground in their course to a new resting place.

March 20. In society all the inspiration of my lonely hours seems to flow back on me, and then first have expression.

Love never degrades its votaries, but lifts them up to higher walks of being. They *over-look* one another. All other charities are swallowed up in this; it is gift and reward both.

We will have no vulgar Cupid for a go-between, to make us the playthings of each other, but rather cultivate an irreconcilable hatred instead of this.

March 21. The world is a fit theatre today in which any part may be acted. There is this moment proposed to me every kind of life that men lead anywhere, or that imagination can paint. By another spring I may be a mail-carrier in Peru, or a South African planter, or a Siberian exile, or a Greenland whaler, or a settler on the Columbia River, or a Canton merchant, or a soldier in Florida, or a mackerel-fisher off Cape Sable, or a Robinson Crusoe in the Pacific, or a silent navigator of any sea. So wide is the choice of parts, what a pity if the part of Hamlet be left out!

I am freer than any planet; no complaint reaches round the world. I can move away from public opinion, from gov-

ernment, from religion, from education, from society. Shall
I be reckoned a ratable poll in the county of Middlesex,
or be rated at one spear under the palm trees of Guinea?
Shall I raise corn and potatoes in Massachusetts, or figs and
olives in Asia Minor? sit out the day in my office in State
Street, or ride it out on the steppes of Tartary? For my
Brobdingnag I may sail to Patagonia; for my Lilliput, to
Lapland. In Arabia and Persia, my day's adventures may surpass the Arabian Nights' Entertainments. I may be a logger
on the head waters of the Penobscot, to be recorded in fable
hereafter as an amphibious river-god, by as sounding a name
as Triton or Proteus; carry furs from Nootka to China, and
so be more renowned than Jason and his golden fleece; or
go on a South Sea exploring expedition, to be hereafter re-
counted along with the periplus of Hanno. I may repeat
the adventures of Marco Polo or Mandeville.

These are but few of my chances, and how many more
things may I do with which there are none to be compared!

March 30. Pray, what things interest me at present? A
long, soaking rain, the drops trickling down the stubble,
while I lay drenched on a last year's bed of wild oats, by
the side of some bare hill, ruminating. These things are
of moment. To watch this crystal globe just sent from heaven
to associate with me. While these clouds and this sombre
drizzling weather shut all in, we two draw nearer and know
one another. The gathering in of the clouds with the last
rush and dying breath of the wind, and then the regular dripping of twigs and leaves the country o'er, the impression of
inward comfort and sociableness, the drenched stubble and
trees that drop beads on you as you pass, their dim outline
seen through the rain on all sides drooping in sympathy with
yourself. These are my undisputed territory. This is Nature's
English comfort. The birds draw closer and are more familiar under the thick foliage, composing new strains on their
roosts against the sunshine.

April 4. We look to windward for fair weather.

April 8. How shall I help myself? By withdrawing into
the garret, and associating with spiders and mice, determin-
ing to meet myself face to face sooner or later. Completely
silent and attentive I will be this hour, and the next, and
forever. The most positive life that history notices has been

a constant retiring out of life, a wiping one's hands of it, seeing how mean it is, and having nothing to do with it.

June 22. . . . When we are shocked at vice we express a lingering sympathy with it. Dry rot, rust, and mildew shock no man, for none is subject to them.

June 23. We Yankees are not so far from right, who answer one question by asking another. Yes and No are lies. A true answer will not aim to establish anything, but rather to set all well afloat. All answers are in the future, and day answereth to day. Do we think we can anticipate them?

In Latin, to respond is to pledge one's self before the gods to do faithfully and honorably, as a man should, in any case. This is good.

June 24. . . . So delicious is plain speech to my ears, as if I were to be more delighted by the whistling of the shot than frightened by the flying of the splinters, I am content, I fear, to be quite battered down and made a ruin of. I outgeneral myself when I direct the enemy to my vulnerable points.

The loftiest utterance of Love is, perhaps, sublimely satirical. Sympathy with what is sound makes sport of what is unsound.

Cliffs. Evening. Though the sun set a quarter of an hour ago, his rays are still visible, darting halfway to the zenith. That glowing morrow in the west flashes on me like a faint presentiment of morning when I am falling asleep. A dull mist comes rolling from the west, as if it were the dust which day has raised. A column of smoke is rising from the woods yonder, to uphold heaven's roof till the light comes again. The landscape, by its patient resting there, teaches me that all good remains with him that waiteth, and that I shall sooner overtake the dawn by remaining here, than by hurrying over the hills of the west.

Morning and evening are as like as brother and sister. The sparrow and thrush sing and the frogs peep for both.

The woods breathe louder and louder behind me. With what hurry-skurry night takes place! The wagon rattling over yonder bridge is the messenger which day sends back to night; but the dispatches are sealed. In its rattle the village seems to say, This one sound, and I have done.

Red, then, is Day's color; at least it is the color of his heel. He is "stepping westward." We only notice him when he comes and when he goes.

With noble perseverance the dog bays the stars yonder. I too, like thee, walk alone in this strange, familiar night, my voice, like thine, beating against its friendly concave; and barking I hear only my own voice. 10 o'clock.

June 25. Let me see no other conflict but with prosperity. If my path run on before me level and smooth, it is all a mirage; in reality it is steep and arduous as a chamois pass. I will not let the years roll over me like a Juggernaut car.

We will warm us at each other's fire. Friendship is not such a cold refining process as a double sieve, but a glowing furnace in which all impurities are consumed.

Men have learned to touch before they scrutinize—to shake hands, and not to stare.

June 26. The best poetry has never been written, for when it might have been, the poet forgot it, and when it was too late remembered it; or when it might have been, the poet remembered it, and when it was too late forgot it.

> The highest condition of art is artlessness.
> Truth is always paradoxical.
> He will get to the goal first who stands stillest.
> There is one let better than any help, and that is— *Let-alone.*
> By sufferance you may escape suffering.
> He who resists not at all will never surrender.
> When a dog runs at you, whistle for him.
> Say, Not so, and you will outcircle the philosophers.
> Stand outside the wall, and no harm can reach you.
The danger is that you be walled in with it.

June 27. I am living this twenty-seventh of June, 1840, a dull, cloudy day and no sun shining. The clink of the smith's hammer sounds feebly over the roofs, and the wind is sighing gently, as if dreaming of cheerfuler days. The farmer is plowing in yonder field, craftsmen are busy in the shops, the trader stands behind the counter, and all works go steadily forward. But I will have nothing to do; I will tell fortune that I play no game with her, and she may reach me in my Asia of serenity and indolence if she can.

July 10. . . . We know men through their eyes. You might say that the eye was always original and unlike another. It is the feature of the individual, and not of the family— in twins still different. All a man's privacy is in his eye, and its expression he cannot alter more than he can alter his character. So long as we look a man in the eye, it seems to rule the other features, and make them, too, original. When I have mistaken one person for another, observing only his form, and carriage, and inferior features, the unlike-ness seemed of the least consequence; but when I caught his eye, and my doubts were removed, it seemed to pervade every feature.

The eye revolves on an independent pivot which we can no more control than our own will. Its axle is the axle of the soul, as the axis of the earth is coincident with the axis of the heavens.

July 12. . . . A wise man will always have his duds picked up, and be ready for whatever may happen, as the prudent merchant, notwithstanding the lavish display of his wares, will yet have them packed or easy to be removed in emergencies. In this sense there is something sluttish in all finery. When I see a fine lady or gentleman dressed to the top of the fashion, I wonder what they would do if an earthquake should happen, or a fire suddenly break out, for they seem to have counted only on fair weather, and that things will go on smoothly and without jostling. Those curls and jewels, so nicely adjusted, expect an unusual defer-ence from the elements.

Our dress should be such as will hang conveniently about us, and fit equally well in good and in bad fortune; such as will approve itself of the right fashion and fabric, whether for the cotillion or the earthquake. . . .

July 19. These two days that I have not written in my Journal, set down in the calendar as the seventeenth and eighteenth of July, have been really an eon in which a Syrian empire might rise and fall. How many Persias have been lost and won in the interim? Night is spangled with fresh stars.

July 27. . . . When bravery is worsted, it joins the peace society.

1841

The problem of making a living plagued Thoreau further, in spite of his efforts to minimize it. In spring he found a temporary solution when Emerson invited him to work at his house as a kind of general-utility man. Thoreau agreed, found the situation acceptable, and stayed at his modest duties for some two years. He felt himself attracted to two sympathetic older women, Emerson's wife, Lidian, and her sister, Mrs. Lucy Brown, as well as to a younger one, Mary Russell, a schoolteacher from Plymouth. He acquired his first disciple, in the form of a young law student named Isaiah Williams, and his strictest critic, in the form of the bluestocking Margaret Fuller, who was helping to edit the Dial. *He published three lyrics in the* Dial. *The amount of quotation in the journal lessens; the amount of description and philosophizing remains substantial. The style of writing becomes more flexible.*

Jan. 24. Sunday. I almost shrink from the arduousness of meeting men erectly day by day.

Be resolutely and faithfully what you are; be humbly what you aspire to be. Be sure you give men the best of your wares, though they be poor enough, and the gods will help you to lay up a better store for the future. Man's noblest gift to man is his sincerity, for it embraces his integrity also. Let him not dole out of himself anxiously, to suit their weaker or stronger stomachs, but make a clean gift of himself, and empty his coffers at once. I would be in society as in the landscape; in the presence of nature there is no reserve, nor effrontery.

Jan. 26. Tuesday. I have as much property as I can command and use. If by a fault in my character I do not derive my just revenues, there is virtually a mortgage on my inheritance. A man's wealth is never entered in the registrar's office. Wealth does not come in along the great thoroughfares, it does not float on the Erie or Pennsylvania canal, but is imported by a solitary track without bustle or competition, from a brave industry to a quiet mind.

Jan. 28. No innocence can quite stand up under suspicion, if it is conscious of being suspected. In the company of one who puts a wrong construction upon your actions, they are apt really to deserve a mean construction. While in that society I can never retrieve myself. Attribute to me a great motive, and I shall not fail to have one; but a mean one, and the fountain of virtue will be poisoned by the suspicion. Show men unlimited faith as the coin with which you will deal with them, and they will invariably exhibit the best wares they have. I would meet men as the friends of all their virtue, and the foes of all their vice, for no man is the partner of his guilt. If you suspect me you will never see me, but all our intercourse will be the politest leave-taking; I shall constantly defer and apologize, and postpone myself in your presence. The self-defender is accursed in the sight of gods and men; he is a superfluous knight, who serves no lady in the land. He will find in the end that he has been fighting windmills, and battered his mace to no purpose. The injured man with querulous tone resisting his fate is like a tree struck by lightning, which rustles its sere leaves the winter through, not having vigor enough [to] cast them off.

As for apologies, I must be off with the dew and the frost, and leave mankind to repair the damage with their gauze screens and straw.

Feb. 4. Thursday. When you are once comfortably seated at a public meeting, there is something unmanly in the sitting on tiptoe and *qui vive* attitude—the involuntarily rising into your throat, as if gravity had ceased to operate—when a lady approaches, with quite god-like presumption, to elicit the miracle of a seat where none is.

Feb. 6. Saturday. One may discover a new side to his most intimate friend when for the first time he hears him speak in public. He will be stranger to him as he is more familiar to the audience. The longest intimacy could not foretell how he would behave then. When I observe my friend's conduct

toward others, then chiefly I learn the traits in his character, and in each case I am unprepared for the issue.

When one gets up to address briefly a strange audience, in
that little he may have opportunity to say he will not quite
do himself injustice. For he will instantly and instinctively
average himself to his audience, and while he is true to his
own character still, he will in a few moments make that
impression which a series of months and years would but
expand. Before he answers, his thought like lightning runs
round the whole compass of his experiences, and he is scrupulous to speak from that which he is and with a more entire truthfulness than usual. How little do we know each other
then! Who can tell how his friend would behave on any
occasion?

. . . The value of the recess in any public entertainment
consists in the opportunity for self-recovery which it offers.
We who have been swayed as one heart, expanding and con-
tracting with the common pulse, find ourselves in the interim, and set us up again, and feel our own hearts beating
in our breasts. We are always a little astonished to see a man
walking across the room, through an attentive audience, with
any degree of self-possession. He makes himself strange to
us. He is a little stubborn withal, and seems to say, "I am
self-sustained and independent as well as the performer, and
am not to be swallowed up in the common enthusiasm. No,
no, there are two of us, and John's as good as Thomas."
In the recess the audience is cut up into a hundred little
coteries, and as soon as each individual life has recovered
its tone and the purposes of health have been answered, it
is time for the performances to commence again.

In a public performer, the simplest actions, which at other
times are left to unconscious nature, as the ascending a
few steps in front of an audience, acquire a fatal importance
and become arduous deeds.

Feb. 7. . . . The eaves are running on the south side of the
house; the titmouse lisps in the poplar; the bells are ringing
for church; while the sun presides over all and makes his
simple warmth more obvious than all else. What shall I do
with this hour, so like time and yet so fit for eternity?
Where in me are these russet patches of ground, and scat-

tered logs and chips in the yard? I do not feel cluttered. I have some notion what the John's-wort and life-everlasting may be thinking about when the sun shines on me as on them and turns my prompt thought into just such a seething shimmer. I lie out indistinct as a heath at noonday. I am evaporating and ascending into the sun.

Feb. 10. . . . I asked a man today if he would rent me some land, and he said he had four acres as good soil "as any outdoors." It was a true poet's account of it. He and I, and all the world, went outdoors to breathe the free air and stretch ourselves. For the world is but outdoors—and we duck behind a panel.

Feb. 11. True help, for the most part, implies a greatness in him who is to be helped as well as in the helper. It takes a god to be helped even. A great person, though unconsciously, will constantly give you great opportunities to serve him, but a mean one will quite preclude all active benevolence. It needs but simply and *greatly* to want it for once, that all true men may contend who shall be foremost to render aid. My neighbor's state must pray to heaven so devoutly yet disinterestedly as he never prayed in words, before my ears can hear. It must ask divinely. But men so cobble and botch their request, that you must stoop as low as they to give them aid. Their meanness would drag down your deed to be a compromise with conscience, and not leave it to be done on the high table-land of the benevolent soul. They would have you doff your bright and knightly armor and drudge for them—serve *them* and not God. But if I am to serve them I must not serve the devil.

What is called charity is no charity, but the interference of a third person. Shall I interfere with fate? Shall I defraud man of the opportunities which God gave him, and so take away his life? Beggars and silent poor cry—how often!— "Get between me and my god." I will not stay to cobble and patch God's rents, but do clean, new work when he has given me my hands full. This almshouse charity is like putting new wine into old bottles, when so many tuns in God's cellars stand empty. We go about mending the times, when we should be building the eternity.

I must serve a strong master, not a weak one. Help implies

a sympathy of energy and effort, else no alleviation will avail.

Feb. 23. . . . The care of the body is the highest exercise of prudence. If I have brought this weakness on my lungs, I will consider calmly and disinterestedly how the thing came about, that I may find out the truth and render justice. Then, after patience, I shall be a wiser man than before.

Let us apply all our wit to the repair of our bodies, as we would mend a harrow, for the body will be dealt plainly and implicitly with. We want no moonshine nor surmises about it. This matter of health and sickness has no fatality in it, but is a subject for the merest prudence. If I know not what ails me, I may resort to amulets and charms and, moonstruck, die of dysentery.

We do wrong to slight our sickness and feel so ready to desert our posts when we are harassed. So much the more should we rise above our condition, and make the most of it, for the fruit of disease may be as good as that of health.

There is a subtle elixir in society which makes it a fountain of health to the sick. We want no consolation which is not the overflow of our friend's health. We will have no condolence who are not dolent ourselves. We would have our friend come and respire healthily before us, with the fragrance of many meadows and heaths in his breath, and we will inhabit his body while our own recruits.

Nothing is so good medicine in sickness as to witness some nobleness in another which will advertise us of health. In sickness it is our faith that ails, and noble deeds reassure us.

That anybody has thought of you on some indifferent occasion frequently implies more good will than you had reason to expect. You have henceforth a higher motive for conduct. We do not know how many amiable thoughts are current.

Feb. 26. Friday. My prickles or smoothness are as much a quality of your hand as of myself. I cannot tell you what I am, more than a ray of the summer's sun. What I am I am, and say not. Being is the great explainer. In the attempt to explain, shall I plane away all the spines, till it is no thistle, but a cornstalk?

If my world is not sufficient without thee, my friend, I will wait till it is and then call thee. You shall come to a palace, not to an almshouse.

My homeliest thought, like the diamond brought from farthest within the mine, will shine with the purest lustre.

Though I write every day, yet when I say a good thing it seems as if I wrote but rarely.

To be great, we do as if we would be tall merely, be longer than we are broad, stretch ourselves and stand on tiptoe. But greatness is well proportioned, unstrained, and stands on the soles of the feet.

Feb. 27. Saturday. Life looks as fair at this moment as a summer's sea, or a blond dress in a saffron light, with its sun and grass and walled towns so bright and chaste, as fair as my own virtue which would adventure therein. Like a Persian city or hanging gardens in the distance, so washed in light, so untried, only to be thridded by clean thoughts. All its flags are flowing, and tassels streaming, and drapery flapping, like some gay pavilion. The heavens hang over it like some low screen, and seem to undulate in the breeze.

Through this pure, unwiped hour, as through a crystal glass, I look out upon the future, as a smooth lawn for my virtue to disport in. It shows from afar as unrepulsive as the sunshine upon walls and cities, over which the passing life moves as gently as a shadow. I see the course of my life, like some retired road, wind on without obstruction into a country maze.

I am attired for the future so, as the sun setting presumes all men at leisure and in contemplative mood—and am thankful that it is thus presented blank and indistinct. It still o'ertops my hope. My future deeds bestir themselves within me and move grandly towards a consummation, as ships go down the Thames. A steady onward motion I feel in me, as still as that, or like some vast, snowy cloud, whose shadow first is seen across the fields. It is the material of all things loose and set afloat that makes my sea.

Feb. 28. Nothing goes by luck in composition. It allows no tricks. The best you can write will be the best you are. Every sentence is the result of a long probation. The author's character is read from title page to end. Of this he never corrects the proofs. We read it as the essential character of a handwriting without regard to the flourishes. And so of the rest of our actions; it runs as straight as a ruled line through them all, no matter how many curvets about it. Our whole life is taxed for the least thing well done; it is its net result. How we eat, drink, sleep, and use our desultory hours, now in these indifferent days, with no eye to observe and no occasion [to] excite us, determines our authority and capacity for the time to come.

March 15. When I have access to a man's barrel of sermons, which were written from week to week, as his life lapsed, though I now know him to live cheerfully and bravely enough, still I cannot conceive what interval there was for laughter and smiles in the midst of so much sadness. Almost in proportion to the sincerity and earnestness of the life will be the sadness of the record. When I reflect that twice a week for so many years he pondered and preached such a sermon, I think he must have been a splenetic and melancholy man, and wonder if his food digested well. It seems as if the fruit of virtue was never a careless happiness.

A great cheerfulness have all great wits possessed, almost a profane levity to such as understood them not, but their religion had the broader basis in proportion as it was less prominent. The religion I love is very laic. The clergy are as diseased, and as much possessed with a devil, as the reformers. They make their topic as offensive as the politician, for our religion is as unpublic and incommunicable as our poetical vein, and to be approached with as much love and tenderness.

March 27. . . . I must not lose any of my freedom by being a farmer and landholder. Most who enter on any profession are doomed men. The world might as well sing a dirge over them forthwith. The farmer's muscles are rigid. He can do one thing long, not many well. His pace seems determined henceforth; he never quickens it. A very rigid Nemesis is his fate. When the right wind blows or a star calls, I can leave this arable and grass ground, without making a will or settling my estate. I would buy a farm as freely as a silken streamer. Let me not think my front windows must face east henceforth because a particular hill slopes that way. My life must undulate still. I will not feel that my wings are clipped when once I have settled on ground which the law calls my own, but find new pinions grown to the old, and talaria to my feet beside.

April 26. Monday. At R. W. E[merson]'s. The charm of the Indian to me is that he stands free and unconstrained in Nature, is her inhabitant and not her guest, and wears her easily and gracefully. But the civilized man has the habits of the house. His house is a prison, in which he finds himself oppressed and confined, not sheltered and protected. He walks as if he sustained the roof; he carries his arms as if the walls would fall in and crush him, and his feet remember the cellar beneath. His muscles are never relaxed. It is rare that he overcomes the house, and learns to sit at home in it, and roof and floor and walls support themselves, as the sky and trees and earth.

It is a great art to saunter.

May 27. Thursday. I sit in my boat on Walden, playing the flute this evening, and see the perch, which I seem to have charmed, hovering around me, and the moon travelling over the bottom, which is strewn with the wrecks of the forest, and feel that nothing but the wildest imagination can conceive of the manner of life we are living. Nature is a wizard. The Concord nights are stranger than the Arabian nights.

We not only want elbow-room, but eye-room in this gray air which shrouds all the fields. Sometimes my eyes see over the county road by daylight to the tops of yonder birches on the hill, as at others by moonlight.

Heaven lies above, because the air is deep.

In all my life hitherto I have left nothing behind.

Aug. 18. . . . Of all the duties of life it is hardest to be in earnest; it implies a good deal both before and behind. I sit here in the barn this flowing afternoon weather, while the school bell is ringing in the village, and find that all the things immediate to be done are very trivial. I could postpone them to hear this locust sing. The cockerels crow and the hens cluck in the yard as if time were dog-cheap. It seems something worth detaining time—the laying of an egg. Cannot man do something to comfort the gods, and not let the world prove such a piddling concern? No doubt they would be glad to sell their shares at a large discount by this time. Eastern Railroad stock promises a better dividend.

Sept. 1. Wednesday. When I observe the effeminate taste of some of my contemporaries in this matter of poetry, and how hardly they bear with certain incongruities, I think if this age were consulted it would not choose granite to be the backbone of the world, but Bristol spar or Brazilian diamonds. But the verses which have consulted the refinements even of a golden age will be found weak and nerveless for an iron one. The poet is always such a Cincinnatus in literature as with republican simplicity to raise all to the chiefest honors of the state.

Each generation thinks to inhabit only a west end of the world, and have intercourse with a refined and civilized Nature, not conceiving of her broad equality and republicanism. They think her aristocratic and exclusive because their own estates are narrow. But the sun indifferently selects his rhymes, and with a liberal taste weaves into his verse the planet and the stubble.

Let us know and conform only to the fashions of eternity.

Sept. 2. Thursday. There is but one obligation, and that is the obligation to obey the highest dictate. None can lay me under another which will supersede this. The gods have given me these years without any incumbrance; society has no mortgage on them. If any man assist me in the way of the world, let him derive satisfaction from the deed itself, for I think I never shall have dissolved my prior obligations to God. Kindness repaid is thereby annulled. I would let his deed lie as fair and generous as it was intended. The truly beneficent never relapses into a creditor; his great kindness is still extended to me and is never done. Of those noble deeds which have me for their object I am only the most fortunate spectator, and would rather be the abettor of their nobleness than stay their tide with the obstructions of impatient gratitude. As true as action and reaction are equal, that nobleness which was as wide as the universe will rebound not on him the individual, but on the world. If any have been kind to me, what more do they want? I cannot make them richer than they are. If they have not been kind, they cannot take from me the privilege which they have not improved. My obligations will be my lightest load, for that gratitude which is of kindred stuff in me, expanding every pore, will easily sustain the pressure. We walk the freest through the air we breathe.

1842

In January Thoreau's brother John died; the blow left an enduring mark. The first shock in fact almost paralyzed Thoreau's writing; there are no journal entries for more than a month after John's death. How far Thoreau recovered we are not sure, since the extant journal ends for all practical purposes in April, with only a few entries surviving for the rest of the year. Notwithstanding, he published his first nature essay in the Dial, *in the guise of an extended book review, and more of his poems, including one to Mary Russell. He began to help too with the editing of the* Dial.

Jan. 8. . . . What offends me most in my compositions is the moral element in them. The repentant say never a brave word. Their resolves should be mumbled in silence. Strictly speaking, morality is not healthy. Those undeserved joys which come uncalled and make us more pleased than grateful are they that sing.

March 11. . . . We can only live healthily the life the gods assign us. I must receive my life as passively as the willow leaf that flutters over the brook. I must not be for myself, but God's work, and that is always good. I will wait the breezes patiently, and grow as Nature shall determine. My fate cannot but be grand so. We may live the life of a plant or an animal, without living an animal life. This constant and universal content of the animal comes of resting quietly in God's palm. I feel as if [I] could at any time resign my life and the responsibility of living into God's hands, and become as innocent, free from care, as a plant or stone.

My life, my life! why will you linger? Are the years short and the months of no account? How often has long delay quenched my aspirations! Can God afford that I should forget him? Is he so indifferent to my career? Can heaven be postponed with no more ado? Why were my ears given to hear those everlasting strains which haunt my life, and yet to be profaned much more by these perpetual dull sounds?

March 17. Thursday. I have been making pencils all day, and then at evening walked to see an old schoolmate who is going to help make the Welland Canal navigable for ships round Niagara. He cannot see any such motives and modes of living as I; professes not to look beyond the securing of certain "creature comforts." And so we go silently different ways, with all serenity, I in the still moonlight through the village this fair evening to write these thoughts in my journal, and he, forsooth, to mature his schemes to ends as good, maybe, but different. So are we two made, while the same stars shine quietly over us. If I or he be wrong, Nature yet consents placidly. She bites her lip and smiles to see how her children will agree. So does the Welland Canal get built, and other conveniences, while I live. Well and good, I must confess. Fast sailing ships are hence not detained.

What means this changing sky, that now I freeze and contract and go within myself to warm me, and now I say it is a south wind, and go all soft and warm along the way? I sometimes wonder if I do not breathe the south wind.

March 21. Who is old enough to have learned from experience?

April 3. . . . . I have just heard the flicker among the oaks on the hillside ushering in a new dynasty. It is the age and youth of time. Why did Nature set this lure for sickly mortals. Eternity could not begin with more security and momentousness than the spring. The summer's eternity is reestablished by this note. All sights and sounds are seen and heard both in time and eternity. And when the eternity of any sight or sound strikes the eye or ear, they are intoxicated with delight.

Sometimes, as through a dim haze, we see objects in their eternal relations; and they stand like Stonehenge and the Pyramids, and we wonder who set them up and what for.

The destiny of the soul can never be studied by the reason, for its modes are not ecstatic. In the wisest calculation or demonstration I but play a game with myself. I am not to be taken captive by myself.

I cannot convince myself. God must convince. I can calculate a problem in arithmetic, but not any morality.

Virtue is incalculable, as it is inestimable. Well, man's destiny is but virtue, or manhood. It is wholly moral, to be learned only by the life of the soul. God cannot calculate it. He has no moral philosophy, no ethics. The reason, before it can be applied to such a subject, will have to fetter and restrict it. How can he, step by step, perform that long journey who has not conceived whither he is bound? How can he expect to perform an arduous journey without interruption who has no passport to the end?

On one side of man is the actual, and on the other the ideal. The former is the province of the reason; it is even a divine light when directed upon it, but it cannot reach forward into the ideal without blindness. The moon was made to rule by night, but the sun to rule by day. Reason will be but a pale cloud, like the moon, when one ray of divine light comes to illumine the soul.

How rich and lavish must be the system which can afford to let so many moons burn all the day as well as the night, though no man stands in need of their light! There is none of that kind of economy in Nature that husbands its stock, but she supplies inexhaustible means to the most frugal methods. The poor may learn of her frugality, and the rich generosity. Having carefully determined the extent of her charity, she establishes it forever; her almsgiving is an annuity. She supplies to the bee only so much wax as is necessary for its cell, so that no poverty could stint it more; but the little economist which fed the Evangelist in the desert still keeps in advance of the immigrant, and fills the cavities of the forest for his repast.

Sept. 29. Today the lark sings again down in the meadow, and the robin peeps, and the bluebirds, old and young, have revisited their box, as if they would fain repeat the summer without the intervention of winter, if Nature would let them.

Beauty is a finer utility whose end we do not see.

Oct. 7. A little girl has just brought me a purple finch or American linnet. These birds are now moving south. It reminds me of the pine and spruce, and the juniper and cedar on whose berries it feeds. It has the crimson hues of the October evenings, and its plumage still shines as if it had caught and preserved some of their tints (beams?). We know it chiefly as a traveller. It reminds me of many things I had forgotten. Many a serene evening lies snugly packed under its wing.

Gower writes like a man of common sense and good parts who has undertaken with steady, rather than high, purpose to do narrative with rhyme. With little or no invention, following in the track of the old fablers, he employs his leisure and his pen-craft to entertain his readers and speak a good word for the right. He has no fire, or rather blaze, though occasionally some brand's end peeps out from the ashes, especially if you approach the heap in a dark day, and if you extend your hands over it you experience a slight warmth there more than elsewhere. In fair weather you may see a slight smoke go up here and there. He narrates what Chaucer sometimes sings. He tells his story with a fair understanding of the original, and sometimes it gains a little in blunt plainness and in point in his hands. Unlike the early Saxon and later English, his poetry is but a plainer and directer speech than other men's prose. He might have been a teamster and written his rhymes on his wagon-seat as he went to mill with a load of plaster.

The banks by retired roadsides are covered with asters, hazels, brakes, and huckleberry bushes, emitting a dry, ripe scent.

Facts must be learned directly and personally, but principles may be deduced from information. The collector of facts possesses a perfect physical organization, the philosopher a perfect intellectual one. One can walk, the other sit; one acts, the other thinks. But the poet in some degree does both, and uses and generalizes the results of both; he generalizes the widest deductions of philosophy.

Oct. 21. The atmosphere is so dry and transparent and, as it were, inflammable at this season that a candle in the grass shines white and dazzling, and purer and brighter the farther off it is. Its heat seems to have been extracted and only its harmless refulgent light left. It is a star dropped down. The ancients were more than poetically true when they called fire Vulcan's flower. Light is somewhat almost moral. The most intense—as the fixed stars and our own sun—has an unquestionable preeminence among the elements. At a certain stage in the generation of all life, no doubt, light as well as heat is developed. It guides to the first rudiments of life. There is a vitality in heat and light.

Men who are felt rather than understood are being most rapidly developed. They stand many deep.

In many parts the Merrimack is as wild and natural as ever, and the shore and surrounding scenery exhibit only the revolutions of nature. The pine stands up erect on its brink, and the alders and willows fringe its edge; only the beaver and the red man have departed.

My friend knows me face to face, but many only venture to meet me under the shield of another's authority, backed by an invisible *corps du réserve* of wise friends and relations. To such I say, "Farewell, we cannot dwell alone in the world."

Sometimes, by a pleasing, sad wisdom, we find ourselves carried beyond all counsel and sympathy. Our friends' words do not reach us.

The truly noble and settled character of a man is not put forward, as the king or conqueror does not march foremost in a procession.

1843

This was in some ways a lost year to Thoreau. From May to December he acted as a tutor in the family of William Emerson on Staten Island. Theoretically he was to be able to teach, write, and win his way into the New York literary market. In actuality he was able to do none of these things to his satisfaction. He could feel no rapport with the William Emerson family, his writing was desultory, and he made little impression in literary New York. On the other hand he continued to learn by helping to edit the Dial. *He also published extensively in it, both poetry and prose, both original pieces and translations. The* Boston Miscellany *printed one of his essays, while the* Democratic Review *printed a sketch and a book review. Whether the journal for this year was thin or thick we do not know; only fragments remain. There are pieces of a journal for 1842–1843 in the Harvard Library, and in the Huntington Library there are pieces of another, which must have run from September 24, 1843, through to January 7, 1844. But they are only pieces, remnants left over when he dismembered the journals for 1843–1844 to use in his other writing. A few are printed in F. B. Sanborn's* The First and Last Journeys of Thoreau *(1905), Vol. I, which is the source of the selections that follow.*

April 12. Thursday. I am pleased with the manner in which Quarles and his contemporaries speak of Nature. The utmost poetry of their expression is after all a sort of gallantry—of a knight to his lady. They do not speak as sincere lovers of Nature or as very conversant with her; but as possessing a thorough respect for her, and a good title to her acquaintance. They can speak of, and to her, well and manfully because their lips are not closed by affection. "The pale faced lady of the black-eyed light [*sic*]," says Quarles. I do not think there was in that age an unusual devotion to Nature; but she certainly held her court then, and all authors were her gentlemen and esquires then. and had always ready an abundance of courtly expressions.

Quarles is always full-mouthed; he is not often weak or shallow, though he is coarse and untasteful. He writes lines which it employs the whole tongue to utter.

He runs in conceits, as well as Herbert. He uses many able-bodied and strong-back words, which have a certain rustic fragrance and force, like countrymen come to town— as if now first devoted to literature, after having served sincere and stern purposes.

Sept. 24. Sunday. Staten Island.

The poet is he that hath fat enough, like bears and marmots, to suck his claws o' winters. He feeds on his own marrow. He hybernates in this world till spring breaks. He records a moment of pure life. Who can see these cities and say that there is any life in them? I walked through New York yesterday, and met no real and living person. I love to think of dormice and all the tribe of dormant creatures, who have such a superfluity of life, while man is pining; enveloped in thick folds of life impervious to winter. I love to think, as I walk over the snowy plain, of those happy dreamers that lie in the sod. The poet is a sort of dormouse; early in the autumn he goes into winter quarters till the sun shall fetch the year about. But most men lead a starved existence, like hawks that would fain keep on the wing and trust to pick up a sparrow now and then.

Sept. 29. Friday. I am winding up my music-box; and, as I pause, meanwhile the strains burst forth like a pent-up fountain of the middle ages. Music is strangely allied to the past. Every era has its strain. It awakens and colors my memories.

The first sparrow of spring! The year beginning with younger hope than ever. The first silvery warblings heard over the bare and dank fields, as if the last flakes of winter tinkled as they fell. What, then, are histories, chronologies, and all written revelations? Flakes of warm sunlight fall on the congealed fields. The brooks and rills sing carols and glees for the spring. The marshhawk already seeks the first stirring life that awakes. The sough of melting snow is heard in all dells, and on all the hillsides, and by the sunny river-banks; and the ice dissolves in the ponds. The earth sends forth, as it were, an inward heat; not yellow like the

sun, but green is the color of *her* flames; and the grass
flames up on the warm hillsides as her spring fire. Methinks
the sight of the first sod of fresh grass in the spring would
make the reformer reconsider his schemes; the faithless and
despairing man revive. Grass is a symbol of perpetual
growth—its blade like a long green ribbon, streaming from
the sod into the summer, checked indeed by the frost, but
anon pushing on again, lifting its last year's spear of withered
hay with the fresh life below. I have seen when early in
spring the clumps of grass stood with their three inches of
new green upholding their withered spears of the last autumn. It is as steady a growth as the rill which leaps out of
the ground—indeed it is almost identical with that; for in the
vigorous fertile days of June when the rills are dry, the
grass-blades are their only channels. And from year to year,
the herds drink this green stream, and the mower cuts
from the out-welling supply—what the several needs require.

So the human life but dies down to the surface of Nature;
but puts forth its green blade to eternity. When the ground
is completely bare of snow, and a few warm days have dried
its surface, it is pleasant to compare the faint tender signs
of the infant year, just peeping forth, with the stately beauty
of the withered vegetation which has withstood the winter.
The various thistles which have not yet sown their seeds;
the graceful reeds and rushes, whose winter is more gay
and stately than their summer, as if not till then was their
beauty ripe. I never tire of admiring their arching, drooping, and sheaflike tops. It is like summer to our winter memories, and one of the forms which art loves to perpetuate—
wild oats perchance, and Life Everlasting, whose autumn has
now arrived. These unexhausted granaries of the winter with
their seeds entertain the earliest birds.

We are obliged to respect that custom which stamps the
loaf of bread with the sheaf of wheat and the sickle. Men
have come at length, after so many centuries, to regard
these gifts properly. The gift of bread even to the poor is
perhaps better received than any other! more religiously
given and taken, and is not liable to be a stone. The manner
in which men consider husbandry is marked, and worthy of
the race. They have slowly learned thus much. Let the despairing race of men know that there is in Nature no sign
of decay, but universal uninterrupted vigor. All waste and
ruin has a speedy period. Who ever detected a wrinkle on

her brow, or a weather seam, or a gray hair on her crown, or a rent in her garment? No one sees Nature who sees her not as young and fresh, without history. We may have such intercourse with her today, as we imagine to constitute the employment of gods. We live here to have intercourse with rivers, forests, mountains—beasts and men. How few do we see conversing with these things!

We think the ancients were foolish who worshipped the sun. I would worship it forever if I had grace to do so. Observe how a New England farmer moves in the midst of Nature—his potato and grain fields; and consider how poets have dreamed that the more religious shepherd lived; and ask which was the wiser, which made the highest use of Nature? As if the Earth were made to yield pumpkins mainly! Did you ever observe that the seasons were ripening another kind of fruit?

Men have a strange taste for death who prefer to go to a museum to behold the cast-off garments of life, rather than handle the life itself. Where is the proper herbarium, the cabinet of shells, the museum of skeletons, but in the meadow where the flowers bloomed, or by the seaside where the tide cast up the fish, or on the hills where the beast laid down his life? Where the skeleton of the traveller reposes in the grass—there may it profitably be studied. What right has mortal man to parade any skeleton on its legs, when we see the gods have unloosed its sinews? what right to imitate heaven with his wires, or to stuff that body with sawdust, which Nature has decreed shall return to dust again?

All the fishes that swim in the ocean can hardly atone for the wrong done by stuffing and varnishing and encasing under glass the relics of one inhabitant of the deep. Go to Italy or Egypt if you would behold these things, where bones are the natural product of the soil which bears tombs and catacombs. Would you live in a dried specimen of a world—a pickled world? Embalming is a sin against heaven and earth—against heaven who has recalled the soul, and set free the servile elements; against earth, who is thus robbed of her dust.

I have had my right-perceiving senses so disturbed in these haunts, as for long to mistake a veritable living man, in the attitude of repose, musing, like myself, as the time and place require, for a stuffed specimen. So are men degraded in consequence.

Oct. 12. Thursday. It is hard to read a contemporary poet critically; for we go within the shallowest verse and inform it with all the life and promise of this day. We are such a near and kind and knowing audience as he will never have again. We go within the fane of the temple and hear the faint music of the worshippers; but posterity will have to stand without and consider the vast proportions and grandeur of the building. It will be solidly and conspicuously great and beautiful, for the multitudes who pass at a distance, as well as for the few pilgrims who enter into its shrine.

The poet will prevail and be popular in spite of his faults, and in spite of his beauties too; he will be careful only that you feel the hammer hit, without regarding the form of its head. No man is enough his own overseer to take cognizance of *all* the particulars which impress men in his actions. The impression will always proceed from a more general influence than he can ever dream of. We may count our steps, but we must not count our breaths. We must be careful not to mix consciousness with the vital functions.

May the gods deliver us from too critical an age—when cross-eyed, near-sighted men are born, who, instead of looking out and bathing their eyes in the deep heaven, introvert them, and think to walk erect and not to stumble by watching their feet, and not by preserving pure hearts.

Oct. 21. Saturday. I have seen such a hollow, glazed life as on a painted floor—which some couples lead; with their basement, parlor with folding doors, a few visitors' cards and the latest Annual; such life only as there is in the shells on the mantelpiece. The very children cry with less inwardness and depth than they do in the cottage. There they do not *live,* it is there they reside. There is no hearth in the centre of that house. The atmosphere of the apartments is not yet peopled with the spirits of its inhabitants; but the voices sound hollow and echo, and we see only the paint and the paper.

Oct. 24. Tuesday. Though I am old enough to have discovered that the dreams of youth are not to be realized in this state of existence, yet I think it would be the next greatest happiness always to be allowed to look under the eyelids of Time and contemplate the Perfect steadily, with the clear understanding that I do not attain to it.

Nov. 1. Wednesday. Though music agitates only a few waves of air, yet it affords an ample field for the imagination. It is a solid ground and palpitating heaven. Science distinguishes its base and its air. There are few things so evanescent and intangible as music; it is like light and heat, in physics—still mooted themes. In aesthetics music occupies the same mysterious place as light and electricity in physics. It seems vain to ask ourselves what music is. If we ponder the question, it is soon changed to, What are we? It is everything but itself. It adorns all things and remains hidden itself. It is unsuspectedly the light which colors all the landscape. It is, as it were, the most subtle ether, the most volatile gas. It is a sovereign electuary which enables us to see all things.

You must store up none of the life in your gift; it is as fatal as to husband your breath. We must *live* all our *life.*

What shall we make of the wonderful beauty of Nature, which enchants us all our youth, and is remembered till our death?—the love we bear to the least woody fibre, or earthly particle, or ray of light? Is not here the true anatomy, where we study our own elements and composition? Why should man love the sunflower, and the color of the walls and trees?

Nov. 2. Thursday. I believe that there is an ideal or real Nature, infinitely more perfect than the actual, as there is an ideal life of man; else where are the glorious summers which in vision sometimes visit my brain? When Nature ceases to be supernatural to a man, what will he do then? Of what worth is human life if its actions are no longer to have this sublime and unexplored scenery? Who will build a cottage and dwell in it with enthusiasm if not in the Elysian fields?

Nov. 4. Saturday. We must look to the West for the growth of a new literature, manners, architecture, etc. Already there is more language there, which is the growth of the soil, than here; good Greekish words there are in abundance—good because necessary and expressive; "diggings," for instance. If you analyze a Greek word you will not get anything simpler, truer, more poetical; and many others, also, which now look so ram-slang-like and colloquial when printed, another generation will cherish and affect as genuine American and standard. Read some western stump-speech, and though it be untoward and rude enough, there will not fail to be some traits of genuine eloquence, and some original and forcible statement, which will remind you of the great orators of antiquity. I am inclined to read the stump-speeches of the West already rather than the Beauties of our Atlantic orators.

Nov. 7. Tuesday. . . . . Let two stand on the highway, and it shall be known that the sun belongs to one rather than to the other; the one will be found to claim, while the other simply retains, possession. The winds blow for one more than another; and on numerous occasions the uncertain or unworthy possessors silently relinquish their right in them. The most doubtful claimants have paid their money and taken a deed of their birthright, but the real owner is forever known to all men wherever he goes, and no one disputes his claim. For he cannot help using and deriving the profit, while to the dishonest possessor an estate is as idle as his parchment deed of it, and that is all he has purchased. Wherever the owner goes, inanimate things will fly to him and adhere.

Nov. 19. Sunday. Pastoral poetry belongs to a highly civilized and refined era. It is the pasture as seen from the hall window—the shepherd of the manor. Its sheep are never actually shorn nor die of the rot. The towering, misty imagination of the poet has descended into the plain and become a lowlander, and keeps flocks and herds. Between the hunting of men and boars and the feeding of sheep is a long interval. Really the shepherd's pipe is no wax-compacted reed, but made of pipe-clay, and nothing but smoke issues from it. Nowadays the sheep take care of themselves for the most part.

The older and grander poems are characterized by the few elements which distinguish the life they describe. Man stands on the moor between the stars and the earth—shrunk to the mere bones and sinews. It is the uncompounded, everlasting life which does not depart with the flesh. The civilized and the uncivilized eras chronicle but the fluctuating condition; the summer or winter lean upon the past estate of man.

Our summer of English poesy, which, like the Greek and Latin before it, seems now well advanced toward its fall, is laden with the fruit and foliage of that season, with all the bright tints of autumn; but the winter of age will scatter its myriad clustering and shading leaves, with their autumnal tints, and leave only the desolate and fibrous boughs to sustain the snow and rime, and creak in the winter's wind.

Man simply lives out his years by the vigor of his constitution. He survives storms and the spear of his foes, and performs a few heroic deeds, and then the cairns answer questions of him. The Scandinavian is not encumbered with modern fashions, but stands free and alert, a naked warrior. Civilization does not much more than dress men. It puts rings on the fingers and watches in the side-pocket.

What do inventors invent for the naked feet and hands? They often only mend the gloves and the shoes which they wear. They make cloth of a finer texture, but they do not toughen the skin.

So when the ancient bards come to narrative and description, they describe character only, not costume, which may change. They knew how to threaten; their threats might have deterred a man. Now there are no such things as vengeance and terror.

1844

Back from Staten Island, Thoreau helped his father with the family pencil-making. He took a summer excursion with Ellery Channing, who was an eccentric offshoot of the noted Channing family. They trekked through the mountains of northwestern Massachusetts and eastern New York State. He accidentally set some of Concord's woods aflame, thereby confirming his townsmen in their low view of him. He published some miscellaneous pieces in the final volume of the Dial. *His journal during this year, like that for the year before, survives only in scattered fragments.*

Jan. 10. Sunday. I believe that no law of mechanics, which is observed and obeyed from day to day, is better established in the experience of men than this—that love never fails to be repaid in its own coin; that just as high as the waters rise in one vessel just so high they will rise in every other into which there is communication, either direct or under ground or from above the stars. Our love is, besides, some such independent fluid element in respect to our vessels, which still obeys only its own, and not our laws, by any means, without regard to the narrow limits to which we would confine it.

Nor is the least object too small for the greatest love to be bestowed upon.

1845

This was the year when Thoreau decided that he would simplify his life by loosening his bonds with civilization. In spring he built a hut close to Walden Pond and on Independence Day took possession of it. In its boxlike confines he began the most successful stint of writing he would ever do. It would cover most of this year and the next and would result in extensive drafts both of A Week on the Concord and Merrimack Rivers *and* Walden. *The journal, starting July 5, again becomes full and rich. It is filled with passages that will later appear, polished, in the two books.*

July 5. Saturday. Walden.

Yesterday I came here to live. My house makes me think of some mountain houses I have seen, which seemed to have a fresher auroral atmosphere about them, as I fancy of the halls of Olympus. I lodged at the house of a saw-miller last summer, on the Catskill Mountains, high up as Pine Orchard, in the blueberry and raspberry region, where the quiet and cleanliness and coolness seemed to be all one—which had their ambrosial character. He was the miller of the Katerskill Falls. They were a clean and wholesome family, inside and out, like their house. The latter was not plastered, only lathed, and the inner doors were not hung. The house seemed high-placed, airy, and perfumed, fit to entertain a travelling god. It was so high, indeed, that all the music, the broken strains, the waifs and accompaniments of tunes, that swept over the ridge of the Catskills, passed through its aisles. Could not man be man in such an abode? And would he ever find out this grovelling life? It was the very light and atmosphere in which the works of Grecian art were composed, and in which they rest. They have appropriated to themselves a loftier hall than mortals ever occupy, at least on a level with the mountain-brows of the world. There was wanting a little of the glare of the lower vales, and in its place a pure twilight as became the precincts of heaven. Yet so equable and calm was the season there that you could not tell whether it was morning or noon or evening. Always there was the sound of the morning cricket.

July 7. I am glad to remember tonight, as I sit by my door, that I too am at least a remote descendant of that heroic race of men of whom there is tradition. I too sit here on the shore of my Ithaca, a fellow-wanderer and survivor of Ulysses. How symbolical, significant of I know not what, the pitch pine stands here before my door! Unlike any glyph I have seen sculptured or painted yet, one of Nature's later designs, yet perfect as her Grecian art. There it is, a done tree. Who can mend it? And now where is the generation of heroes whose lives are to pass amid these our northern pines, whose exploits shall appear to posterity pictured amid these strong and shaggy forms? Shall there be only arrows and bows to go with these pines on some pipe-stone quarry at length? There is something more respectable than railroads in these simple relics of the Indian race. What hieroglyphs shall we add to the pipe-stone quarry?

1845. . . . . There is a memorable interval between the written and the spoken language, the language read and the language heard. The one is transient, a sound, a tongue, a dialect, and all men learn it of their mothers. It is loquacious, fragmentary—raw material. The other is a reserved, select, matured expression, a deliberate word addressed to the ear of nations and generations. The one is natural and convenient, the other divine and instructive. The clouds flit here below, genial, refreshing with their showers and gratifying with their tints—alternate sun and shade, a grosser heaven adapted to our trivial wants; but above them repose the blue firmament and the stars. The stars are written words and stereotyped on the blue parchment of the skies; the fickle clouds that hide them from our view, which we on this side need, though heaven does not, these are our daily colloquies, our vaporous, garrulous breath.

1845. . . . . I have carried an apple in my pocket tonight—a sopsivine, they call it—till, now that I take my handkerchief out, it has got so fine a fragrance that it really seems like a friendly trick of some pleasant demon to entertain me with. It is redolent of sweet-scented orchards, of innocent, teeming harvests. I realize the existence of a goddess Pomona, and that the gods have really intended that men should feed divinely, like themselves, on their own nectar and ambrosia. They have so painted this fruit, and freighted it with such a fragrance, that it satisfies much more than an animal appetite. Grapes, peaches, berries, nuts, etc., are likewise provided for those who will sit at their sideboard. I have felt, when partaking of this inspiring diet, that my appetite was an indifferent consideration; that eating became a sacrament, a method of communion, an ecstatic exercise, a mingling of bloods, and [a] sitting at the communion table of the world; and so have not only quenched my thirst at the spring but the health of the universe.

The indecent haste and grossness with which our food is swallowed have cast a disgrace on the very act of eating itself. But I do believe that, if this process were rightly conducted, its aspect and effects would be wholly changed, and we should receive our daily life and health, Antæus-like, with an ecstatic delight, and, with upright front, an innocent and graceful behavior, take our strength from day to day. This fragrance of the apple in my pocket has, I confess, deterred me from eating of it. I am more effectually fed by it another way.

Aug. . . . . All nature is classic and akin to art. The sumach and pine and hickory which surround my house remind me of the most graceful sculpture. Sometimes their tops, or a single limb or leaf, seems to have grown to a distinct expression as if it were a symbol for me to interpret. Poetry, painting, and sculpture claim at once and associate with themselves those perfect specimens of the art of nature—leaves, vines, acorns, pine cones, etc. The critic must at last stand as mute though contented before a true poem as before an acorn or a vine leaf. The perfect work of art is received again into the bosom of nature whence its material proceeded, and that criticism which can only detect its unnaturalness has no longer any office to fulfill. The choicest maxims that have come down to us are more beautiful or integrally wise than they are wise to our understandings. This wisdom which we are inclined to pluck from their stalk is the point only of a single association. Every natural form—palm leaves and acorns, oak leaves and sumach and dodder—are [*sic*] untranslatable aphorisms.

Aug. 23. . . . Why not live a hard and emphatic life, not to be avoided, full of adventures and work, learn much in it, travel much, though it be only in these woods? I sometimes walk across a field with unexpected expansion and long-missed content, as if there were a field worthy of me. The usual daily boundaries of life are dispersed, and I see in what field I stand.

When on my way this afternoon, Shall I go down this long hill in the rain to fish in the pond? I ask myself. And I say to myself: Yes, roam far, grasp life and conquer it, learn much and live. Your fetters are knocked off; you are really free. Stay till late in the night; be unwise and daring. See many men far and near, in their fields and cottages before the sun sets, though as if many more were to be seen. And yet each *rencontre* shall be so satisfactory and simple that no other shall seem possible. Do not repose every night as villagers do. The noble life is continuous and unintermitting. At least, live with a longer radius. Men come home at night only from the next field or street, where their household echoes haunt, and their life pines and is sickly because it breathes its own breath. Their shadows morning and evening reach farther than their daily steps. But come home from far, from ventures and perils, from enterprise and discovery and crusading, with faith and experience and character. Do not rest much. Dismiss prudence, fear, conformity. Remember only what is promised. Make the day light you, and the night hold a candle, though you be falling from heaven to earth "from morn to dewy eve a summer's day."

1845. . . . The mythologies, those vestiges of ancient poems, the world's inheritance, still reflecting some of their original hues, like the fragments of clouds tinted by the departed sun, the wreck of poems, a retrospect as [of] the loftiest fames—what survives of oldest fame—some fragment will still float into the latest summer day and ally this hour to the morning of creation. These are the materials and hints for a history of the rise and progress of the race. How from the condition of ants it arrived at the condition of men, how arts were invented gradually—let a thousand surmises shed some light on this story. We will not be confined by historical, even geological, periods, which would allow us to doubt of a progress in human events. If we rise above this wisdom for the day, we shall expect that this morning of the race, in which they have been supplied with the simplest necessaries —with corn and wine and honey and oil and fire and articulate speech and agricultural and other arts—reared up by degrees from the condition of ants to men, will be succeeded by a day of equally progressive splendor; that, in the lapse of the divine periods, other divine agents and godlike men will assist to elevate the race as much above its present condition.

1845–46. . . . It is worth the while to have lived a primitive wilderness life at some time, to know what are, after all, the necessaries of life and what methods society has taken to supply them. I have looked over the old daybooks of the merchants with the same view—to see what it was shopmen bought. They are the grossest groceries. Salt is perhaps the most important article in such a list, and most commonly bought at the stores, of articles commonly thought to be necessaries—salt, sugar, molasses, cloth, etc.—by the farmer. You will see why stores or shops exist, not to furnish tea and coffee, but salt, etc. Here's the rub, then.

I see how I could supply myself with every other article which I need, without using the shops, and to obtain this might be the fit occasion for a visit to the seashore. Yet even salt cannot strictly speaking be called a necessary of human life, since many tribes do not use it.

1846

This was another significant year. Though Thoreau spent less time at his hut than he had before, it remained the retreat where he did some of his most fruitful writing. In July he spent a night in the Concord jail because he had declined repeatedly to pay a poll tax. He was let out the next morning when someone paid it, but Thoreau never forgot the experience. It confirmed his contempt for government and fueled his lecture, and then his essay, on civil disobedience. Later in summer he traveled to Maine again, this time with a better purpose than looking for a job. He hiked through the Maine woods and found them a pleasure and an inspiration. Only a few pages of the journal survive, of which the passages below are a sample.

March 13. The song sparrow and blackbird heard today. The snow going off. The ice in the pond one foot thick.

March 26. The change from foul weather to fair, from dark, sluggish hours to serene, elastic ones, is a memorable crisis which all things proclaim. The change from foulness to serenity is instantaneous. Suddenly an influx of light, though it was late, filled my room. I looked out and saw that the pond was already calm and full of hope as on a summer evening, though the ice was dissolved but yesterday. There seemed to be some intelligence in the pond which responded to the unseen serenity in a distant horizon. I heard a robin in the distance—the first I had heard this spring— repeating the assurance. The green pitch [pine] suddenly looked brighter and more erect, as if now entirely washed and cleansed by the rain. I knew it would not rain any more. A serene summer-evening sky seemed darkly reflected in the pond, though the clear sky was nowhere visible overhead. It was no longer the end of a season, but the beginning.

The pines and shrub oaks, which had before drooped and cowered the winter through with myself, now recovered their several characters and in the landscape revived the expression of an immortal beauty. Trees seemed all at once to be fitly grouped, to sustain new relations to men and to one another. There was somewhat cosmical in the arrangement of nature. O the evening robin, at the close of a New England day! If I could ever find the twig he sits upon! . . .

1847

Thoreau finished the manuscript of the Week *to his satis-*
faction and then tried to get it published. By the time the
year ended, four firms had declined to print it without sub-
sidy. In September Thoreau tired of living in his hut and
returned to Concord. The next month Emerson sailed for
London, leaving his household in charge of Thoreau. He
again lived at the Emersons' and acted again as the universal
helper. He published an article in Graham's Magazine, *thanks*
to the efforts of the New York editor Horace Greeley,
whose interest he had aroused. He pressed ahead with his
work on Walden. *He became acquainted with the great*
Swiss naturalist Louis Agassiz, who had taken a post at
Harvard, and began to send him unusual specimens of fish
and reptiles. Again only a few dated pages of the journal
survive. The selections reprinted below come from a muti-
lated journal for the Walden period, from mid-1845 to mid-
1847; they are put under this year for convenience. Among
them are a number of Thoreau's pungent observations.

1845–47. . . . To live to a good old age such as the ancients
reached, serene and contented, dignifying the life of man,
leading a simple, epic country life in these days of confusion and turmoil—that is what Wordsworth has done. Re-
taining the tastes and the innocence of his youth. There is
more wonderful talent, but nothing so cheering and world-
famous as this.

The life of man would seem to be going all to wrack
and pieces, and no instance of permanence and the ancient natural health, notwithstanding Burns, and Coleridge,
and Carlyle. It will not do for men to die young; the greatest
genius does not die young. Whom the gods love most do
indeed die young, but not till their life is matured, and their

years are like those of the oak, for they are the products
half of nature and half of God. What should nature do
without old men, not children but men?

The life of men, not to become a mockery and a jest,
should last a respectable term of years. We cannot spare
the age of those old Greek Philosophers. They live long
who do not live for a near end, who still forever look to
the immeasurable future for their manhood.

1845–47. . . . From all points of the compass, from the
earth beneath and the heavens above, have come these in-
spirations and been entered duly in the order of their arrival
in the journal. Thereafter, when the time arrived, they were
winnowed into lectures, and again, in due time, from lectures into essays. And at last they stand, like the cubes
of Pythagoras, firmly on either basis; like statues on their
pedestals, but the statues rarely take hold of hands. There is
only such connection and series as is attainable in the galleries. And this affects their immediate practical and popular influence.

1845–47. . . . King James loved his old shoes best. Who
does not? Indeed these new clothes are often won and worn
only after a most painful birth. At first movable prisons,
oyster-shells which the tide only raises, opens, and shuts,
washing in what scanty nutriment may be afloat. How many
men walk over the limits, carrying their limits with them?
In the stocks they stand, not without gaze of multitudes,
only without rotten eggs, in torturing boots, the last wedge
but one driven. Why should we be startled at death? Life
is constant putting off of the mortal coil—coat, cuticle,
flesh and bones, all old clothes.

1845–47. . . . Moles nesting in your cellar and nibbling
every third potato. A whole rabbit-warren only separated from
you by the flooring. To be saluted when you stir in the dawn
by the hasty departure of Monsieur—thump, thump, thump,
striking his head against the floor-timbers. Squirrels and
field mice that hold to a community of property in your
stock of chestnuts.

The blue jays suffered few chestnuts to reach the ground,
resorting to your single tree in flocks in the early morning,
and picking them out of the burs at a great advantage.

The crop of blackberries small; berries not yet grown.
Ground-nuts not dug.

1845–47. . . . Bread I made pretty well for a while, while I remembered the rules; for I studied this out methodically, going clear back to the primitive days and first invention of the unleavened kind, and coming gradually down through that lucky accidental souring of the dough which taught men the leavening process, and all the various fermentations thereafter, till you get to "good, sweet, wholesome bread," the staff of life. I went on very well mixing rye and flour and Indian and potato with success, till one morning I had forgotten the rules, and thereafter scalded the yeast—killed it out—and so, after the lapse of a month, was glad after all to learn that such palatable staff of life could be made out of the dead and scalt creature and risings that lay flat.

1845–47. . . . The way to compare men is to compare their respective ideals. The actual man is too complex to deal with.

Carlyle is an earnest, honest, heroic worker as literary man and sympathizing brother of his race.

Idealize a man, and your notion takes distinctness at once.

Carlyle's talent is perhaps quite equal to his genius.

Striving [?] to live in reality—not a general critic, philosopher, or poet.

Wordsworth, with very feeble talent, has not so great and admirable as unquestionable and persevering genius.

Heroism, heroism is his word—his thing.

He would realize a brave and adequate human life, and die hopefully at last.

Emerson again is a critic, poet, philosopher, with talent not so conspicuous, not so adequate to his task; but his field is still higher, his task more arduous. Lives a far more intense life; seeks to realize a divine life; his affections and intellect equally developed. Has advanced farther, and a new heaven opens to him. Love and Friendship, Religion, Poetry, the Holy are familiar to him. The life of an Artist; more variegated, more observing, finer perception; not so robust, elastic; practical enough in his own field; faithful, a judge of men. There is no such general critic of men and things, no such trustworthy and faithful man. More of the divine realized in him than in any. A poetic critic, reserving the unqualified nouns for the gods.

1845–47. . . . How many an afternoon has been stolen from more profitable, if not more attractive, industry—afternoons when a good run of custom might have been expected on the main street, such as tempt the ladies out a-shopping—spent, I say, by me away in the meadows, in the well-nigh hopeless attempt to set the river on fire or be set on fire by it, with such tinder as I had, with such flint as I was. Trying at least to make it flow with milk and honey, as I had heard of, or liquid gold, and drown myself without getting wet—a laudable enterprise, though I have not much to show for it.

So many autumn days spent outside the town, trying to hear what was in the wind, to hear it and carry it express. I well-nigh sunk all my capital in it, and lost my own breath into the bargain, by running in the face of it. Depend upon it, if it had concerned either of the parties, it would have appeared in the yeoman's gazette, the *Freeman,* with other earliest intelligence.

For many years I was self-appointed inspector of snow-storms and rain-storms, and did my duty faithfully, though I never received one cent for it.

Surveyor, if not of higher ways, then of forest paths and all across-lot routes, keeping many open ravines bridged and passable at all seasons, where the public heel had testified to the importance of the same, all not only without charge, but even at considerable risk and inconvenience. Many a mower would have forborne to complain had he been aware of the invisible public good that was in jeopardy.

1848

It was a mixed year. At the end of July Thoreau came home from the Emersons', Emerson himself having returned from Europe. Though he worked a little in the family business he still failed to find it to his taste. He liked surveying better and took steps to drum up clients; he even had an advertising handbill printed. The major literary event of his year was the publication in the Union Magazine, under the title of "Ktaadn and the Maine Woods," of five excerpts from his writing on his outdoor experience in Maine. He lectured early and late—in January before the Concord Lyceum on the idea of civil disobedience and in November at Salem about some of his experiences during his Walden sojourn. He acquired a devoted admirer in H. G. O. Blake of Worcester, to whom he thereafter addressed many highflown letters. Nothing of the journal remains for us to see.

1849

Improved by Thoreau after its initial rejections, the Week *appeared on May 30. James Munroe & Co. published it with the help of a guarantee from Thoreau. Though the book received some respectful attention it was a commercial failure. It cost Thoreau $290 and earned him $15. Ironically, the pencil and graphite business grew better but Thoreau begrudged the time it took. "Civil Disobedience" appeared in May also, in a short-lived magazine called* Aesthetic Papers, *under the title of "Resistance to Civil Government." Other events of the year included the death of his sister Helen and his first excursion to Cape Cod. He lectured four times. So far as his journalizing is concerned this is the last of the years that are missing in whole or part. Soon there will be such abundance that we will hardly know how to pick and choose.*

1850

Thoreau made his second visit to Cape Cod and, along with Ellery Channing, his first and most important excursion to Canada. He surveyed, lectured (five times in all), and wrote. He went to Fire Island to look for the body of Margaret Fuller, drowned when her ship foundered within sight of shore. In his journal he wrote up his visit to Canada and then probably cut the pages out and used them as the basis for what ultimately became A Yankee in Canada, *issued in book form after his death. Men and birds, crickets and cows, find their way onto the pages of the journal. The description of nature is increasingly exact and detailed; the speculations about life diminish.*

June 4. . . . Today, June fourth, I have been tending a burning in the woods. Ray was there. It is a pleasant fact that you will know no man long, however low in the social scale, however poor, miserable, intemperate, and worthless he may appear to be, a mere burden to society, but you will find at last that there is something which he understands and can do better than any other. I was pleased to hear that one man had sent Ray as the one who had had the most experience in setting fires of any man in Lincoln. He had experience and skill as a burner of brush.

You must burn against the wind always, and burn slowly. When the fire breaks over the hoed line, a little system and perseverance will accomplish more toward quelling it than any man would believe. It fortunately happens that the experience acquired is oftentimes worth more than the wages. When a fire breaks out in the woods, and a man fights it too near and on the side, in the heat of the moment, without the systematic cooperation of others, he is disposed to think it a desperate case, and that this relentless fiend will

95

run through the forest till it is glutted with food; but let the company rest from their labors a moment, and then proceed more deliberately and systematically, giving the fire a wider berth, and the company will be astonished to find how soon and easily they will subdue it. The woods themselves furnish one of the best weapons with which to contend with the fires that destroy them—a pitch pine bough. It is the best instrument to thrash it with. There are few men who do not love better to give advice than to give assistance.

However large the fire, let a few men go to work deliberately but perseveringly to rake away the leaves and hoe off the surface of the ground at a convenient distance from the fire, while others follow with pine boughs to thrash it with when it reaches the line, and they will finally get round it and subdue it, and will be astonished at their own success.

A man who is about to burn his field in the midst of woods should rake off the leaves and twigs for the breadth of a rod at least, making no large heaps near the outside, and then plow around it several furrows and break them up with hoes, and set his fire early in the morning, before the wind rises.

As I was fighting the fire today, in the midst of the roaring and crackling—for the fire seems to snort like a wild horse—I heard from time to time the dying strain, the last sigh, the fine, clear, shrill scream of agony, as it were, of the trees breathing their last, probably the heated air or the steam escaping from some chink. At first I thought it was some bird, or a dying squirrel's note of anguish, or steam escaping from the tree. You sometimes hear it on a small scale in the log on the hearth. When a field is burned over, the squirrels probably go into the ground. How foreign is the yellow pine to the green woods—and what business has it here?

The fire stopped within a few inches of a partridge's nest today, June fourth, whom we took off in our hands and found thirteen creamy-colored eggs. I started up a woodcock when I went to a rill to drink, at the westernmost angle of R. W. E.'s wood-lot.

June 5. . . . Tonight, June fifth, after a hot day, I hear the first peculiar summer breathing of the frogs.

When all is calm, a small whirlwind will suddenly lift up the blazing leaves and let them fall beyond the line, and set all the woods in a blaze in a moment. Or some slight almost invisible cinder, seed of fire, will be wafted from the burnt district on to the dry turf which covers the surface and fills the crevices of many rocks, and there it will catch as in tinder, and smoke and smoulder, perchance, for half an hour, heating several square yards of ground where yet no fire is visible, until it spreads to the leaves and the wind fans it into a blaze.

Men go to a fire for entertainment. When I see how eagerly men will run to a fire, whether in warm or in cold weather, by day or by night, dragging an engine at their heels, I am astonished to perceive how good a purpose the love of excitement is made to serve. What other force, pray, what offered pay, what disinterested neighborliness could ever effect so much? No, these are boys who are to be dealt with, and these are the motives that prevail. There is no old man or woman dropping into the grave but covets excitement.

Nov. 8. The stillness of the woods and fields is remarkable at this season of the year. There is not even the creak of a cricket to be heard. Of myriads of dry shrub oak leaves, not one rustles. Your own breath can rustle them, yet the breath of heaven does not suffice to. The trees have the aspect of waiting for winter. The autumnal leaves have lost their color; they are now truly sere, dead, and the woods wear a sombre color. Summer and harvest are over. The hickories, birches, chestnuts, no less than the maples, have lost their leaves. The sprouts, which had shot up so vigorously to repair the damage which the choppers had done, have stopped short for the winter. Everything stands silent and expectant. If I listen, I hear only the note of a chickadee —our most common and I may say native bird, most identified with our forests—or perchance the scream of a jay, or perchance from the solemn depths of these woods I hear tolling far away the knell of one departed. Thought rushes in to fill the vacuum. As you walk, however, the partridge still bursts away. The silent, dry, almost leafless, certainly fruitless woods. You wonder what cheer that bird can find in them. The partridge bursts away from the foot of a shrub oak like its own dry fruit, immortal bird! This sound still startles us. Dry goldenrods, now turned gray and white, lint our clothes as we walk. And the drooping, downy seedvessels of the epilobium remind us of the summer. Perchance you will meet with a few solitary asters in the dry fields, with a little color left. The sumach is stripped of everything but its cone of red berries.

Nov. 19. The first really cold day. I find, on breaking off a shrub oak leaf, a little life at the foot of the leaf-stalk, so that a part of the green comes off. It has not died quite down to the point of separation, as it will do, I suppose, before spring. Most of the oaks have lost their leaves except on the lower branches, as if they were less exposed and less mature there, and felt the changes of the seasons less. The leaves have either fallen or withered long since, yet I found this afternoon, cold as it is—and there has been snow in the neighborhood—some sprouts which had come up this year from the stump of a young black-looking oak, covered still with handsome fresh red and green leaves, very large and unwithered and unwilted. It was on the south side of Fair Haven in a warm angle, where the wood was cut last winter and the exposed edge of the still standing wood running north and south met the cliff at right angles and served for a fence to keep off the wind. There were one or two stumps here whose sprouts had fresh leaves which transported me back to October. Yet the surrounding shrub oak leaves were as dry and dead as usual. There were also some minute birches only a year old, their leaves still freshly yellow, and some young wild apple trees apparently still growing, their leaves as green and tender as in summer. The goldenrods, one or more species of the white and some yellow ones, were many of them still quite fresh, though elsewhere they are all whitish and dry. I saw one whose top rose above the edge of a rock, and so much of it was turned white and dry; but the lower part of its raceme was still yellow. Some of the white species seemed to have started again as if for another spring. They had sprung up freshly a foot or more, and were budded to blossom, fresh and green. And sometimes on the same stem were old and dry and white downy flowers, and fresh green blossom-buds not yet expanded. I saw there some *pale* blue asters still bright, and the mullein leaves still large and green, one green to its top. And I discovered that when I put my hand on the mullein leaves they felt decidedly warm, but the radical leaves of the goldenrods felt cold and clammy. There was also the columbine, its leaves still alive and green; and I was pleased to smell the pennyroyal which I had bruised, though this dried up long ago. Each season is thus drawn out and lingers in certain localities, as the birds and insects know very well. If you penetrate to some warm recess under a cliff in the woods, you will be astonished at the amount of summer life that still flourishes there. No doubt more of the summer's life than we are aware thus slips by and outmaneuvers the winter, gliding from fence to fence. I have no doubt that a diligent search in proper places would discover many more of our summer flowers thus lingering till the snow came, than we suspect. It is as if the plant made no preparation for winter.

Now that the grass is withered and the leaves are withered or fallen, it begins to appear what is evergreen: the partridge [-berry] and checkerberry, and wintergreen leaves even, are more conspicuous.

The old leaves have been off the pines now for a month.

I once found a kernel of corn in the middle of a deep wood by Walden, tucked in behind a lichen on a pine, about as high as my head, either by a crow or a squirrel. It was a mile at least from any corn field.

Several species plainly linger till the snow comes.

Nov. 20. It is a common saying among country people that if you eat much fried hasty pudding it will make your hair curl. My experience, which was considerable, did not confirm this assertion.

Nov. 24. Plucked a buttercup on Bear Hill today.

I have certain friends whom I visit occasionally, but I commonly part from them early with a certain bitter-sweet sentiment. That which we love is so mixed and entangled with that we hate in one another that we are more grieved and disappointed, aye, and estranged from one another, by meeting than by absence. Some men may be my acquaintances merely, but one whom I have been accustomed to regard, to idealize, to have dreams about as a friend, and mix up intimately with myself, can never degenerate into an acquaintance. I must know him on that higher ground or not know him at all. We do not confess and explain, because we would fain be so intimately related as to understand each other without speech. Our friend must be broad. His must be an atmosphere coextensive with the universe, in which we can expand and breathe. For the most part we are smothered and stifled by one another. I go and see my friend and try his atmosphere. If our atmospheres do not mingle, if we repel each other strongly, it is of no use to stay.

Nov. 28. . . . It is remarkable, but nevertheless true, as far as my observation goes, that women, to whom we commonly concede a somewhat finer and more sibylline nature, yield a more implicit obedience even to their animal instincts than men. The nature in them is stronger, the reason weaker. There are, for instance, many young and middle-aged men among my acquaintance—shoemakers, carpenters, farmers, and others—who have scruples about using animal food, but comparatively few girls or women. The latter, even the most refined, are the most intolerant of such reforms. I think that the reformer of the severest, as well as finest, class will find more sympathy in the intellect and philosophy of man than in the refinement and delicacy of woman. It is, perchance, a part of woman's conformity and easy nature. Her savior must not be too strong, stern, and intellectual, but charitable above all things.

Dec. 1. It is quite mild and pleasant today. I saw a little green hemisphere of moss which looked as if it covered a stone, but, thrusting my cane into it, I found it was nothing but moss, about fifteen inches in diameter and eight or nine inches high. When I broke it up, it appeared as if the annual growth was marked by successive layers half an inch deep each. The lower ones were quite rotten, but the present year's quite green, the intermediate white. I counted fifteen or eighteen. It was quite solid, and I saw that it continued solid as it grew by branching occasionally, just enough to fill the newly gained space, and the tender extremities of each plant, crowded close together, made the firm and compact surface of the bed. There was a darker line separating the growths, where I thought the surface had been exposed to the winter. It was quite saturated with water, though firm and solid.

Dec. 2. The woodpeckers' holes in the apple trees are about a fifth of an inch deep or just through the bark and half an inch apart. They must be the decaying trees that are most frequented by them, and probably their work serves to relieve and ventilate the tree and, as well, to destroy its enemies.

The barberries are shrivelled and dried. I find yet cranberries hard and not touched by the frost.

1851

Thoreau lectured about Cape Cod, about Walden, and about "The Wild." Never a popular lecturer, he nevertheless continued to receive an occasional invitation. The year was marked by no publications, but there was a gratifying amount of writing, much of it apparently preserved in the journal.

Jan. 2. Saw at Clinton last night a room at the gingham mills which covers one and seven-eighths acres and contains 578 looms, not to speak of spindles, both throttle and mule. The rooms all together cover three acres. They were using between three and four hundred horsepower, and kept an engine of two hundred horsepower, with a wheel twenty-three feet in diameter and a band ready to supply deficiencies, which have not often occurred. Some portion of the machinery—I think it was where the cotton was broken up, lightened up, and mixed before being matted together—revolved eighteen hundred times in a minute.

I first saw the pattern room where patterns are made by a hand loom. There were two styles of warps ready for the woof or filling. The operator must count the threads of the woof, which in the mill is done by the machinery. It was the ancient art of weaving, the shuttle flying back and forth, putting in the filling. As long as the warp is the same, it is but one "style," so called.

The cotton should possess a long staple and be clean and free from seed. The Sea Island cotton has a long staple and is valuable for thread. Many bales are thoroughly mixed to make the goods of one quality. The cotton is then torn to pieces and thoroughly lightened up by cylinders armed with hooks and by fans; then spread, a certain weight on a square yard, and matted together, and torn up and matted together again two or three times over; then the matted cotton fed to a cylindrical card, a very thin web of it, which is gathered into a copper trough, making six (the six-card machines) flat, rope-like bands, which are united into one at the railway head and drawn. And this operation of uniting and drawing or stretching goes on from one machine to another until the thread is spun, which is then dyed (calico is printed after being woven)—having been wound off on to reels and so made into skeins—dyed and dried by steam; then, by machinery, wound on to spools for the warp and the woof. From a great many spools the warp is drawn off over cylinders and different-colored threads properly mixed and arranged. Then the ends of the warp are drawn through the harness of the loom by hand. The operator knows the succession of red, blue, green, etc., threads, having the numbers given her, and draws them through the harness accordingly, keeping count. Then the woof is put in, or it is *woven!!* Then the inequalities or nubs are picked off by girls. If *they* discover any imperfection, they tag it, and if necessary the wages of the weaver are reduced. Now, I think, it is passed over a red-hot iron cylinder, and the fuzz singed off, then washed with wheels with cold water; then the water forced out by centrifugal force within horizontal wheels. Then it is starched, the ends stitched together by machinery; then stretched smooth, dried, and ironed by machinery; then measured, folded, and packed.

This the agent, Forbes, says is the best gingham mill in this country. The goods are better than the imported. The English have even stolen their name Lancaster Mills, calling them "Lancasterian."

The machinery is some of it peculiar, part of the throttle spindles (?) for instance.

The coach-lace mill, only place in this country where it is made by machinery; made of thread of different materials, as cotton, worsted, linen, as well as colors, the raised figure produced by needles inserted woof fashion. Well worth examining further. Also pantaloon stuffs made in same mill and dyed after being woven, the woolen not taking the same dye with the cotton; hence a slight parti-colored appearance. These goods are sheared, i.e. a part of the nap taken off, making them smoother. Pressed between pasteboards.

The Brussels carpets made at the carpet factory said to be the best in the world. Made like coach lace, only wider.

Erastus (?) Bigelow inventor of what is new in the above

machinery; and, with his brother and another, owner of the carpet factory.

I am struck by the fact that no work has been shirked when a piece of cloth is produced. Every thread has been counted in the finest web; it has not been matted together. The operator has succeeded only by patience, perseverance, and fidelity.

Jan. 7. . . . Science does not embody all that men know, only what is for men of science. The woodman tells me how he caught trout in a box trap, how he made his trough for maple sap of pine logs, and the spouts of sumach or white ash, which have a large pith. He can relate his facts to human life.

The knowledge of an unlearned man is living and luxuriant like a forest, but covered with mosses and lichens and for the most part inaccessible and going to waste; the knowledge of the man of science is like timber collected in yards for public works, which still supports a green sprout here and there, but even this is liable to dry rot.

I felt my spirits rise when I had got off the road into the open fields, and the sky had a new appearance. I stepped along more buoyantly. There was a warm sunset over the wooded valleys, a yellowish tinge on the pines. Reddish dun-colored clouds like dusky flames stood over it. And then streaks of blue sky were seen here and there. The life, the joy, that is in blue sky after a storm! There is no account of the blue sky in history. Before I walked in the ruts of travel; now I adventured. This evening a fog comes up from the south.

Feb. 9. The last half of January was warm and thawy. The swift streams were open, and the muskrats were seen swimming and diving and bringing up clams, leaving their shells on the ice. We had now forgotten summer and autumn, but had already begun to anticipate spring. Fishermen improved the warmer weather to fish for pickerel through the ice. Before it was only the autumn landscape with a thin layer of snow upon it; we saw the withered flowers through it; but now we do not think of autumn when we look on this snow. That earth is effectually buried. It is midwinter. Within a few days the cold has set in stronger than ever, though the days are much longer now. Now I travel across the fields on the crust which has frozen since the January thaw, and I can cross the river in most places. It is easier to get about the country than at any other season—easier than in summer, because the rivers and meadows are frozen and there is no high grass or other crops to be avoided; easier than in December before the crust was frozen.

I have heard that there is a Society for the Diffusion of Useful Knowledge. It is said that knowledge is power and the like. Methinks there is equal need of a Society for the Diffusion of Useful Ignorance, for what is most of our boasted so-called knowledge but a conceit that we know something, which robs us of the advantages of our actual ignorance.

For a man's ignorance sometimes is not only useful but beautiful, while his knowledge is oftentimes worse than useless, beside being ugly. In reference to important things, whose knowledge amounts to more than a consciousness of his ignorance? Yet what more refreshing and inspiring knowledge than this?

How often are we wise as serpents without being harmless as doves!

Feb. 16. Do we call this the land of the free? What is it to be free from King George the Fourth and continue the slaves of prejudice? What is it [to] be born free and equal, and not to live? What is the value of any political freedom, but as a means to moral freedom? Is it a freedom to be slaves or a freedom to be free, of which we boast? We are a nation of politicians, concerned about the outsides of freedom, the means and outmost defenses of freedom. It is our children's children who may perchance be essentially free. We tax ourselves unjustly. There is a part of us which is not represented. It is taxation without representation. We quarter troops upon ourselves. In respect to virtue or true manhood, we are essentially provincial, not metropolitan—mere Jonathans. We are provincial, because we do not find at home our standards; because we do not worship truth but the reflection of truth; because we are absorbed in and narrowed by trade and commerce and agriculture, which are but means and not the end. We are essentially provincial, I say, and so is the English Parliament. Mere country bumpkins they betray themselves, when any more important question arises for them to settle. Their natures are subdued to what they work in!

April. . . . When I read the account of the carrying back
of the fugitive into slavery, which was read last Sunday
evening, and read also what was not read here, that the
man who made the prayer on the wharf was Daniel Foster
of *Concord,* I could not help feeling a slight degree of pride
because, of all the towns in the Commonwealth, Concord
was the only one distinctly named as being represented in
that new tea-party, and, as she had a place in the first, so
would have a place in this, the last and perhaps next most
important chapter of the History of Massachusetts. But my
second feeling, when I reflected how short a time that gentleman has resided in this town, was one of doubt and shame,
because the *men* of Concord in recent times have done
nothing to entitle them to the honor of having their town
named in such a connection.

I hear a good deal said about trampling this law under
foot. Why, one need not go out of his way to do that. This
law lies not at the level of the head or the reason. Its natural
habitat is in the dirt. It was bred and has its life only in
the dust and mire, on a level with the feet; and he who
walks with freedom, unless, with a sort of quibbling and
Hindu mercy, he avoids treading on every venomous reptile,
will inevitably tread on it, and so trample it under foot.

It has come to this, that the friends of liberty, the friends
of the slave, have shuddered when they have understood
that his fate has been left to the legal tribunals, so-called,
of the country to be decided. The people have no faith that
justice will be awarded in such a case. The judge may de-
cide this way or that; it is a kind of accident at best. It is
evident that he is not a competent authority in so important
a case. I would not trust the life of my friend to the judges
of all the Supreme Courts in the world put together, to be
sacrificed or saved by precedent. I would much rather trust
to the sentiment of the people, which would itself be a
precedent to posterity. In their vote you would get something
worth having at any rate, but in the other case only the
trammelled judgment of an individual, of no significance,
be it which way it will.

April. . . . As for measures to be adopted, among others
I would advise abolitionists to make as earnest and vigorous
and persevering an assault on the press, as they have already made, and with effect too, on the church. The church
has decidedly improved within a year or two, aye, even

within a fortnight; but the press is, almost without exception, corrupt. I believe that in this country the press exerts a greater and a more pernicious influence than the church. We are not a religious people, but we are a nation of politicians. We do not much care for, we do not read, the Bible, but we do care for and we do read the newspaper. It is a bible which we read every morning and every afternoon, standing and sitting, riding and walking. It is a bible which every man carries in his pocket, which lies on every table and counter, which the mail and thousands of missionaries are continually dispersing. It is the only book which America has printed, and is capable of exerting an almost inconceivable influence for good or for bad. The editor is [a] preacher whom you voluntarily support. Your tax is commonly one cent, and it costs nothing for pew hire. But how many of these preachers preach the truth? I repeat the testimony of many an intelligent traveller, as well as my own convictions, when I say that probably no country was ever ruled by so mean a class of tyrants as are the editors of the periodical press in *this* country.

April 30. . . . I observe that the *New York Herald* advertises situations wanted by "respectable young women" by the column, but never by respectable young men, rather "intelligent" and "smart" ones; from which I infer that the public opinion of New York does not require young men to be respectable in the same sense in which it requires young women to be so.

May 1. . . . In regard to purity, I do not know whether I am much worse or better than my acquaintances. If I confine my thought to myself, I appear, whether by constitution or by education, irrevocably impure, as if I should be shunned by my fellow-men if they knew me better, as if I were of two inconsistent natures; but again, when I observe how the mass of men speak of woman and of chastity —with how little love and reverence—I feel that so far I am unaccountably better than they. I think that none of my acquaintances has a greater love and admiration for chastity than I have. Perhaps it is necessary that one should actually stand low himself in order to reverence what is high in others.

All distant landscapes seen from hilltops are veritable pictures, which will be found to have no actual existence to him who travels to them. " 'Tis distance lends enchantment to the view." It is the bare landscape without this depth of atmosphere to glass it. The distant river-reach seen in the north from the Lincoln Hill, high in the horizon, like the ocean stream flowing round Homer's shield, the rippling waves reflecting the light, is unlike the same seen near at hand. Heaven intervenes between me and the object. By what license do I call it Concord River. It redeems the character of rivers to see them thus. They were worthy then of a place on Homer's shield.

As I looked today from Mt. Tabor in Lincoln to the Waltham hill, I saw the same deceptive slope, the near hill melting into the further inseparably, indistinguishably; it was one gradual slope from the base of the near hill to the summit of the further one, a succession of copse-woods, but I knew that there intervened a valley two or three miles wide, studded with houses and orchards and drained by a considerable stream. When the shadow of a cloud passed over the nearer hill, I could distinguish its shaded summit against the side of the other.

May 12. . . . If I have got false teeth, I trust that I have not got a false conscience. It is safer to employ the dentist than the priest to repair the deficiencies of nature.

By taking the ether the other day I was convinced how far asunder a man could be separated from his senses. You are told that it will make you unconscious, but no one can imagine what it is to be unconscious—how far removed from the state of consciousness and all that we call "this world"—until he has experienced it. The value of the experiment is that it does give you experience of an interval as between one life and another—a greater space than you ever travelled. You are a sane mind without organs—groping for organs—which if it did not soon recover its old senses would get new ones. You expand like a seed in the ground. You exist in your roots, like a tree in the winter. If you have an inclination to travel, take the ether; you go beyond the furthest star.

It is not necessary for them to take ether, who in their sane and waking hours are ever translated by a thought; nor for them to see with their hindheads, who sometimes see from their foreheads; nor listen to the spiritual knockings, who attend to the intimations of reason and conscience.

May 24. Saturday. Our most glorious experiences are a kind of regret. Our regret is so sublime that we may mistake it for triumph. It is the painful, plaintively sad surprise of our Genius remembering our past lives and contemplating what is possible. It is remarkable that men commonly never refer to, never hint at, any crowning experiences when the common laws of their being were unsettled and the divine and eternal laws prevailed in them. Their lives are not revolutionary; they never recognize any other than the local and temporal authorities. It is a regret so divine and inspiring, so genuine, based on so true and distinct a contrast, that it surpasses our proudest boasts and the fairest expectations.

My most sacred and memorable life is commonly on awaking in the morning. I frequently awake with an atmosphere about me as if my unremembered dreams had been divine, as if my spirit had journeyed to its native place, and, in the act of reentering its native body, had diffused an elysian fragrance around.

June 7. My practicalness is not to be trusted to the last. To be sure, I go upon my legs for the most part, but, being hard-pushed and dogged by a superficial common sense which is bound to near objects by beaten paths, I am off the handle, as the phrase is—I begin to be transcendental and show where my heart is. I am like those guinea-fowl which Charles Darwin saw at the Cape de Verd Islands. He says, "They avoided us like partridges on a rainy day in September, running with their heads cocked up; and if pursued, they readily took to the wing." Keep your distance, do not infringe on the interval between us, and I will pick up lime and lay real terrestrial eggs for you, and let you know by cackling when I have done it.

When I have been asked to speak at a temperance meeting, my answer has been, "I am too transcendental to serve you in your way." They would fain confine me to the rumsellers and rum-drinkers, of whom I am not one, and whom I know little about.

It is a certain fairyland where we live. You may walk out in any direction over the earth's surface, lifting your horizon, and everywhere your path, climbing the convexity of the globe, leads you between heaven and earth, not away from the light of the sun and stars and the habitations of men. I wonder that I ever get five miles on my way, the walk is so crowded with events and phenomena. How many questions there are which I have not put to the inhabitants!

One of those gentle, straight-down rainy days, when the rain begins by spotting the cultivated fields as if shaken from a pepper-box; a fishing day, when I see one neighbor after another, having donned his oil-cloth suit, walking or riding past with a fish-pole, having struck work—a day and an employment to make philosophers of them all.

June 11. . . . The woodland paths are never seen to such advantage as in a moonlight night, so embowered, still opening before you almost against expectation as you walk; you are so completely in the woods, and yet your feet meet no obstacles. It is as if it were not a path, but an open, winding passage through the bushes, which your feet find.

Now I go by the spring, and when I have risen to the same level as before, find myself in the warm stratum again.

The woods are about as destitute of inhabitants at night as the streets. In both there will be some nightwalkers. There are but few wild creatures to seek their prey. The greater part of its inhabitants have retired to rest.

Ah, that life that I have known! How hard it is to remember what is most memorable! We remember how we itched, not how our hearts beat. I can sometimes recall to mind the quality, the immortality, of my youthful life, but in memory is the only relation to it.

The very cows have now left their pastures and are driven home to their yards. I meet no creature in the fields.

I hear the night-warbler breaking out as in his dreams, made so from the first for some mysterious reason.

Our spiritual side takes a more distinct form, like our shadow which we see accompanying us.

I do not know but I feel less vigor at night, my legs will not carry me so far; as if the night were less favorable to muscular exertion—weakened us, somewhat as darkness turns plants pale. But perhaps my experience is to be referred to being already exhausted by the day, and I have never tried the experiment fairly. Yet sometimes after a hard day's work I have found myself unexpectedly vigorous. It was so hot summer before last that the Irish laborers on the railroad worked by night instead of day for a while, several of them having been killed by the heat and cold water. I do not know but they did as much work as ever by day. Yet me-thinks Nature would not smile on such labors.

Only the Hunter's and Harvest moons are famous, but I think that each full moon deserves to be and has its own character well marked. One might be called the Midsummer-Night Moon.

The wind and water are still awake. At night you are sure to hear what wind there is stirring. The wind blows, the river flows, without resting. There lies Fair Haven Lake, undistinguishable from fallen sky. The pines seem forever foreign, at least to the civilized man—not only their aspect but their scent, and their turpentine.

So still and moderate is the night! No scream is heard, whether of fear or joy. No great comedy nor tragedy is being enacted. The chirping of crickets is the most universal, if not the loudest, sound. There is no French Revolution in Nature, no excess. She is warmer or colder by a degree or two.

By night no flowers, at least no variety of colors. The pinks are no longer pink; they only shine faintly, reflecting more light. Instead of flowers underfoot, stars overhead.

My shadow has the distinctness of a second person, a certain black companion bordering on the imp, and I ask, "Who is this?" which I see dodging behind me as I am about to sit down on a rock.

No one, to my knowledge, has observed the minute differences in the seasons. Hardly two nights are alike. The rocks do not feel warm tonight, for the air is warmest; nor does the sand particularly. A book of the seasons, each page of which should be written in its own season and out-of-doors, or in its own locality wherever it may be.

When you get into the road, though far from the town, and feel the sand under your feet, it is as if you had reached your own gravel walk. You no longer hear the whippoorwill, nor regard your shadow, for here you expect a fellow-traveller. You catch yourself walking merely. The road leads your steps and thoughts alike to the town. You see only the path, and your thoughts wander from the objects which are presented to your senses. You are no longer in place. It is like conformity—walking in the ways of men.

June 13. Walked to Walden last night (moon not quite full) by railroad and upland wood-path, returning by Wayland road. Last full moon the elms had not leaved out—cast no heavy shadows—and their outlines were less striking and rich in the streets at night.

I noticed night before night before last from Fair Haven how valuable was some water by moonlight, like the river and Fair Haven Pond, though far away, reflecting the light with a faint glimmering sheen, as in the spring of the year. The water shines with an inward light like a heaven on earth. The silent depth and serenity and majesty of water! Strange that men should distinguish gold and diamonds, when these precious elements are so common. I saw a distant river by moonlight, making no noise, yet flowing, as by day, still to the sea, like melted silver reflecting the moonlight. Far away it lay encircling the earth. How far away it may look in the night, and even from a low hill how miles away down in the valley! As far off as paradise and the delectable country! There is a certain glory attends on water by night. By it the heavens are related to the earth, undistinguishable from a sky beneath you. And I forgot to say that after I reached the road by Potter's bars—or further, by Potter's Brook—I saw the moon suddenly reflected full from a pool. A puddle from which you may see the moon reflected, and the earth dissolved under your feet. The magical moon with attendant stars suddenly looking up with mild lustre from a window in the dark earth.

I observed also the same night a halo about my shadow in the moonlight, which I referred to the accidentally lighter color of the surrounding surface; I transferred my shadow to the darkest patches of grass, and saw the halo there equally. It serves to make the outlines of the shadow more distinct.

But now for last night. A few fireflies in the meadow. Do they shine, though invisibly, by day? Is their candle lighted by day? It is not nightfall till the whippoorwills begin to sing.

As I entered the Deep Cut, I was affected by beholding the first faint reflection of genuine and unmixed moonlight on the eastern sand-bank while the horizon, yet red with day, was tingeing the western side. What an interval between those two lights! The light of the moon—in what age of the world does that fall upon the earth? The moonlight was as the earliest and dewy morning light, and the daylight tinge reminded me much more of the night. There were the old and new dynasties opposed, contrasted, and an interval between, which time could not span. Then is night, when the daylight yields to the nightlight. It suggested an interval, a distance not recognized in history. Nations have flourished in that light.

When I had climbed the sand-bank on the left, I felt the warmer current or stratum of air on my cheek, like a blast from a furnace.

The white stems of the pines, which reflected the weak light, standing thick and close together while their lower branches were gone, reminded me that the pines are only larger grasses which rise to a chaffy head, and we the insects that crawl between them. They are particularly grass-like.

June 22. . . . My pulse must beat with Nature. After a hard day's work without a thought, turning my very brain into a mere tool, only in the quiet of evening do I so far recover my senses as to hear the cricket, which in fact has been chirping all day. In my better hours I am conscious of the influx of a serene and unquestionable wisdom which partly unfits, and if I yielded to it more rememberingly would wholly unfit me, for what is called the active business of life, for that furnishes nothing on which the eye of reason can rest. What is that other kind of life to which I am thus continually allured? which alone I love? Is it a life for this world? Can a man feed and clothe himself gloriously who keeps only the truth steadily before him? who calls in no evil to his aid? Are there duties which necessarily interfere with the serene perception of truth? Are our serene moments mere foretastes of heaven—joys gratuitously vouchsafed to us as a consolation—or simply a transient realization of what might be the whole tenor of our lives?

To be calm, to be serene! There is the calmness of the lake when there is not a breath of wind; there is the calmness of a stagnant ditch. So is it with us. Sometimes we are clarified and calmed healthily, as we never were before in our lives, not by an opiate, but by some unconscious obedience to the all-just laws, so that we become like a still lake of purest crystal and without an effort our depths are revealed to ourselves. All the world goes by us and is reflected in our deeps. Such clarity! obtained by such pure means! by simple living, by honesty of purpose. We live and rejoice. I awoke into a music which no one about me heard. Whom shall I thank for it? The luxury of wisdom! the luxury of virtue! Are there any intemperate in these things? I feel my Maker blessing me. To the sane man the world is a musical instrument. The very touch affords an exquisite pleasure.

July 2. . . . Many large trees, especially elms, about a house are a surer indication of old family distinction and worth than any evidence of wealth. Any evidence of care bestowed on these trees secures the traveller's respect as for a nobler husbandry than the raising of corn and potatoes.

I passed a regular country dooryard this forenoon, the unpainted one-story house, long and low with projecting stoop, a deep grass-plot unfenced for yard, hens and chickens scratching amid the chip dirt about the door—this last the main feature, relics of wood-piles, sites of the wooden towers.

The nightshade has bloomed and the prinos, or winterberry.

July 5. . . . I am interested in those fields in the woods where the potato is cultivated, growing in the light, dry, sandy soil, free from weeds; now in blossom, the slight vine not crowded in the hill. I think they do not promise many potatoes, though mealy and wholesome like nuts. Many fields have now received their last hoeing, and the farmers' work seems to be soon over with them. What a pleasant interview he must have had with them! What a liberal education with these professors! Better than a university. It is pleasing to consider man's cultivating this plant thus assiduously, without reference to any crop it may yield him, as if he were to cultivate johnswort in like manner. What influences does he receive from this long intercourse.

The flowers of the umbelled pyrola, or common wintergreen, are really very handsome now, dangling red from their little umbels like jewelry—especially the unexpanded buds with their red calyx-leaves against the white globe of petals.

There is a handsome wood-path on the east side of White Pond. The shadows of the pine stems and branches falling across the path, which is perfectly red with pine-needles, make a very handsome carpet. Here is a small road running north and south along the edge of the wood, which would be a good place to walk by moonlight.

The calamint grows by the lane beyond Seven-Star Lane; now in blossom.

As we come over Hubbard's Bridge between 5 and 6 P.M., the sun getting low, a cool wind blowing up the valley, we sit awhile on the rails which are destined for the new railing. The light on the Indian hill is very soft and glorious, giving the idea of the most wonderful fertility. The most barren hills are gilded like waving grain fields. What a paradise to sail by! The cliffs and woods up the stream are nearer and have more shadow and actuality about them. This retired bridge is a favorite spot with me. I have witnessed many a fair sunset from it.

July 6. . . . There is some advantage in being the humblest, cheapest, least dignified man in the village, so that the very stable boys shall damn you. Methinks I enjoy that advantage to an unusual extent. There is many a coarsely well-meaning fellow, who knows only the skin of me, who addresses me familiarly by my Christian name. I get the whole good of him and lose nothing myself. There is "Sam" [Staples], the jailer—whom I never call Sam, however— who exclaimed last evening: "Thoreau, are you going up the street pretty soon? Well, just take a couple of these handbills along and drop one in at Hoar's piazza and one at Holbrook's, and I'll do as much for you another time." I am not above being used, aye abused, sometimes.

July 9. . . . Coming out of town—willingly as usual—when I saw that reach of Charles River just above the depot, the fair, still water this cloudy evening suggesting the way to eternal peace and beauty, whence it flows, the placid, lakelike fresh water, so unlike the salt brine, affected me not a little. I was reminded of the way in which Wordsworth so coldly speaks of some natural visions or scenes "giving him pleasure." This is perhaps the first vision of elysium on this route from Boston. And just then I saw an encampment of Penobscots, their wigwams appearing above the railroad fence, they, too, looking up the river as they sat on the ground, and enjoying the scene. What can be more impressive than to look up a noble river just at evening—one, perchance, which you have never explored—and behold its placid waters, reflecting the woods and sky, lapsing inaudibly toward the ocean; to behold as a lake, but know it as a river, tempting the beholder to explore it and his own destiny at once? Haunt of waterfowl. This was above the factories—all that I saw. That water could never have flowed under a factory. How *then* could it have reflected the sky?

July 10. A gorgeous sunset after rain, with horizontal bars of clouds, red sashes to the western window, barry clouds hanging like a curtain over the window of the west, damask. First there is a low arch of the storm clouds in the west, under which is seen the clearer, fairer, serener sky and more distant sunset clouds, and under all, on the horizon's edge, heavier, massive dark clouds, not to be distinguished from the mountains. How many times I have seen this kind of sunset—the most gorgeous sight in nature! From the hill behind Minott's I see the birds flying against this red sky, the sun having set; one looks like a bat. Now between two stupendous mountains of the low stratum under the evening red, clothed in slightly rosaceous amber light, through a magnificent gorge, far, far away, as perchance may occur in pictures of the Spanish coast viewed from the Mediterranean, I see a city, the eternal city of the west, the phantom city, in whose streets no traveller has trod, over whose pavements the horses of the sun have already hurried, some Salamanca of the imagination. But it lasts only for a moment, for now the changing light has wrought such changes in it that I see the resemblance no longer.

July 16. . . . I think that no experience which I have today comes up to, or is comparable with, the experiences of my boyhood. And not only this is true, but as far back as I can remember I have unconsciously referred to the experiences of a previous state of existence. "For life is a forgetting," etc. Formerly, methought, Nature developed as I developed, and grew up with me. My life was ecstasy. In youth, before I lost any of my senses, I can remember that I was all alive, and inhabited my body with inexpressible satisfaction; both its weariness and its refreshment were sweet to me. This earth was the most glorious musical instrument, and I was audience to its strains. To have such sweet impressions made on us, such ecstasies begotten of the breezes! I can remember how I was astonished. I said to myself—I said to others —"There comes into my mind such an indescribable, infinite, all-absorbing, divine, heavenly pleasure, a sense of elevation and expansion, and [I] have had nought to do with it. I perceive that I am dealt with by superior powers.

This is a pleasure, a joy, an existence which I have not procured myself. I speak as a witness on the stand, and tell what I have perceived." The morning and the evening were sweet to me, and I led a life aloof from society of men. I wondered if a mortal had ever known what I knew. I looked in books for some recognition of a kindred experience, but, strange to say, I found none. Indeed, I was slow to discover that other men had had this experience, for it had been possible to read books and to associate with men on other grounds. The maker of me was improving me. When I detected this interference I was profoundly moved. For years I marched as to a music in comparison with which the military music of the streets is noise and discord. I was daily intoxicated, and yet no man could call me intemperate. With all your science can you tell how it is, and whence it is, that light comes into the soul?

Methinks this is the first of dog-days. The air in the distance has a peculiar blue mistiness, or furnace-like look, though, as I have said, it is not sultry yet. It is not the season for distant views. Mountains are not *clearly* blue now. The air is the opposite to what it is in October and November. You are not inclined to travel. It is a world of orchards and small-fruits now, and you can stay at home if the well has cool water in it. The black thimble-berry is an honest, homely berry, now drying up as usual. I used to have a pleasant time stringing them on herd's-grass stems, tracing the wallsides for them. It is pleasant to walk through these elevated fields, terraced upon the side of the hill so that the eye of the walker looks off into the blue cauldron of the air at his own level. Here the haymakers have just gone to tea—at 5 o'clock, the farmer's hour, before the afternoon is ended, while he still thinks much work may still be done before night. He does not wait till he is strongly reminded of the night. In the distance some burdened fields are black with haycocks. Some thoughtless and cruel sportsman has killed twenty-two young partridges not much bigger than robins, against the laws of Massachusetts and humanity. At the Corner Bridge the white lilies are budded. Green apples are now so large as to remind me of coddling and the autumn again. The season of fruits is arrived. The dog's-bane has a pretty, delicate bell-like flower. The Jersey tea abounds. I see the marks of the scythes in the fields, showing the breadth of each swath the mowers cut. Cool springs are now a desideratum. The geranium still hangs on. Even the creeping vines love the brooks, and I see where one slender one has struggled down and dangles into the current, which rocks it to and fro. Filberts are formed, and you may get the berry stains out of your hands with their husks, if you have any. Nightshade is in blossom. Came through the pine plains behind James Baker's, where late was open pasture, now open pitch pine woods, only here and there the grass has given place to a carpet of pine needles. These are among our pleasantest woods—open, level, with blackberry vines interspersed and flowers, as lady's-slippers, earlier, and pinks on the outskirts. Each tree has room enough. And now I hear the wood thrush from the shade, who loves these pine woods as well as I. I pass by Walden's scalloped shore. The epilobium reflects a pink gleam up the vales and down the hills. The chewink jingles on a bush's top. Why will the Irishman drink of a puddle by the railroad instead of digging a well? How shiftless! What death in life! He cannot be said to live who does not get pure water.

July 19. Here I am thirty-four years old [his birthday was July 12], and yet my life is almost wholly unexpanded. How much is in the germ! There is such an interval between my ideal and the actual in many instances that I may say I am unborn. There is the instinct for society, but no society. Life is not long enough for one success. Within another thirty-four years that miracle can hardly take place. Methinks my seasons revolve more slowly than those of nature; I am differently timed. I am contented. This rapid revolution of nature, even of nature in me, why should it hurry me? Let a man step to the music which he hears, however measured. Is it important that I should mature as soon as an apple tree? aye, as soon as an oak? May not my life in nature, in proportion as it is supernatural, be only the spring and infantile portion of my spirit's life? Shall I turn my spring to summer? May I not sacrifice a hasty and petty completeness here to entireness there? If my curve is large, why bend it to a smaller circle? My spirit's unfolding observes not the pace of nature. The society which I was made for is not here. Shall I, then, substitute for the anticipation of that this poor reality? I would [rather] have the unmixed expectation of that than this reality. If life is a waiting, so be it. I will not be shipwrecked on a vain reality. What were any reality which I can substitute? Shall I with pains erect a heaven of blue glass over myself, though when it is done I shall be sure to gaze still on the true ethereal heaven far above, as if the former were not—that still distant sky o'erarching that blue expressive eye of heaven? I am enamored of the blue-eyed arch of heaven.

July 21. . . . Men are very generally spoiled by being so civil and well-disposed. You can have no profitable conversation with them, they are so conciliatory, determined to agree with you. They exhibit such long-suffering and kindness in a short interview. I would meet with some provoking strangeness, so that we may be guest and host and refresh one another. It is possible for a man wholly to disappear and be merged in his manners. The thousand and one gentlemen whom I meet, I meet despairingly and but to part from them, for I am not cheered by the hope of any rudeness from them. A cross man, a coarse man, an eccentric man, a silent, a man who does not drill well—of him there is some hope. Your gentlemen, they are all alike. They utter their opinions as if it was not a man that uttered them. It is "just as you please"; they are indifferent to everything. They will talk with you for nothing. The interesting man will rather avoid [you], and it is a rare chance if you get so far as talk with him. The laborers whom I know, the loafers, fishers, and hunters, I can spin yarns with profitably, for it is hands off; they are they and I am I still; they do not come to me and quarter themselves on me for a day or an hour to be treated politely, they do not cast themselves on me for entertainment, they do not approach me with a flag of truce. They do not go out of themselves to meet me. I am never electrified by my gentleman; he is not an electric eel, but one of the common kind that slip through your hands, however hard you clutch them, and leave them covered with slime. He is a man, every inch of him; is worth a groom.

July 23. . . . 8 A.M. A comfortable breeze blowing. Methinks I can write better in the afternoon, for the novelty of it, if I should go abroad this morning. My genius makes distinctions which my understanding cannot, and which my senses do not report. If I should reverse the usual—go forth and saunter in the fields all the forenoon, then sit down in my chamber in the afternoon, which it is so unusual for me to do—it would be like a new season to me, and the novelty of it [would] inspire me. The wind has fairly blown me outdoors; the elements were so lively and active, and I so sympathized with them, that I could not sit while the wind went by. And I am reminded that we should especially improve the summer to live out-of-doors. When we may so easily, it behooves us to break up this custom of sitting in the house, for it is but a custom, and I am not sure that it has the sanction of common sense. A man no sooner gets up than he sits down again. Fowls leave their perch in the morning, and beasts their lairs, unless they are such as go abroad only by night. The cockerel does not take up a new perch *in the barn,* and he is the embodiment of health and common sense. Is the literary man to live always or chiefly sitting in a chamber through which nature enters by a window only? What is the use of the summer?

You must walk so gently as to hear the finest sounds, the faculties being in repose. Your mind must not perspire. True, out of doors my thought is commonly drowned, as it were, and shrunken, pressed down by stupendous piles of light ethereal influences, for the pressure of the atmosphere is still fifteen pounds to a square inch. I can do little more than preserve the equilibrium and resist the pressure of the atmosphere. I can only nod like the rye-heads in the breeze. I expand more surely in my chamber, as far as expression goes, as if that pressure were taken off; but here outdoors is the place to store up influences.

July 25. Friday. Started for Clark's Island at 7 A.M.

At 9 A.M. took the Hingham boat and was landed at Hull. There was a pleasure party on board, apparently boys and girls belonging to the South End, going to Hingham. There was a large proportion of ill-dressed and ill-mannered boys of Irish extraction. A sad sight to behold! Little boys of twelve years, prematurely old, sucking cigars! I felt that if I were their mothers I should whip them and send them to bed. Such children should be dealt with as for stealing or impurity. The opening of this valve for the safety of the city!

Aug. 5. . . . I hear now from Bear Garden Hill—I rarely walk by moonlight without hearing—the sound of a flute, or a horn, or a human voice. It is a performer I never see by day; should not recognize him if pointed out; but you may hear his performance in every horizon. He plays but one strain and goes to bed early, but I know by the character of that single strain that he is deeply dissatisfied with the man-

ner in which he spends his day. He is a slave who is pur-
chasing his freedom. He is Apollo watching the flocks of
Admetus on every hill, and this strain he plays every evening to remind him of his heavenly descent. It is all that
saves him—his one redeeming trait. It is a reminiscence; he
loves to remember his youth. He is sprung of a noble family. He is highly related, I have no doubt; was tenderly nur-
tured in his infancy, poor hind as he is. That noble strain he
utters, instead of any jewel on his finger, or precious locket
fastened to his breast, or purple garments that came with
him. The elements recognize him, and echo his strain. All
the dogs know him their master, though lords and ladies,
rich men and learned, know him not. He is the son of a
rich man, of a famous man who served his country well.
He has heard his sire's stories. I thought of the time when
he would discover his parentage, obtain his inheritance and
sing a strain suited to the morning hour. He cherishes hopes.
I never see the man by day who plays that clarionet.

Aug. 17. For a day or two it has been quite cool, a coolness that was felt even when sitting by an open window in
a thin coat on the west side of the house in the morning, and
you naturally sought the sun at that hour. The coolness concentrated your thought, however. As I could not command a
sunny window, I went abroad on the morning of the fifteenth
and lay in the sun in the fields in my thin coat, though it
was rather cool even there. I feel as if this coolness would
do me good. If it only makes my life more pensive! Why
should pensiveness be akin to sadness? There is a certain
fertile sadness which I would not avoid, but rather earnestly
seek. It is positively joyful to me. It saves my life from
being trivial. My life flows with a deeper current, no longer
as a shallow and brawling stream, parched and shrunken by
the summer heats. This coolness comes to condense the dews
and clear the atmosphere. The stillness seems more deep
and significant. Each sound seems to come from out a greater thoughtfulness in nature, as if nature had acquired some
character and mind. The cricket, the gurgling stream, the
rushing wind amid the trees, all speak to me soberly yet en-
couragingly of the steady onward progress of the universe.
My heart leaps into my mouth at the sound of the wind in
the woods. I, whose life was but yesterday so desultory and
shallow, suddenly recover my spirits, my spirituality, through
my hearing. I see a goldfinch go twittering through the still,

louring day, and am reminded of the peeping flocks which
will soon herald the thoughtful season. Ah! if I could so live
that there should be no desultory moment in all my life! that
in the trivial season, when small fruits are ripe, my fruits
might be ripe also! that I could match nature always with
my moods! that in each season when some part of nature
especially flourishes, then a corresponding part of me may
not fail to flourish! Ah, I would walk, I would sit and sleep,
with natural piety! What if I could pray aloud or to myself
as I went along by the brooksides a cheerful prayer like the
birds! For joy I could embrace the earth; I shall delight to be
buried in it. And then to think of those I love among men,
who will know that I love them though I tell them not! I
sometimes feel as if I were rewarded merely for expecting
better hours. I did not despair of worthier moods, and now
I have occasion to be grateful for the flood of life that is
flowing over me. I am not so poor: I can smell the ripening
apples; the very rills are deep; the autumnal flowers, the
Trichostema dichotomum—not only its bright blue flower
above the sand, but its strong wormwood scent which belongs to the season—feed my spirit, endear the earth to me,
make me value myself and rejoice; the quivering of pigeons'
wings reminds me of the tough fibre of the air which they
rend. I thank you, God. I do not deserve anything, I am unworthy of the least regard; and yet I am made to rejoice.
I am impure and worthless, and yet the world is gilded for
my delight and holidays are prepared for me, and my path
is strewn with flowers. But I cannot thank the Giver; I cannot even whisper my thanks to those human friends I have.
It seems to me that I am more rewarded for my expectations
than for anything I do or can do. Ah, I would not tread on
a cricket in whose song is such a revelation, so soothing
and cheering to my ear! Oh, keep my senses pure! And why
should I speak to my friends? for how rarely is it that I am I;
and are they, then, they? We will meet, then, far away. The
seeds of the summer are getting dry and falling from a thousand nodding heads. If I did not know you through thick
and thin, how should I know you at all? Ah, the very
brooks seem fuller of reflections than they were! Ah, such
provoking sibylline sentences they are! The shallowest is all
at once unfathomable. How can that depth be fathomed
where a man may see himself reflected? The rill I stopped
to drink at I drink in more than I expected. I satisfy and
still provoke the thirst of thirsts. Nut Meadow Brook where it

crosses the road beyond Jenny Dugan's that was. I do not drink in vain. I mark that brook as if I had swallowed a water snake that would live in my stomach. I have swallowed something worth the while. The day is not what it was before I stooped to drink. Ah, I shall hear from that draught! It is not in vain that I have drunk. I have drunk an arrowhead. It flows from where all fountains rise.

Aug. 18. . . . How impossible it is to give that soldier a good education, without first making him virtually a deserter.

Aug. 19. . . . The poet must be continually watching the moods of his mind, as the astronomer watches the aspects of the heavens. What might we not expect from a long life faithfully spent in this wise? The humblest observer would see some stars shoot. A faithful description as by a disinterested person of the thoughts which visited a certain mind in threescore years and ten, as when one reports the number and character of the vehicles which pass a particular point. As travellers go round the world and report natural objects and phenomena, so faithfully let another stay at home and report the phenomena of his own life—catalogue stars, those thoughts whose orbits are as rarely calculated as comets. It matters not whether they visit my mind or yours—whether the meteor falls in my field or in yours— only that it come from heaven. (I am not concerned to express that kind of truth which Nature has expressed. Who knows but I may suggest some things to her? Time was when she was indebted to such suggestions from another quarter, as her present advancement shows. I deal with the truths that recommend themselves to me—please me—not those merely which any system has voted to accept.) A meteorological journal of the mind. You shall observe what occurs in your latitude, I in mine.

Aug. 21. . . . There is some advantage, intellectually and spiritually, in taking wide views with the bodily eye and not pursuing an occupation which holds the body prone. There is some advantage, perhaps, in attending to the general features of the landscape over studying the particular plants and animals which inhabit it. A man may walk abroad and no more see the sky than if he walked under a shed. The poet is more in the air than the naturalist, though they may walk side by side. Granted that you are out-of-doors; but what if the outer door *is* open, if the inner door is shut! You must walk sometimes perfectly free, not prying nor inquisitive, not bent upon seeing things. Throw away a whole day for a single expansion, a single inspiration of air.

Aug. 23. . . . P.M. Walk to Annursnack and back over stone bridge.

I sometimes reproach myself because I do not find anything attractive in certain mere trivial employments of men —that I skip men so commonly, and their affairs—the professions and the trades—do not elevate them at least in my thought and get some material for poetry out of them directly. I will not avoid, then, to go by where these men are repairing the stone bridge—see if I cannot see poetry in that, if that will not yield me a reflection. It is narrow to be confined to woods and fields and grand aspects of Nature only. The greatest and wisest will still be related to men. Why not see men standing in the sun and casting a shadow, even as trees? May not some light be reflected from them as from the stems of trees? I will try to enjoy them as animals, at least. They are perhaps better animals than men. Do not neglect to speak of men's low life and affairs with sympathy, though you ever so speak as to suggest a contrast between them and the ideal and divine. You may be excused if you are always pathetic, but do not refuse to recognize.

Resolve to read no book, to take no walk, to undertake no enterprise, but such as you can endure to give an account of to yourself. Live thus deliberately for the most part.

Aug. 26. . . . I perceive that some farmers are cutting turf now. They require the driest season of the year. There is something agreeable to my thoughts in thus burning a part of the earth, the stock of fuel is so inexhaustible. Nature looks not mean and niggardly, but like an ample loaf. Is not he a rich man who owns a peat meadow? It is to enjoy the luxury of wealth. It must be a luxury to sit around the fire in winter days and nights and burn these dry slices of the meadow which contain roots of all herbs. You dry and burn the very earth itself. It is a fact kindred with salt-licks. The meadow is strewn with the fresh bars, bearing the marks of the fork, and the turf-cutter is wheeling them out with his barrow. To sit and see the world aglow and try to imagine how it would seem to have it so destroyed!

Woodchucks are seen tumbling into their holes on all sides.

Aug. 31. . . . With what sober joy I stand to let the water drip from me and feel my fresh vigor, who have been bathing in the same tub which the muskrat uses! Such a medicated bath as only nature furnishes. A fish leaps, and the dimple he makes is observed now. How ample and generous was nature! My inheritance is not narrow. Here is no other this evening. Those resorts which I most love and frequent, numerous and vast as they are, are as it were given up to me, as much as if I were an autocrat or owner of the world, and by my edicts excluded men from my territories. Perchance there is some advantage here not enjoyed in older countries. There are said to be two thousand inhabitants in Concord, and yet I find such ample space and verge, even miles of walking every day in which I do not meet nor see a human being, and often not very recent traces of them. So much of man as there is in your mind, there will be in your eye. Methinks that for a great part of the time, as much as it is possible, I walk as one possessing the advantages of human culture, fresh from society of men, but turned loose into the woods, the only man in nature, walking and meditating to a great extent as if man and his customs and institutions were not. The catbird, or the jay, is sure of the whole of your ear now. Each noise is like a stain on pure glass. The rivers now, these great blue subterranean heavens, reflecting the supernal skies and red-tinted clouds.

Sept. 2. . . . We cannot write well or truly but what we write with gusto. The body, the senses, must conspire with the mind. Expression is the act of the whole man, that our speech may be vascular. The intellect is powerless to express thought without the aid of the heart and liver and of every member. Often I feel that my head stands out too dry, when it should be immersed. A writer, a man writing, is the scribe of all nature; he is the corn and the grass and the atmosphere writing. It is always essential that we love to do what we are doing, do it with a heart. The maturity of the mind, however, may perchance consist with a certain dryness.

Sept. 3. . . . It is a very remarkable and significant fact that, though no man is quite well or healthy, yet every one believes practically that health is the rule and disease the exception, and each invalid is wont to think himself in a minority, and to postpone somewhat of endeavor to another state of existence. But it may be some encouragement to men to know that in this respect they stand on the same platform, that disease is, in fact, the *rule* of our terrestrial life and the prophecy of a *celestial* life. Where is the coward who despairs because he is sick? Every one may live either the life of Achilles or of Nestor. Seen in this light, our life with all its diseases will look healthy, and in one sense the more healthy as it is the more diseased. Disease is not the accident of the individual, nor even of the generation, but of life itself. In some form, and to some degree or other, it is one of the permanent conditions of life. It is, nevertheless, a cheering fact that men affirm health unanimously, and esteem themselves miserable failures. Here was no blunder. They gave us life on exactly these conditions, and methinks we shall live it with more heart when we perceive clearly that these are the terms on which we have it. Life is a warfare, a struggle, and the diseases of the body answer to the troubles and defeats of the spirit. Man begins by quarrelling with the animal in him, and the result is immediate disease. In proportion as the spirit is the more ambitious and persevering, the more obstacles it will meet with. It is as a seer that man asserts his disease to be exceptional.

Sept. 4. . . . It had been a warm day, especially warm to the head. I do not perspire as in the early summer, but am sensible of the ripening heat, more as if by contact. Suddenly the wind changed to east, and the atmosphere grew more and more hazy and thick on that side, obstructing the view, while it was yet clear in the west. I thought it was the result of the cooler air from over the sea meeting and condensing the vapor in the warm air of the land. That was the haze, or thin, dry fog which some call smoke. It gradually moved westward and affected the prospect on that side somewhat. It was a very thin fog invading all the east. I felt the cool air from the ocean, and it was very refreshing. I opened my bosom and my mouth to inhale it. Very delicious and invigorating.

Sept. 11. Every artisan learns positively something by his trade. Each craft is familiar with a few simple, well-known, well-established facts, not requiring any genius to discover, but mere use and familiarity. You may go by the man at his work in the street every day of your life, and though he is

there before you, carrying into practice certain essential information, you shall never be the wiser. Each trade is in
fact a craft, a cunning, a covering an ability; and its methods
are the result of a long experience. There sits a stone-mason,
splitting Westford granite for fence posts. Egypt has perchance taught New England something in this matter. His
hammer, his chisels, his wedges, his shims or half-rounds, his
iron spoon—I suspect that these tools are hoary with age
as with granite dust. He learns as easily where the best
granite comes from as he learns how to erect that screen to
keep off the sun. He knows that he can drill faster into a
large stone than a small one, because there is less jar and
yielding. He deals in stone as the carpenter in lumber. In
many of his operations only the materials are different. His
work is slow and expensive. Nature is here hard to be overcome. He wears up one or two drills in splitting a single
stone. He must sharpen his tools oftener than the carpenter.
He fights with granite. He knows the temper of the rocks.
He grows stony himself. His tread is ponderous and steady
like the fall of a rock. And yet by patience and art he splits
a stone as surely as the carpenter or woodcutter a log. So
much time and perseverance will accomplish. One would say
that mankind had much less moral than physical energy,
that any day you see men following the trade of splitting
rocks, who yet shrink from undertaking apparently less arduous moral labors, the solving of moral problems. See how
surely he proceeds. He does not hesitate to drill a dozen
holes, each one the labor of a day or two for a savage; he
carefully takes out the dust with his iron spoon; he inserts
his wedges, one in each hole, and protects the sides of the
holes and gives resistance to his wedges by thin pieces of
half-round iron (or shims); he marks the red line which he
has drawn, with his chisel, carefully cutting it straight; and
then how carefully he drives each wedge in succession,
fearful lest he should not have a good split!

The habit of looking at men in the gross makes their lives
have less of human interest for us. But though there are
crowds of laborers before us, yet each one leads his little epic
life each day. There is the stone-mason, who, methought,
was simply a stony man that hammered stone from breakfast
to dinner, and dinner to supper, and then went to his slum-
bers. But he, I find, is even a man like myself, for he feels
the heat of the sun and has raised some boards on a frame
to protect him. And now, at mid-forenoon, I see his wife

and child have come and brought him drink and meat for his lunch and to assuage the stoniness of his labor, and sit to chat with him.

There are many rocks lying there for him to split from end to end, and he will surely do it. This only at the command of luxury, since stone posts are preferred to wood. But how many moral blocks are lying there in every man's yard, which he surely will not split nor earnestly endeavor to split. There lie the blocks which will surely get split, but here lie the blocks which will surely not get split. Do we say it is too hard for human faculties? But does not the mason dull a basketful of steel chisels in a day, and yet, by sharpening them again and tempering them aright, succeed? Moral effort! Difficulty to be overcome!!! Why, men work in stone, and sharpen their drills when they go home to dinner!

Sept. 20. 3 P.M. To Cliffs via Bear Hill.

As I go through the fields, endeavoring to recover my tone and sanity and to perceive things truly and simply again, after having been perambulating the bounds of the town all the week, and dealing with the most commonplace and worldly minded men, and emphatically *trivial* things, I feel as if I had committed suicide in a sense. I am again forcibly struck with the truth of the fable of Apollo serving King Admetus, its universal applicability. A fatal coarseness is the result of mixing in the trivial affairs of men. Though I have been associating even with the *select* men of this and the surrounding towns, I feel inexpressibly begrimed. My Pegasus has lost his wings; he has turned a reptile and gone on his belly. Such things are compatible only with a cheap and superficial life.

Sept. 22. . . . . Yesterday and today the stronger winds of autumn have begun to blow, and the telegraph harp has sounded loudly. I heard it especially in the Deep Cut this afternoon, the tone varying with the tension of different parts of the wire. The sound proceeds from near the posts, where the vibration is apparently more rapid. I put my ear to one of the posts, and it seemed to me as if every pore of the wood was filled with music, labored with the strain—as if every fibre was affected and being seasoned or timed, rearranged according to a new and more harmonious law. Every swell and change or inflection of tone pervaded and seemed to proceed from the wood, the divine tree or wood, as if its very substance was transmuted. What a recipe for preserving wood, perchance—to keep it from rotting—to fill its pores with music! How this wild tree from the forest, stripped of its bark and set up here, rejoices to transmit this music! When no music proceeds from the wire, on applying my ear I hear the hum within the entrails of the wood—the oracular tree acquiring, accumulating, the prophetic fury.

The resounding wood! How much the ancients would have made of it! To have a harp on so great a scale, girdling the very earth, and played on by the winds of every latitude and longitude, and that harp were, as it were, the manifest blessing of heaven on a work of man's! Shall we not add a tenth Muse to the immortal Nine? And that the invention thus divinely honored and distinguished—on which the Muse has condescended to smile—is this magic medium of communication for mankind!

Sept. 24. . . . What can be handsomer for a picture than our river scenery now? Take this view from the first Conantum Cliff. First this smoothly shorn meadow on the west side of the stream, with all the swaths distinct, sprinkled with apple trees casting heavy shadows black as ink, such as can be seen only in this clear air, this strong light, one cow wandering restlessly about in it and lowing; then the blue river, scarcely darker than and not to be distinguished from the sky, its waves driven southward, or up-stream, by the wind, making it appear to flow that way, bordered by willows and button-bushes; then the narrow meadow beyond, with varied lights and shades from its waving grass, which for some reason has not been cut this year, though so dry, now at length each grass-blade bending south before the wintry blast, as if bending for aid in that direction; then the hill rising sixty feet to a terrace-like plain covered with shrub oaks, maples, etc., now variously tinted, clad all in a livery of gay colors, every bush a feather in its cap; and further in the rear the wood-crowned Cliff some two hundred feet high, where gray rocks here and there project from amidst the bushes, with its orchard on the slope; and to the right of the Cliff the distant Lincoln hills in the horizon. The landscape so handsomely colored, the air so clear and wholesome; and the surface of the earth is so pleasingly varied, that it seems rarely fitted for the abode of man.

Sept. 26. . . . Most New England biographies and journals
—John Adams's not excepted—affect me like opening of the
tombs.

Sept. 27. . . . We of Massachusetts boast a good deal of
what we do for the education of our people, of our district-
school system; and yet our district schools are as it were but
infant-schools, and we have no system for the education of
the great mass who are grown up. I have yet to learn that
one cent is spent by this town, this political community
called Concord, directly to educate the great mass of its
inhabitants who have long since left the district school; for the
Lyceum, important as it is comparatively, though absolutely
trifling, is supported by individuals. There are certain refining and civilizing influences, as works of art, journals and
books, and scientific instruments, which this community is
amply rich enough to purchase, which would educate this
village, elevate its tone of thought, and, if it alone improved these opportunities, easily make it the centre of
civilization in the known world, put us on a level as to opportunities at once with London and Arcadia, and secure us
a culture at once superior to both. Yet we spend sixteen thousand dollars on a Town House, a hall for our political
meetings mainly, and nothing to educate ourselves who are
grown up. Pray is there nothing in the market, no advantages, no intellectual food worth buying? Have Paris and London and New York and Boston nothing to dispose of which
this village might try and appropriate to its own use? Might
not this great villager adorn his villa with a few pictures and
statues, enrich himself with a choice library as available,
without being cumbrous, as any in the world, with scientific
instruments for such as have a taste to use them? Yet we are
contented to be countrified, to be provincial. I am astonished
to find that in this nineteenth century, in this land of
free schools, we spend absolutely nothing as a town on
our own education, cultivation, civilization. Each town, like
each individual, has its own character—some more, some
less, cultivated. I know many towns so mean-spirited and
benighted that it would be a disgrace to belong to them. I
believe that some of our New England villages within thirty
miles of Boston are as boorish and barbarous communities
as there are on the face of the earth. And how much superior are the best of them? If London has any refinement,
any information to sell, why should we not buy it? Would

not the town of Carlisle do well to spend sixteen thousand dollars on its own education at once, if it could only find a schoolmaster for itself? It has one man, as I hear, who takes the *North American Review*. That will never civilize them, I fear. Why should not the town itself take the London and Edinburgh Reviews, and put itself in communication with whatever sources of light and intelligence there are in the world? Yet Carlisle is very little behind Concord in these respects. I do not know but it spends its proportional part on education. How happens it that the only libraries which the towns possess are the district-school libraries—books for children only, or for readers who must needs be written down to? Why should they not have a library, if not so extensive, yet of the same stamp and more select than the British Museum? It is not that the town cannot well afford to buy these things, but it is unaspiring and ignorant of its own wants. It sells milk, but it only builds larger barns with the money which it gets for its milk. . . .

Sept. 28. . . . . The railroads as much as anything appear to have unsettled the farmers. Our young Concord farmers and their young wives, hearing this bustle about them, seeing the world all going by as it were—some daily to the cities about their business, some to California—plainly cannot make up their minds to live the quiet, retired, old-fashioned, country-farmer's life. They are impatient if they live more than a mile from a railroad. . . .

Oct. 1. 5 P.M. Just put a fugitive slave, who has taken the name of Henry Williams, into the cars for Canada. He escaped from Stafford County, Virginia, to Boston last October; has been in Shadrach's place at the Cornhill Coffee-House; had been corresponding through an agent with his master, who is his father, about buying himself, his master asking six hundred dollars, but he having been able to raise only five hundred dollars. Heard that there were writs out for two Williamses, fugitives, and was informed by his fellow-servants and employer that Augerhole Burns and others of the police had called for him when he was out. Accordingly fled to Concord last night on foot, bringing a letter to our family from Mr. Lovejoy of Cambridge and another which Garrison had formerly given him on another occasion. He lodged with us, and waited in the house till funds were collected with which to forward him. Intended to dispatch

him at noon through to Burlington, but when I went to buy
his ticket, saw one at the depot who looked and behaved so
much like a Boston policeman that I did not venture that
time. An intelligent and very well-behaved man, a mulatto.

Oct. 4. . . . [George] Minott is, perhaps, the most poetical farmer—who most realizes to me the poetry of the
farmer's life—that I know. He does nothing with haste and
drudgery, but as if he loved it. He makes the most of his
labor, and takes infinite satisfaction in every part of it. He
is not looking forward to the sale of his crops or any pecuniary profit, but he is paid by the constant satisfaction
which his labor yields him. He has not too much land to
trouble him—too much work to do—no hired man nor boy
—but simply to amuse himself and live. He cares not so
much to raise a large crop as to do his work well. He knows
every pin and nail in his barn. If another linter is to be
floored, he lets no hired man rob him of that amusement,
but he goes slowly to the woods and, at his leisure, selects
a pitch pine tree, cuts it, and hauls it or gets it hauled to
the mill; and so he knows the history of his barn floor.
   Farming is an amusement which has lasted him longer
than gunning or fishing. He is never in a hurry to get his
garden planted and yet [it] is always planted soon enough,
and none in the town is kept so beautifully clean.
   He always prophesies a failure of the crops, and yet is
satisfied with what he gets. His barn floor is fastened down
with oak pins, and he prefers them to iron spikes, which
he says will rust and give way. He handles and amuses
himself with every ear of his corn crop as much as a child
with its playthings, and so his small crop goes a great way.
He might well cry if it were carried to market. The seed
of weeds is no longer in his soil.
   He loves to walk in a swamp in windy weather and hear
the wind groan through the pines. He keeps a cat in his barn
to catch the mice. He indulges in no luxury of food or
dress or furniture, yet he is not penurious but merely
simple. If his sister dies before him, he may have to go
to the almshouse in his old age; yet he is not poor,
for he does not want riches. He gets out of each manipu-
lation in the farmers' operations a fund of entertainment
which the speculating drudge hardly knows. With never-
failing rheumatism and trembling hands, he seems yet to
enjoy perennial health. . . .

Oct. 9. Heard two screech owls in the night. Boiled a quart of acorns for breakfast, but found them not so palatable as raw, having acquired a bitterish taste, perchance from being boiled with the shells and skins; yet one would soon get accustomed to this.

Oct. 10. . . . Ah, I yearn toward thee, my friend, but I have not confidence in thee. We do not believe in the same God. I am not thou; thou art not I. We trust each other today, but we distrust tomorrow. Even when I meet thee unexpectedly, I part from thee with disappointment. Though I enjoy thee more than other men, yet I am more disappointed with thee than with others. I know a noble man; what is it hinders me from knowing him better? I know not how it is that our distrust, our hate, is stronger than our love. Here I have been on what the world would call friendly terms with one fourteen years, have pleased my imagination sometimes with loving him; and yet our hate is stronger than our love. Why are we related, yet thus unsatisfactorily? We almost are a sore to one another. Ah, I am afraid because thy relations are not my relations. Because I have experienced that in some respects we are strange to one another, strange as some wild creature. Ever and anon there will come the consciousness to mar our love that, change the theme but a hair's breadth, and we are tragically strange to one another. We do not know what hinders us from coming together. But when I consider what my friend's relations and acquaintances are, what his tastes and habits, then the difference between us gets named. I see that all these friends and acquaintances and tastes and habits are indeed my friend's self. In the first place, my friend is prouder than I am—and I am very proud, perchance.

Oct. 12. . . . I love very well this cloudy afternoon, so sober and favorable to reflection after so many bright ones. What if the clouds shut out the heavens, provided they concentrate my thoughts and make a more celestial heaven below! I hear the crickets plainer; I wander less in my thoughts, am less dissipated; am aware how shallow was the current of my thoughts before. Deep streams are dark, as if there were a cloud in their sky; shallow ones are bright and sparkling, reflecting the sun from their bottoms. The very wind on my cheek seems more fraught with meaning.

Many maples around the edges of the meadows are now quite bare, like smoke.

I seem to be more constantly merged in nature; my intellectual life is more obedient to nature than formerly, but perchance less obedient to spirit. I have less memorable seasons. I exact less of myself. I am getting used to my meanness, getting to accept my low estate. O if I could be discontented with myself! If I could feel anguish at each descent!

Oct. 13. Drizzling, misty showers still, with a little misty sunshine at intervals. The trees have lost many of their leaves in the last twenty-four hours. The sun has got so low that it will do to let his rays in on the earth; the cattle do not need their shade now, nor men. Warmth is more desirable now than shade.

The alert and energetic man leads a more intellectual life in winter than in summer. In summer the animal and vegetable in him are perfected as in a torrid zone; he lives in his senses mainly. In winter cold reason and not warm passion has her sway; he lives in thought and reflection; he lives a more spiritual, a less sensual, life. If he has passed a merely sensual summer, he passes his winter in a torpid state like some reptiles and other animals.

The mind of man in the two seasons is like the atmosphere of summer compared with the atmosphere of winter. He depends more on himself in winter—on his own resources—less on outward aid. Insects, it is true, disappear for the most part, and those animals which depend upon them; but the nobler animals abide with man the severity of winter. He migrates into his mind, to perpetual summer. And to the healthy man the winter of his discontent never comes.

Nov. 1. . . . It is a rare qualification to be able to state a fact simply and adequately, to digest some experience cleanly, to say "yes" and "no" with authority, to make a square edge, to conceive and suffer the truth to pass through us living and intact, even as a waterfowl an eel, as it flies over the meadows, thus stocking new waters. First of all a man must see, before he can say. Statements are made but partially. Things are said with reference to certain conventions or existing institutions, not absolutely. A fact truly and absolutely stated is taken out of the region of common sense and acquires a mythologic or universal significance. Say it

and have done with it. Express it without expressing yourself. See not with the eye of science, which is barren, nor
of youthful poetry, which is impotent. But taste the world
and digest it. It would seem as if things got said but
rarely and by chance. As you *see,* so at length will you *say.*
When facts are seen superficially, they are seen as they lie in
relation to certain institutions, perchance. But I would have
them expressed as more deeply seen, with deeper references;
so that the hearer or reader cannot recognize them or ap-
prehend their significance from the platform of common life,
but it will be necessary that he be in a sense translated in
order to understand them; when the truth respecting his
things shall naturally exhale from a man like the odor of
the muskrat from the coat of the trapper. At first blush a
man is not capable of reporting truth; he must be drenched
and saturated with it first. What was *enthusiasm* in the young
man must become *temperament* in the mature man. Without excitement, heat, or passion, he will survey the world
which excited the youth and threw him off his balance. As all
things are significant, so all words should be significant.
It is a fault which attaches to the speaker, to speak flippantly
or superficially of anything. Of what use are words which
do not move the hearer—are not oracular and fateful? A style
in which the matter is all in all, and the manner nothing at all.

Nov. 11. . . . When I have been confined to my chamber
for the greater part of several days by some employment, or
perchance by the ague, till I felt weary and house-worn,
I have been conscious of a certain softness to which I am
otherwise and commonly a stranger, in which the gates were
loosened to some emotions; and if I were to become a confirmed invalid, I see how some sympathy with mankind and
society might spring up. Yet what is my softness good for,
even to tears. It is not I, but nature in me. I laughed at
myself the other day to think that I cried while reading a
pathetic story. I was no more affected in spirit than I frequently am, methinks. The tears were merely a phenomenon
of the bowels, and I felt that that expression of my sympathy, so unusual with me, was something mean, and such
as I should be ashamed to have the subject of it understand.
I had a cold in my head withal, about those days. I found
that I had some bowels, but then it was because my bowels
were out of order.

Nov. 13. To Fair Haven Hill.

A cold and dark afternoon, the sun being behind clouds in the west. The landscape is barren of objects, the trees being leafless, and so little light in the sky for variety. Such a day as will almost oblige a man to eat his own heart. A day in which you must hold on to life by your teeth. You can hardly ruck up any skin on Nature's bones. The sap is down; she won't peel. Now is the time to cut timber for yokes and ox-bows, leaving the tough bark on—yokes for your own neck. Finding yourself yoked to Matter and to Time. Truly a hard day, hard times these! Not a mosquito left. Not an insect to hum. Crickets gone into winter quarters. Friends long since gone there, and you left to walk on frozen ground, with your hands in your pockets. Ah, but is not this a glorious time for your deep inward fires? And will not your green hickory and white oak burn clear in this frosty air? Now is not your manhood taxed by the great Assessor? Taxed for having a soul, a ratable soul. A day when you cannot pluck a flower, cannot dig a parsnip, nor pull a turnip, for the frozen ground! What do the thoughts find to live on? What avails you now the fire you stole from heaven? Does not each thought become a vulture to gnaw your vitals? No Indian summer have we had this November. I see but few traces of the perennial spring. Now is there nothing, not even the cold beauty of ice crystals and snowy architecture, nothing but the echo of your steps over the frozen ground, no voice of birds nor frogs. You are dry as a farrow cow. The earth will not admit a spade. All fields lie fallow. Shall not your mind? True, the freezing ground is being prepared for immeasurable snows, but there are brave thoughts within you that shall remain to rustle the winter through like white oak leaves upon your boughs, or like scrub oaks that remind the traveller of a fire upon the hillsides; or evergreen thoughts, cold even in midsummer, by their nature shall contrast the more fairly with the snow. Some warm springs shall still tinkle and fume, and send their column of vapor to the skies.

The walker now fares like cows in the pastures, where is no grass but hay; he gets nothing but an appetite. If we must return to hay, pray let us have that which has been stored in barns, which has not lost its sweetness. The poet needs to have more stomachs than the cow, for for him no fodder is stored in barns. He relies upon his instinct, which teaches him to paw away the snow to come at the withered grass.

Methinks man came very near being made a dormant creature, just as some of these animals. The ground squirrel, for
instance, which lays up vast stores, is yet found to be half
dormant, if you dig him out. Now for the oily nuts of
thought which you have stored up.

The mountains are of an uncommonly dark blue today.
Perhaps this is owing, not only to the greater clearness of
the atmosphere, which brings them nearer, but to the absence of the leaves! They are many miles nearer for it. A
little mistiness occasioned by warmth would set them further
off and make them fainter.

Just spent a couple of hours (eight to ten) with Miss Mary
Emerson [aunt of R. W. Emerson] at Holbrook's. The
wittiest and most vivacious woman that I know, certainly
that woman among my acquaintance whom it is most profitable to meet, the least frivolous, who will most surely
provoke to good conversation and the expression of what
is in you. She is singular, among women at least, in being
really and perseveringly interested to know what thinkers
think. She relates herself surely to the intellectual where
she goes. It is perhaps her greatest praise and peculiarity
that she, more surely than any other woman, gives her
companion occasion to utter his best thoughts. In spite of
her own biases, she can entertain a large thought with hos-
pitality, and is not prevented by any intellectuality in it, as
women commonly are. In short, she is a genius, as woman
seldom is, reminding you less often of her sex than any
woman whom I know. In that sense she is capable of a
masculine appreciation of poetry and philosophy. I never
talked with any other woman who I thought accompanied
me so far in describing a poetic experience. Miss Fuller is
the only woman I think of in this connection, and of her
rather from her fame than from any knowledge of her.
Miss Emerson expressed tonight a singular want of respect
for her own sex, saying that they were frivolous almost
without exception, that woman was the weaker vessel, etc.;
that into whatever family she might go, she depended more
upon the "clown" for society than upon the lady of the
house. Men are more likely to have opinions of their own.

Nov. 14. . . . In the evening went to a party. It is a bad
place to go to—thirty or forty persons, mostly young wom-
en, in a small room, warm and noisy. Was introduced to two

young women. The first one was as lively and loquacious as a chickadee; had been accustomed to the society of watering places, and therefore could get no refreshment out of such a dry fellow as I. The other was said to be pretty-looking. but I rarely look people in their faces, and, moreover, I could not hear what she said, there was such a clacking—could only see the motion of her lips when I looked that way. I could imagine better places for conversation, where there should be a certain degree of silence surrounding you, and less than forty talking at once. Why, this afternoon, even, I did better. There was old Mr. Joseph Hosmer and I ate our luncheon of cracker and cheese together in the woods. I heard all he said, though it was not much, to be sure, and he could hear me. And then he talked out of such a glorious repose, taking a leisurely bite at the cracker and cheese between his words; and so some of him was communicated to me, and some of me to him, I trust.

These parties, I think, are a part of the machinery of modern society, that young people may be brought together to form marriage connections.

What is the use of going to see people whom yet you never see, and who never see you? I begin to suspect that it is not necessary that we should see one another.

Some of my friends make singular blunders. They go out of their way to talk with certain young women of whom they think, or have heard, that they are pretty, and take pains to introduce me to them. That may be a reason why they should look at them, but it is not a reason why they should talk with them. I confess that I am lacking a sense, perchance, in this respect, and I derive no pleasure from talking with a young woman half an hour simply because she has regular features. The society of young women is the most unprofitable I have ever tried. They are so light and flighty that you can never be sure whether they are there or not there. I prefer to talk with the more staid and settled, *settled for life,* in every sense.

Nov. 16. Sunday. It is remarkable that the highest intellectual mood which the world tolerates is the perception of the truth of the most ancient revelations, now in some respects out of date; but any direct revelation, any original thoughts, it hates like virtue. The fathers and the mothers of the town would rather hear the young man or young woman at their tables express reverence for some old statement of the truth than utter a direct revelation themselves. They don't want to have any prophets born into their families— damn them! So far as thinking is concerned, surely original thinking is the divinest thing. Rather we should reverently watch for the least motions, the least scintillations, of thought in this sluggish world, and men should run to and fro on the occasion more than at an earthquake. We check and repress the divinity that stirs within us, to fall down and worship the divinity that is dead without us. I go to see many a good man or good woman, so called, and utter freely that thought which alone it was given to me to utter; but there was a man who lived a long, long time ago, and his name was Moses, and another whose name was Christ, and if your thought does not, or does not appear to, coincide with what they said, the good man or the good woman has no ears to hear you. They think they love God! It is only his old clothes, of which they make scarecrows for the children. Where will they come nearer to God than in those very children?

Nov. 20. It is often said that melody can be heard farther than noise, and the finest melody farther than the coarsest. I think there is truth in this, and that accordingly those strains of the piano which reach me here in my attic stir me so much more than the sounds which I should hear if I were below in the parlor, because they are so much purer and diviner melody. They who sit farthest off from the noisy and bustling world are not at pains to distinguish what is sweet and musical, for that alone can reach them; that chiefly comes down to posterity.

Hard and steady and engrossing labor with the hands, especially out of doors, is invaluable to the literary man and serves him directly. Here I have been for six days surveying in the woods, and yet when I get home at evening, somewhat weary at last, and beginning to feel that I have nerves, I find myself more susceptible than usual to the finest influences, as music and poetry. The very air can intoxicate me, or the least sight or sound, as if my finer senses had acquired an appetite by their fast.

Dec. 12. . . . I have been surveying for twenty or thirty days, living coarsely, even as respects my diet—for I find that that will always alter to suit my employment—indeed, leading a quite trivial life; and tonight, for the first time, had made a fire in my chamber and endeavored to return to myself. I wished to ally myself to the powers that rule the universe. I wished to dive into some deep stream of thoughtful and devoted life, which meandered through retired and fertile meadows far from towns. I wished to do again, or for once, things quite congenial to my highest inmost and most sacred nature, to lurk in crystalline thought like the trout under verdurous banks, where stray mankind should only see my bubble come to the surface. I wished to live, ah! as far away as a man can think. I wished for leisure and quiet to let my life flow in its proper channels, with its proper currents; when I might not waste the days, might establish daily prayer and thanksgiving in my family; might do my own work and not the work of Concord and Carlisle, which would yield me better than money.

Dec. 17. . . . The winter morning is the time to see the woods and shrubs in their perfection, wearing their snowy and frosty dress. Even he who visits them half an hour after sunrise will have lost some of their most delicate and fleeting beauties. The trees wear their snowy burden but coarsely after midday, and it no longer expresses the character of the tree. I observed that early in the morning every pine needle was covered with a frosty sheath, but soon after sunrise it was all gone. You walk in the pitch pine wood as under a penthouse. The stems and branches of the trees look black by contrast. You wander zigzag through the aisles of the wood, where stillness and twilight reign.

Improve every opportunity to express yourself in writing, as if it were your last.

I do not know but a pine wood is as substantial and as memorable a fact as a friend. I am more sure to come away from it cheered, than from those who come nearest to being my friends. It is unfortunate for the chopper and the walker when the cold wind comes from the same side with the sun, for then he cannot find a warm recess in which to sit. It is pleasant to walk now through open and stately white pine woods. Their plumes do not hold so much snow commonly, unless where their limbs rest or are weighed down on to a neighboring tree. It is cold but still in their midst, where the snow is untracked by man, and ever and anon you see the snow-dust, shone on by the sun, falling from their tops and, as it strikes the lower limbs, producing in-

numerable new showers. For, as after a rain there is a second
rain in the woods, so after a light snow there is a second
snow in the woods, when the wind rises. The branches of
the white pine are more horizontal than those of the pitch,
and the white streaks of snow on them look accordingly. I
perceive that the young black oaks and the red oaks, too,
methinks, still keep their leaves as well as the white. This
piercing wind is so nearly from the west this afternoon that,
to stand at once in a sheltered and a sunny place, you must
seek the south-southeast side of the woods.

What slight but important distinctions between one creature and another! What little, but essential, advantages one
enjoys over another! I noticed this afternoon a squirrel's nest
high in the fork of a white pine. Thither he easily ascends,
but many creatures strive in vain to get at him.

The lower branches of the hemlock point down, and even
trail on the ground, the whole tree making a perfect canopy.

When they who have aspired to be friends cease to sympathize, it is the part of religion to keep asunder.

One of the best men I know often offends me by uttering
made words—the very best words, of course, or dinner
speeches, most smooth and gracious and fluent repartees,
a sort of talking to Buncombe, a dash of polite conversation,
a graceful bending, as if I were Master Slingsby of promising
parts, from the University. O would you but be simple
and downright! Would you but cease your palaver! It is the
misfortune of being a gentleman and famous. The conversation of gentlemen after dinner! One of the best of men and
wisest, to whom this diabolical formality will adhere. Repeating himself, shampooing himself! Passing the time of day,
as if he were just introduced! No words are so tedious.
Never a natural or simple word or yawn. It produces an
appearance of phlegm and stupidity in me the auditor. I
am suddenly the closest and most phlegmatic of mortals,
and the conversation comes to naught. Such speeches as an
ex-Member of Congress might make to an ex-Member of Parliament.

To explain to a friend is to suppose that you are not intelligent of one another. If you are not, to what purpose will
you explain?

My acquaintances will sometimes wonder why I will impoverish myself by living aloof from this or that company,
but greater would be the impoverishment if I should associate
with them.

Dec. 20. . . . . Our country is broad and rich, for here, within twenty miles of Boston, I can stand in a clearing in the woods and look a mile or more, over the shrub oaks, to the distant pine copses and horizon of uncut woods, without a house or road or cultivated field in sight.

Dec. 24. It spits snow this afternoon.

Dec. 25. . . . . A wind is now blowing the light snow which fell a day or two ago into drifts, especially on the lee, now the south, side of the walls, the outlines of the drifts corresponding to the chinks in the walls and the eddies of the wind. The snow glides, unperceived for the most part, over the open fields without rising into the air (unless the ground is elevated), until it reaches an opposite wall, which it sifts through and is blown over, blowing off from it like steam when seen in the sun. As it passes through the chinks, it does not drive straight onward, but curves gracefully upwards into fantastic shapes, somewhat like the waves which curve as they break upon the shore; that is, as if the snow that passes through a chink were one connected body, detained by the friction of its lower side. It takes the form of saddles and shells and porringers. It builds up a fantastic alabaster wall behind the first—a snowy sierra. It is wonderful what sharp turrets it builds up—builds up, i.e. by accumulation though seemingly by attrition, though the curves upward to a point like the prows of ancient vessels look like sharp carving, or as if the material had been held before the blowpipe. So what was blown up into the air gradually sifts down into the road or field, and forms the slope of the sierra. Astonishingly sharp and thin overhanging eaves it builds, even this dry snow, where it has the least suggestion from a wall or bank—less than a mason ever springs his brick from. This is the architecture of the snow. On high hills exposed to wind and sun, it curls off like the steam from a damp roof in the morning. Such sharply defined forms it takes as if the core had been the flames of gaslights.

Dec. 30. . . . . This afternoon, being on Fair Haven Hill, I heard the sound of a saw, and soon after from the Cliff saw two men sawing down a noble pine beneath, about forty rods off. I resolved to watch it till it fell, the last of a dozen or more which were left when the forest was cut and for fifteen years have waved in solitary majesty over the sprout-land. I saw them like beavers or insects gnawing at the trunk of this noble tree, the diminutive manikins with their cross-cut saw which could scarcely span it. It towered up a hundred feet as I afterward found by measurement, one of the tallest probably in the township and straight as an arrow, but slanting a little toward the hillside, its top seen against the frozen river and the hills of Conantum. I watch closely to see when it begins to move. Now the sawers stop, and with an axe open it a little on the side toward which it leans, that it may break the faster. And now their saw goes again. Now surely it is going; it is inclined one quarter of the quadrant, and, breathless, I expect its crashing fall. But no, I was mistaken; it has not moved an inch; it stands at the same angle as at first. It is fifteen minutes yet to its fall. Still its branches wave in the wind, as if it were destined to stand for a century, and the wind soughs through its needles as of yore; it is still a forest tree, the most majestic tree that waves over Musketaquid. The silvery sheen of the sunlight is reflected from its needles; it still affords an inaccessible crotch for the squirrel's nest; not a lichen has forsaken its mast-like stem, its raking mast—the hill is the hulk. Now, now's the moment! The manikins at its base are fleeing from their crime. They have dropped the guilty saw and axe. How slowly and majestically it starts! as if it were only swayed by a summer breeze, and would return without a sigh to its location in the air. And now it fans the hillside with its fall, and it lies down to its bed in the valley, from which it is never to rise, as softly as a feather, folding its green mantle about it like a warrior, as if, tired of standing, it embraced the earth with silent joy, returning its elements to the dust again. But hark! there you only saw, but did not hear. There now comes up a deafening crash to these rocks, advertising you that even trees do not die without a groan. It rushes to embrace the earth, and mingle its elements with the dust. And now all is still once more and forever, both to eye and ear.

1852

The noted newspaper editor Horace Greeley appointed himself Thoreau's unofficial literary agent; his efforts failed to result in any publications in 1852 but were better rewarded later on. Meanwhile, if Thoreau's life could ever be said to settle into a routine, this was the year it did so. His walking, his lecturing, his surveying, and his writing all continued. By now his self-training as a writer was showing its full effect. He wrote easily, copiously, and often very well indeed. The journal includes passages of description that are better than anyone else has penned.

Jan. 7. . . . This afternoon, in dells of the wood and on the lee side of the woods, where the wind has not disturbed it, the snow still lies on the trees as richly as I ever saw it. It was just moist enough to stick. The pitch pines wear it best, their plumes hang down like the feathers of the ostrich or the tail of the cassowary, so purely white—I am sorry that I cannot say *snowy* white, for in purity it is like nothing but itself. From contrast with the dark needles and stems of the trees, whiter than ever on the ground. Even the bare apple tree limbs and twigs in the hollows support each a little ridge of snow, a collar of snow, five or six inches high. The trees are bent under the weight into a great variety of postures—arches, etc. Their branches and tops are so consolidated by the burden of snow, and they stand in such new attitudes, the tops often like canopies or parasols, agglomerated, that they remind me of the pictures of palms and other Oriental trees. . . .

Jan. 11. . . . We sometimes find ourselves living fast—unprofitably and coarsely even—as we catch ourselves eating our meals in unaccountable haste. But in one sense we cannot live too leisurely. Let me not live as if time was short. Catch the pace of the seasons; have leisure to attend to every phenomenon of nature, and to entertain every thought that comes to you. Let your life be a leisurely progress through the realms of nature, even in guest quarters.

Jan. 13. . . . Here I am on the Cliffs at half past 3 or 4 o'clock. The snow more than a foot deep over all the land. Few if any leave the beaten paths. A few clouds are floating overhead, downy and dark. Clear sky and bright sun, and yet no redness. Remarkable, yet admirable, moderation that this should be confined to the morning and evening. Greeks were they who did it. A mother-o'-pearl tint is the utmost they will give you at midday, and this but rarely. Singular enough, twenty minutes later, looking up, I saw a long, light-textured cloud stretching from north to south, with a dunnish mass and an enlightened border, with its under edge toward the west all beautiful mother-o'-pearl, as remarkable as a rainbow, stretching over half the heavens; and underneath it, in the west, were flitting mother-o'-pearl clouds, which change their loose-textured form and melt rapidly away, never any so fast, even while I write. Before I can complete this sentence, I look up and they are gone, like smoke or rather the steam from the engine in the winter air. Even a considerable cloud, like a fabulous Atlantis or unfortunate isle in the Hesperian sea, is dissolved and dispersed in a minute or two, and nothing is left but the pure ether. Then another comes by magic, is born out of the pure blue empyrean, with beautiful mother-o'-pearl tints, where not a shred of vapor was to be seen before, not enough to stain a glass or polished steel blade. It grows more light and porous; the blue deeps are seen through it here and there; only a few flocks are left; and now these too have disappeared, and no one knows whither it is gone. You are compelled to look at the sky, for the earth is invisible.

Jan. 15. We have heard a deal about English comfort. But may you not trace these stories home to some wealthy Sardanapalus who was able to pay for obsequious attendance and for every luxury? How far does it describe merely the tact and selfishness of the wealthy class? Ask the great mass of Englishmen and travellers, whose vote alone is conclusive, concerning the comfort they enjoyed in second and third class accommodations in steamboats and railroads and eating and lodging houses. Lord Somebody-or-other may have made himself comfortable, but the very style of his living makes it necessary that the great majority of his countrymen should be uncomfortable.

Jan. 17. . . . The other day, the fourteenth, as I was passing the further Garfield house beyond Holden's, with my pantaloons, as usual, tucked into my boots (there was no path beyond Holden's), I heard some persons in Garfield's shed, but did not look round, and when I had got a rod or two beyond, I heard some one call out impudently from the shed, quite loud, something like "Holloa, mister! what do you think of the walking?" I turned round directly and saw three men standing in the shed. I was resolved to discomfit them—that they should prove their manhood, if they had any, and find something to say, though they had nothing before, that they should make amends to the universe by feeling cheap. They should either say to my face and eye what they had said to my back, or they should feel the meanness of having to change their tone. So I called out, looking at one, "Do you wish to speak to me, sir?" No answer. So I stepped a little nearer and repeated the question, when one replied, "Yes, sir." So I advanced with alacrity up the path they had shovelled. In the meanwhile one ran into the house. I thought I had seen the nearest one [before]. He called me by name, faintly and with hesitation, and held out his hand half unconsciously, which I did not decline, and I inquired gravely if he wished to say anything to me. He could only wave me to the other and mutter, "My brother." I approached *him* and repeated the question. He looked as if he were shrinking into a nutshell; a pitiable object he was. He looked away from me while he began to frame some business, some surveying, that he might wish to have done. I saw that he was drunk, that his brother was ashamed of him, and I turned my back on him in the outset of this indirect but drunken apology.

. . . It appears to me that at a very early age the mind of man, perhaps at the same time with his body, ceases to be elastic. His intellectual power becomes something defined and limited. He does not think expansively, as he would stretch himself in his growing days. What was flexible sap hardens into heart-wood, and there is no further change. In the season of youth, methinks, man is capable of intellectual effort and performance which surpass all rules and bounds; as the youth lays out his whole strength without fear or prudence and does not feel his limits. It is the transition from poetry to prose. The young man can run and leap; he has not learned exactly how far, he knows no limits. The grown man does not exceed his daily labor. He has no strength to waste.

Jan. 20. . . . The farmers nowadays can cart out peat and muck over the frozen meadows. Somewhat analogous, methinks, the scholar does; drives in with tight-braced energy and winter cheer on to his now firm meadowy grounds, and carts, hauls off, the virgin loads of fertilizing soil which he threw up in the warm, soft summer. We now bring our muck out of the meadows, but it was thrown up first in summer. The scholar's and the farmer's work are strictly analogous. Easily he now conveys, sliding over the snow-clad ground, great loads of fuel and of lumber which have grown in many summers, from the forest to the town. *He* deals with the dry hay and cows, the spoils of summer meads and fields, stored in his barns, doling it out from day to day, and manufactures milk for men. When I see the farmer driving into his barnyard with a load of muck, whose blackness contrasts strangely with the white snow, I have the thoughts which I have described. He is doing like myself. My barnyard is my journal.

Jan. 21. . . . I never realized so distinctly as this moment that I am peacefully parting company with the best friend I ever had, by each pursuing his proper path. I perceive that it is possible that we may have a better *understanding* now than when we were more at one. Not expecting such essential agreement as before. Simply our paths diverge.

Jan. 24. . . . I see in the woods the woodman's embers, which have melted a circular hole in the snow, where he warms his coffee at noon. But these days the fire does not melt the snow over a space three feet across.

These woods! Why do I not feel their being cut more sorely? Does it not affect me nearly? The axe can deprive me of much. Concord is sheared of its pride. I am certainly the less attached to my native town in consequence. One, and a main, link is broken. I shall go to Walden less frequently.

Jan. 29. . . . Heard C. [Ellery Channing] tonight. It was a bushel of nuts. Perhaps the most original lecture I ever heard. Ever so unexpected, not to be foretold, and so sententious that you could not look at him and take his thought at the same time. You had to give your undivided attention to the thoughts, for you were not assisted by set phrases or modes of speech intervening. There was no sloping up or down to or from his points. It was all genius, no talent. It required more close attention, more abstraction from surrounding circumstances, than any lecture I have heard. For, well as I know C., he more than any man disappoints my expectation. When I see him in the desk, hear him, I cannot realize that I ever saw him before. He will be strange, unexpected, to his best acquaintance. I cannot associate the lecturer with the companion of my walks. It was from so original and peculiar a point of view, yet just to himself in the main, that I doubt if three in the audience apprehended a tithe that he said. It was so hard to hear that doubtless few made the exertion. A thick succession of mountain passes and no intermediate slopes and plains. Other lectures, even the best, in which so much space is given to the elaborate development of a few ideas, seemed somewhat meagre in comparison. Yet it would be how much more glorious if talent were added to genius, if there [were] a just arrangement and development of the thoughts, and each step were not a leap, but he ran a space to take a yet higher leap!

Jan. 30. . . . Nature allows of no universal secrets. The more carefully a secret is kept on one side of the globe, the larger the type it is printed in on the other. Nothing is too pointed, too personal, too immodest, for her to blazon. The relations of sex, transferred to flowers, become the study of ladies in the drawing room. While men wear fig leaves, she grows the *Phallus impudicus* and *P. caninus* and other phallus-like fungi.

Jan. 31. . . . One woman whom I visit sometimes thinks I am conceited, and yet wonders that I do not visit her oftener. If I were sure she was right perhaps I should. . . .

Feb. 1. . . . If I have not succeeded in my friendships, it was because I demanded more of them and did not put up with what I could get; and I got no more partly because I gave so little.

. . . The recent rush to California and the attitude of the world, even of its philosophers and prophets, in relation to it appears to me to reflect the greatest disgrace on mankind. That so many are ready to get their living by the lottery of gold-digging without contributing any value to society, and that the great majority who stay at home justify them in this both by precept and example! It matches the infatuation of the Hindus who have cast themselves under the car of Juggernaut. I know of no more startling development of the morality of trade and all the modes of getting a living than the rush to California affords. Of what significance the philosophy, or poetry, or religion of a world that will rush to the lottery of California gold-digging on the receipt of the first news, to live by luck, to get the means of commanding the labor of others less lucky, i.e. of slave-holding, without contributing any value to society? And that is called enterprise, and the devil is only a little more enterprising! The philosophy and poetry and religion of such a mankind are not worth the dust of a puffball. The hog that *roots* his own living, and so makes manure, would be ashamed of such company. If I could command the wealth of all the worlds by lifting my finger, I would not pay such a price for it. It makes God to be a moneyed gentleman who scatters a handful of pennies in order to see mankind scramble for them. Going to California. It is only three thousand miles nearer to hell. I will resign my life sooner than live by luck. The world's raffle. A subsistence in the domains of nature a thing to be raffled for! No wonder that they gamble there. I never heard that they did anything else there. What a comment, what a satire, on our institutions! . . .

Feb. 8. Mrs. Buttrick says that she has five cents for making a shirt, and that if she does her best she can make one in a day.

Feb. 9. . . . Met Sudbury Haines on the river before the Cliffs, come a-fishing. Wearing an old coat, much patched, with many colors. He represents the Indian still. The very patches in his coat and his improvident life do so. I feel that he is as essential a part, nevertheless, of our community as the lawyer in the village. He tells me that he caught three pickerel here the other day that weighed seven pounds all together. It is the old story. The fisherman is a natural storyteller. No man's imagination plays more pranks than his, while he is tending his reels and trotting from one to another, or watching his cork in summer. He is ever waiting for the sky to fall. He has sent out a venture. He has a ticket in the lottery of fate, and who knows what it may draw? He ever expects to catch a bigger fish yet. He is the most patient and believing of men. Who else will stand so long in wet places? When the haymaker runs to shelter, he takes down his pole and bends his steps to the river, glad to have a leisure day. He is more like an inhabitant of nature. The weather concerns him. He is an observer of her phenomena.

Feb. 13. Talking with Rice this afternoon about the bees which I discovered the other day, he told me something about his bee-hunting. He and Pratt go out together once or twice a year. He takes a little tin box with a little refined sugar and water about the consistency of honey, or some honey in the comb, which comes up so high only in the box as to let the lid clear a bee's back, also some little bottles of paint—red, blue, white, etc.—and a compass properly prepared to line the bees with, the sights perhaps a foot apart. Then they ride off (this is in the fall) to some extensive wood, perhaps the west side of Sudbury. They go to some buckwheat field or a particular species of late goldenrod which especially the bees frequent at that season, and they are sure to find honey-bees enough. They catch one by putting the box under the blossoms and then covering him with the lid, at the same time cutting off the stalk of the flower. They then set down the box, and after a while raise the lid slightly to see if the bee is feeding: if so, they take off the lid, knowing that he will not fly away till he gets ready, and catch another; and so on till they get a sufficient number. Then they thrust sticks into their little paint bottles, and, with these, watching their opportunity, they give the bees each a spot

of a particular color on his body—they spot him distinctly—
and then, lying about a rod off, not to scare them, and watching them carefully all the while, they wait till one has filled
his sac, and prepares to depart to his hive. They are careful
to note whether he has a red or a blue jacket or what color.
He rises up about ten feet and then begins to circle rapidly
round and round with a hum, sometimes a circle twenty
feet in diameter before he has decided which way to steer,
and then suddenly shoots off in a beeline to his hive. The
hunters lie flat on their backs and watch him carefully all
the while. If blue-jacket steers toward the open land where
there are known to be hives, they forthwith leave out of the
box all the blue-jackets, and move off a little and open the
box in a new place to get rid of that family. And so they
work till they come to a bee, red-jacket perhaps, that steers
into the wood or swamp or in a direction to suit them. They
take the point of compass exactly, and wait perhaps till red-
jacket comes back, that they may ascertain his course more
exactly, and also judge by the time it has taken for him to
go and return, using their watches, how far off the nest is,
though sometimes they are disappointed in their calculations,
for it may take the [bee] more or less time to crawl into
its nest, depending on its position in the tree. By the third
journey he will commonly bring some of his companions.
Our hunters then move forward a piece, from time to time
letting out a bee to make sure of their course. After the
bees have gone and come once, they generally steer straight
to their nest at once without circling round first. Sometimes
the hunters, having observed this course carefully on the
compass, go round a quarter of a circle and, letting out another bee, observe the course from that point, knowing that
where these two lines intersect must be the nest. Rice thinks
that a beeline does not vary more than fifteen or twenty feet
from a straight one in going half a mile. They frequently
trace the bees thus to their hives more than a mile.

He said that the last time he went out the wind was so
strong that the bees made some leeway just as a bullet will,
and he could not get the exact course to their hives. He has
a hive of bees over in Sudbury, and he every year sows
some buckwheat for them. He has visited this buckwheat
when in blossom when there was more than one bee to
every six inches square, and out of curiosity has caught a
number of the bees and, letting them out successively, has
calculated by the several courses they took whose hives they

came from in almost every instance, though some had come more than two miles and others belonged to his own hive close by.

Feb. 18. . . . I have a commonplace-book for facts and another for poetry, but I find it difficult always to preserve the vague distinction which I had in my mind, for the most interesting and beautiful facts are so much the more poetry and that is their success. They are *translated* from earth to heaven. I see that if my facts were sufficiently vital and significant—perhaps transmuted more into the substance of the human mind—I should need but one book of poetry to contain them all.

March 15. This afternoon I throw off my outside coat. A mild spring day. I must hie to the Great Meadows. The air is full of bluebirds. The ground almost entirely bare. The villagers are out in the sun, and every man is happy whose work takes him outdoors. I go by Sleepy Hollow toward the Great Fields. I lean over a rail to hear what is in the air, liquid with the bluebirds' warble. My life partakes of infinity. The air is as deep as our natures. Is the drawing in of this vital air attended with no more glorious results than I witness? The air is a velvet cushion against which I press my ear. I go forth to make new demands on life. I wish to begin this summer well; to do something in it worthy of it and of me; to transcend my daily routine and that of my townsmen; to have my immortality now, that it be in the *quality* of my daily life; to pay the greatest price, the greatest tax, of any man in Concord, and enjoy the most!! I will give all I am for *my* nobility. I will pay all my days for *my* success. I pray that the life of this spring and summer may ever lie fair in my memory. May I dare as I have never done! May I persevere as I have never done! May I purify myself anew as with fire and water, soul and body! May my melody not be wanting to the season! May I gird myself to be a hunter of the beautiful, that naught escape me! May I attain to a youth never attained! I am eager to report the glory of the universe; may I be worthy to do it; to have got through with regarding human values, so as not to be distracted from regarding divine values. It is reasonable that a man should be something worthier at the end of the year than he was at the beginning.

Yesterday's rain, in which I was glad to be drenched, has

advanced the spring, settled the ways, and the old footpath and the brook and the plank bridge behind the hill are suddenly uncovered, which have [been] buried so long; as if we had returned to our earth after an absence, and took pleasure in finding things so nearly in the state in which we left them.

We go out without our coats, saunter along the street, look at the aments of the willow beginning to appear and the swelling buds of the maple and the elm. The Great Meadows are water instead of ice. I see the ice on the bottom in white sheets. And now one great cake rises amid the bushes (behind Peter's). I see no ducks.

April 1. . . . We have had a good solid winter, which has put the previous summer far behind us; intense cold, deep and lasting snows, and clear, tense winter sky. It is a good experience to have gone through with.

April 3. . . . The bluebird carries the sky on his back.

April 12. . . . I am made somewhat sad this afternoon by the coarseness and vulgarity of my companion, because he is one with whom I have made myself intimate. He inclines latterly to speak with coarse jesting of facts which should always be treated with delicacy and reverence. I lose my respect for the man who can make the mystery of sex the subject of a coarse jest, yet, when you speak earnestly and seriously on the subject, is silent. I feel that this is to be truly irreligious. Whatever may befall me, I trust that I may never lose my respect for purity in others. The subject of sex is one on which I do not wish to meet a man at all unless I *can* meet him on the most inspiring ground—if his view degrades, and does not elevate. I would preserve purity in act and thought, as I would cherish the memory of my mother.

April 16. . . . As I turned round the corner of Hubbard's Grove, saw a woodchuck, the first of the season, in the middle of the field, six or seven rods from the fence which bounds the wood, and twenty rods distant. I ran along the fence and cut him off, or rather overtook him, though he started at the same time. When I was only a rod and a half off, he stopped, and I did the same; then he ran again, and I ran up within three feet of him, when he stopped again, the fence being between us. I squatted down and surveyed him at my leisure. His eyes were dull black and rather inobvious, with a faint chestnut (?) iris, with but little expression and that more of resignation than of anger. The general aspect was a coarse grayish brown, a sort of grisel (?). A lighter brown next the skin, then black or very dark brown and tipped with whitish rather loosely. The head between a squirrel and a bear, flat on the top and dark brown, and darker still or black on the tip of the nose. The whiskers black, two inches long. The ears very small and roundish, set far back and nearly buried in the fur. Black feet, with long and slender claws for digging. It appeared to tremble, or perchance shivered with cold. When I moved, it gritted its teeth quite loud, sometimes striking the under jaw against the other chatteringly, sometimes grinding one jaw on the other, yet as if more from instinct than anger. Whichever way I turned, that way it headed. I took a twig a foot long and touched its snout, at which it started forward and bit the stick, lessening the distance between us to two feet, and still it held all the ground it gained. I played with it tenderly awhile with the stick, trying to open its gritting jaws. Ever its long incisors, two above and two below, were presented. But I thought it would go to sleep if I stayed long enough. It did not sit upright as sometimes, but *standing* on its fore feet with its head down, i.e. half sitting, half standing. We sat looking at one another about half an hour, till we began to feel mesmeric influences. When I was tired, I moved away, wishing to see him run, but I could not start him. He would not stir as long as I was looking at him or could see him. I walked round him; he turned as fast and fronted me still. I sat down by his side within a foot. I talked to him *quasi* forest lingo, baby-talk, at any rate in a conciliatory tone, and thought that I had some influence on him. He gritted his teeth less. I chewed checkerberry leaves and presented them to his nose at last without a grit; though I saw that by so much gritting of the teeth he had worn them rapidly and they were covered with a fine white powder, which, if you measured it thus, would have made his anger terrible. He did not mind any noise I might make. With a little stick I lifted one of his paws to examine it, and held it up at pleasure. I turned him over to see what color he was beneath (darker or more purely brown), though he turned himself back again sooner than I could have wished. His tail was also all brown, though not very dark, rat-tail like, with loose hairs standing out on all sides like a caterpillar brush. He had a rather mild look. I spoke kindly to him. I reached checkerberry leaves to his mouth. I stretched my hands over him, though he turned up his head and still gritted a little. I laid my hand on him, but immediately took it off again, instinct not being wholly overcome. If I had had a few fresh bean leaves, thus in advance of the season, I am sure I should have tamed him completely. It was a frizzly tail. His is a humble, terrestrial color like a partridge's, well concealed where dead wiry grass rises above darker brown or chestnut dead leaves—a modest color. If I had had some food, I should have ended with stroking him at my leisure. Could easily have wrapped him in my handkerchief. He was not fat nor particularly lean. I finally had to leave him without seeing him move from the place. A large, clumsy, burrowing squirrel. *Arctomys,* bearmouse. I respect him as one of the natives. He lies there, by his color and habits so naturalized amid the dry leaves, the withered grass, and the bushes. A sound nap, too, he has enjoyed in his native fields, the past winter. I think I might learn some wisdom of him. His ancestors have lived here longer than mine. He is more thoroughly acclimated and naturalized than I. Bean leaves the red man raised for him, but he can do without them.

April 24. . . . I know two species of men. The vast majority are men of society. They live on the surface; they are interested in the transient and fleeting; they are like driftwood on the flood. They ask forever and only the news, the froth and scum of the eternal sea. They use policy; they make up for want of matter with manner. They have many letters to write. Wealth and the approbation of men is to them success. The enterprises of society are something final and sufficing for them. The world advises them, and they listen to its advice. They live wholly an evanescent life, creatures of circumstance. It is of prime importance to them who is the president of the day. They have no knowledge of truth, but by an exceedingly dim and transient instinct, which stereotypes the church and some other institutions. They dwell, they are ever, right in my face and eyes like gnats; they are like motes, so near the eyes that, looking beyond, they appear like blurs; they have their being between my eyes and the end of my nose. The *terra firma* of my existence lies far beyond, behind them and their improvements. If they write, the best of them deal in "elegant literature." Society, man, has no prize to offer me that can tempt me; not one. That which interests a town or city or any large number of men is always something trivial, as politics. It is impossible for me to be interested in what interests men generally. Their pursuits and interests seem to me frivolous. When I am most myself and see the clearest, men are least to be seen; . . . and that they are seen at all is the proof of imperfect vision. These affairs of men are so narrow as to afford no vista, no distance; it is a shallow foreground only, no large extended views to be taken. Men put to me frivolous questions: When did I come? where am I going? That was a more pertinent question—what I lectured for?—which one auditor put once to another. What an ordeal it were to make men pass through, to consider how many ever put to you a vital question! Their knowledge of something better gets no further than what is called religion and spiritual knockings.

May 8. . . . No tarts that I ever tasted at any table possessed such a refreshing, cheering, encouraging acid that literally put the heart in you and set you on edge for this world's experiences, bracing the spirit, as the cranberries I have plucked in the meadows in the spring. They cut the winter's phlegm, and now I can swallow another year of this world without other sauce. Even on the Thanksgiving table they are comparatively insipid, have lost as much flavor as beauty, are never so beautiful as in water.

May 18. . . . The landscape is most beautiful looking toward the sun (in the orchard on Fair Haven) at four. First, there is this green slope on which I sit, looking down between the rows of apple trees just being clothed with tender green—sometimes underneath them to the sparkling water, or over through them, or seeing them against the sky. Secondly, the outline of this bank or hill is drawn against the water far below; the river still high, a beautifully bright sheen on the water there, though it is elsewhere a dull slaty-blue color, a sober rippled surface. A fine sparkling shimmer in front, owing to the remarkable clearness of the atmosphere (clarified by the May storm?). Thirdly, on either side of the wood beyond the river are patches of bright, tender, yellowish, velvety green grass in meadows and on hillsides. It is like a short furred mantle now and bright as if it had the sun on it. Those great fields of green affect me as did those early green blades by the Corner Spring—like a fire flaming up from the earth. The earth proves itself well alive even in the skin. No scurf on it, only a browner color on the barren tops of hills. Fourthly, the forest, the dark-green pines, wonderfully distinct, near and erect, with their distinct dark stems, spiring tops, regularly disposed branches, and silvery light on their needles. They seem to wear an aspect as much fresher and livelier as the other trees—though their growth can hardly be perceptible yet—as if they had been washed by the rains and the air. They are now being invested with the light, sunny, yellowish-green of the deciduous trees. This tender foliage, putting so much light and life into the landscape, is the remarkable feature at this date. The week when the deciduous trees are generally and conspicuously expanding their leaves. The various tints of gray oaks and yellowish-green birches and aspens and hickories, and the red or scarlet tops where maple keys are formed (the blossoms are now over)—these last the high color (rosaceous?) in the bouquet. And fifthly, I detect a great stretch of high-backed, mostly bare, grassy pasture country between this and the Nashua, spotted with pines and forests, which I had formerly taken for forest uninterrupted. And finally, sixthly, Wachusett rising in the background, slightly veiled in bluish mist —toward which all these seem to slope gradually upward— and those grassy hillsides in the foreground, seen but as patches of bare grassy ground on a spur of that distant mountain.

May 19. Up to about the fourteenth of May I watched the progress of the season very closely—though not so carefully the earliest birds—but since that date, both from poor health and multiplicity of objects, I have noted little but what fell under my observation. . . .

June 9. . . . For a week past we have had *washing* days. The grass waving, and trees having leaved out, their boughs wave and feel the effect of the breeze. Thus new life and motion is imparted to the trees. The season of waving boughs; and the lighter under sides of the new leaves are exposed. This is the first half of June. Already the grass is not so fresh and liquid-velvety a green, having much of it blossom[ed] and some even gone to seed, and it is mixed with reddish ferns and other plants, but the general leafiness, shadiness, and waving of grass and boughs in the breeze characterize the season. The wind is not quite agreeable, because it prevents your hearing the birds sing. Meanwhile the crickets are strengthening their quire. The weather is very clear, and the sky bright. The river shines like silver. Methinks this is a traveller's month. The locust in bloom. The waving, undulating rye. The deciduous trees have filled up the intervals between the evergreens, and the woods are bosky now.

A child loves to strike on a tin pan or other ringing vessel with a stick, because, its ears being fresh, sound, attentive, and percipient, it detects the finest music in the sound, at which all nature assists. Is not the very cope of the heavens the sounding board of the infant drummer? So clear and unprejudiced ears hear the sweetest and most soul-stirring melody in tinkling cowbells and the like (dogs baying the moon), not to be referred to association, but intrinsic in the sound itself; those cheap and simple sounds which men despise because their ears are dull and debauched. Ah, that I were so much a child that I could unfailingly draw music from a quart pot! Its little ears tingle with the melody. To it there is music in sound alone.

June 11. . . . As I climbed the Cliffs, when I jarred the foliage, I perceived an exquisite perfume which I could not trace to its source. Ah, those fugacious universal fragrances of the meadows and woods! Odors rightly mingled!

June 12. . . . The critchicrotches are going to seed. . . .

June 15. . . . I hear the scream of a great hawk, sailing with a ragged wing against the high wood-side, apparently to scare his prey and so detect it—shrill, harsh, fitted to excite terror in sparrows and to issue from his split and curved bill. I see his open bill the while against the sky. Spit with force from his mouth with an undulatory quaver imparted to it from his wings or motion as he flies. A hawk's ragged wing will grow whole again, but so will not a poet's.

June 19. . . . It requires considerable skill in crossing a country to avoid the houses and too cultivated parts—somewhat of the engineer's or gunner's skill—so to pass a house, if you must go near it through high grass—pass the enemy's lines where houses are thick—as to make a hill or wood screen you—to shut every window with an apple tree. For that route which most avoids the houses is not only the one in which you will be least molested, but it is by far the most agreeable. . . .

June 20. . . . Lying with my window open, these warm, even sultry nights, I hear the sonorously musical trump of the bullfrogs from time to time, from some distant shore of the river, as if the world were given up to them. By those villagers who live on the street they are never seen and rarely heard by day, but in the quiet sultry nights their notes ring from one end of the town to another. It is as if you had waked up in the infernal regions. I do not know for a time in what world I am. It affects my morals, and all questions take a new aspect from this sound. At night bullfrogs lie on the pads and answer to one another all over North America; undoubtedly there is an incessant and uninterrupted chain of sound, *troomp, troomp, troomp,* from the Atlantic to the Pacific (*vide* if they reach so far west), further than Britain's morning gun. It is the snoring music of nature at night. When you wake thus at midnight and hear this sonorous trump from far in the horizon, you need not go to Dante for an idea of the infernal regions. It requires the night air, this sound. . . .

June 25. . . . One man lies in his words, and gets a bad reputation; another in his manners, and enjoys a good one.

. . . 8:30 P.M. To Conantum.
Moon half full. Fields dusky; the evening star and one other bright one near the moon. It is a cool but pretty still night. Methinks I am less thoughtful than I was last year at this time. The flute I now hear from the Depot Field does not find such caverns to echo and resound in my mind— no such answering depths. Our minds should echo at least as many times as a Mammoth Cave to every musical sound. It should awaken reflections in us. I hear not many crickets. Some children calling their kitten home by some endearing name. Now his day's work is done, the laborer plays his flute—only possible at this hour. Contrasted with his work, what an accomplishment! Some drink and gamble. He plays

some well-known march. But the music is not in the tune; it is in the sound. It does not proceed from the trading nor political world. He practices this ancient art. There are light, vaporous clouds overhead; dark, fuscous ones in the north. The trees are turned black. As candles are lit on earth, stars are lit in the heavens. I hear the bullfrog's trump from afar.

Now I turn down the Corner road. At this quiet hour the evening wind is heard to moan in the hollows of your face, mysterious, spirit-like, conversing with you. It can be heard now only. The whippoorwill sings. I hear a laborer going home, coarsely singing to himself. Though he has scarcely had a thought all day, killing weeds, at this hour he sings or talks to himself. His humble, earthy contentment gets expression. It is kindred in its origin with the notes or music of many creatures. A more fit and natural expression of his mood, this humming, than conversation is wont to be. The fireflies appear to be flying, though they may be stationary on the grass stems, for their perch and the nearness of the ground are obscured by the darkness, and now you see one here and then another there, as if it were one in motion. Their light is singularly bright and glowing to proceed from a living creature. Nature loves variety in all things, and so she adds glowworms to fireflies, though I have not noticed any this year. The great story of the night is the moon's adventures with the clouds. What innumerable encounters she has had with them! When I enter on the moonlit causeway, where the light is reflected from the glistening alder leaves, and their deep, dark, liquid shade beneath strictly bounds the firm damp road and narrows it, it seems like autumn. The rows of willows completely fence the way and appear to converge in perspective, as I had not noticed by day. The bullfrogs are of various tones. Some horse in a distant pasture whinnies; dogs bark; there is that dull, dumping sound of frogs, as if a bubble containing the lifeless sultry air of day burst on the surface, a belching sound. When two or more bullfrogs trump together, it is a ten-pound-ten note. In Conant's meadow I hear the gurgling of unwearied water, the trill of a toad, and go through the cool, primordial liquid air that has settled there. As I sit on the great doorstep, the loose clapboards on the old house rattle in the wind weirdly, and I seem to hear some wild mice running about on the floor, and sometimes a loud crack from some weary timber trying to change its position.

On Conantum-top, all white objects like stones are observed, and dark masses of foliage, at a distance even. How
distant is day and its associations! The light, dry cladonia
lichens on the brows of hills reflect the moonlight well,
looking like rocks. The night wind comes cold and whisper-
ing, murmuring weirdly from distant mountain-tops. No
need to climb the Andes or Himalayas, for brows of lowest
hills are highest mountain-tops in cool moonlight nights. Is
it a cuckoo's chuckling note I heard? Occasionally there is
something enormous and monstrous in the size and distance of objects. A rock, is it? or an elephant asleep? Are these
trees on an upland or a lowland? Or do they skirt the
brink of a sea-beach? When I get there, shall I look off
over the sea? The whiteweed is the only obvious flower. I
see the tops of the rye wave, and grain fields are more interesting than by day. The water is dull-colored, hardly more
bright than a rye field. There is dew only in the low
grounds. What were the firefly's light, if it were not for darkness? The one implies the other.

June 26. . . . . I have a faint recollection of pleasure derived from smoking dried lily stems before I was a man. I
had commonly a supply of these. I have never smoked anything more noxious. . . .

. . . The American's taste for architecture, whether Grecian
or Gothic, is like his taste for olives and wine, though the
last may be made of logwood. Consider the beauty of New
York architecture—and there is no very material difference
between this and Baalbec—a vulgar adornment of what is
vulgar. To what end pray is so much stone hammered? An
insane ambition to perpetuate the memory of themselves by
the amount of hammered stone they leave. Such is the glory
of nations. What if equal pains were taken to smooth and
polish their manners? Is not the builder of more consequence
than the material? One sensible act will be more memorable
than a monument as high as the moon. I love better to see
stones in place. The grandeur of Thebes was a vulgar
grandeur. She was not simple, and why should I be imposed
on by the hundred gates of her prison? More sensible is a
rod of stone wall that bounds an honest man's field than
a hundred-gated Thebes that has mistaken the true end of
life, that places hammered marble before honesty. The

religion and civilization which are barbaric and heathenish build splendid temples, but Christianity does not. It needs no college-bred architect. . . .

July 1. . . . How well-behaved are cows! When they approach me reclining in the shade, from curiosity, or to receive a whisp of grass, or to share the shade, or to lick the dog held up, like a calf—though just now they ran at him to toss him—they do not obtrude. Their company is acceptable, for they can endure the longest pause; they have not got to be entertained. They occupy the most eligible lots in the town. I love to see some pure white about them; they suggest the more neatness.

Borrowed Brigham the wheelwright's boat at the Corner Bridge. He was quite ready to lend it, and took pains to shave down the handle of a paddle for me, conversing the while on the subject of spiritual knocking, which he asked if I had looked into—which made him the slower. An obliging man, who understands that I am abroad viewing the works of Nature and not loafing, though he makes the pursuit a semireligious one, as are all more serious ones to most men. All that is not sporting in the field, as hunting and fishing, is of a religious or else love-cracked character. Another hard-featured but talkative character at the bridge inquired, as I was unlocking the boat, if I knew anything that was good for the rheumatism; but I answered that I had heard of so many and had so little faith in any that I had forgotten them all.

July 4. . . . I looked down on the river behind Dodd's at 2:30 P.M., a slate-colored stream with a scarcely perceptible current, with a male and female shore; the former, more abrupt, of button-bushes and willows, the other, flat, of grass and pickerel-weed alone. Beyond the former, the water being deep, extends a border or fringe of green and purplish pads lying perfectly flat on the surface, but on the latter side the pads extend a half a rood or a rod beyond the pickerel-weed—shining pads reflecting the light, dotted with white or yellow lilies. This sort of ruff does the river wear, and so the land is graduated off to water. A tender place in Nature, an exposed vein, and Nature making a feint to bridge it quite over with a paddy film, with red-winged blackbirds liquidly warbling and whistling on the willows, and kingbirds on the elms and oaks; these pads, if there is any wind, rippling with the water and helping to smooth and allay it. It looks tender and exposed, as if it were naturally subterranean, and now, with these shields of pads, held scalelike by long threads from the bottom, she makes a feint to bridge it. So floats the Musketaquid over its segment of the sphere.

July 5. . . . How perfect an invention is glass! There is a fitness in glass windows which reflect the sun morning and evening, windows, the doorways of light, thus reflecting the rays of that luminary with a splendor only second to itself. This invention one would say was anticipated in the arrangement of things. The sun rises with a salute and leaves the world with a farewell to our windows. To have, instead of opaque shutters or dull horn or paper, a material like solidified air, which reflects the sun thus brightly! It is inseparable from our civilization and enlightenment. It is encouraging that this intelligence and brilliancy or splendor should belong to the dwellings of men, and not to the cliffs and micaceous rocks and lakes exclusively.

. . . How cheering it is to behold a full spring bursting forth directly from the earth, like this of Tarbell's, from clean gravel, copiously, in a thin sheet; for it descends at once, where you see no opening, cool from the caverns of the earth, and making a considerable stream. Such springs, in the sale of lands, are not valued for as much as they are worth. I lie almost flat, resting my hands on what offers, to drink at this water where it bubbles, at the very udders of Nature, for man is never weaned from her breast while this life lasts. How many times in a single walk does he stoop for a draught!

July 6. . . . I am disappointed that [Edmund] Hosmer, the most intelligent farmer in Concord, and perchance in Middlesex, who admits that he has property enough for his use without accumulating more, and talks of leaving off hard work, letting his farm, and spending the rest of his days easier and better, cannot yet think of any method of employing himself but in work with his hands; only he would have a little less of it. Much as he is inclined to speculation in conversation—giving up any work to it for the time—and long-headed as he is, he talks of working for a neighbor for a day now and then and taking his dollar. He "would not like to spend his time sitting on the mill-dam." He has not even planned an essentially better life.

July 9. . . . Bathing is an undescribed luxury. To feel the wind blow on your body, the water flow on you and lave you, is a rare physical enjoyment this hot day. The water is remarkably warm here, especially in the shallows —warm to the hand, like that which has stood long in a kettle over a fire. The pond water being so warm made the water of the brook feel very cold; and this kept close on the bottom of the pond for a good many rods about the mouth of the brook, as I could feel with my feet; and when I thrust my arm down where it was only two feet deep, my arm was in the warm water of the pond, but my hand in the cold water of the brook. . . .

July 10. . . . 2 P.M. To the North River. . . .
There are but few fishes to be seen. They have, no doubt, retreated to the deepest water. In one somewhat muddier place, close to the shore, I came upon an old pout cruising with her young. She dashed away at my approach, but the fry remained. They were of various sizes from a third of an inch to an inch and a half long, quite black and pout-shaped, except that the head was most developed in the smallest. They were constantly moving about in a somewhat circular, or rather lenticular, school, about fifteen or eighteen inches in diameter, and I estimated that there were at least a thousand of them. Presently the old pout came back and took the lead of her brood, which followed her, or rather gathered about her, like chickens about a hen; but this mother had so many children she didn't know what to do. Her maternal yearnings must be on a great scale. When one half of the divided school found her out, they came down upon her and completely invested her like a small cloud. She was soon joined by another smaller pout, apparently her mate, and all, both old and young, began to be very familiar with me; they came round my legs and felt them with their feelers, and the old pouts nibbled my toes, while the fry half concealed my feet. Probably if I had been standing on the bank with my clothes on they would have been more shy. Ever and anon the old pouts dashed aside to drive away a passing bream or perch. The larger

one kept circling about her charge, as if to keep them together within a certain compass. If any of her flock were lost
or devoured she could hardly have missed them. I wondered if there was any calling of the roll at night—whether
she, like a faithful shepherdess, ever told her tale under
some hawthorn in the river's dales. Ever ready to do battle
with the wolves that might break into her fold. The young
pouts are protected then for a season by the old. Some had
evidently been hatched before the others. One of these large
pouts had a large velvet-black spot which included the right
pectoral fin, a kind of disease which I have often observed
on them.

July 12. . . . The mower, perchance, cuts some plants which
I have never seen in flower.

July 18. . . . No one has ever put into words what the
odor of water-lilies expresses. A sweet and innocent purity.
The perfect purity of the flower is not to be surpassed.
They now begin to shut up. Looking toward the sun, I
cannot see them, cannot distinguish lilies from the sun
reflected from the pads.

July 23. . . . Twenty minutes after seven, I sit at my
window to observe the sun set. The lower clouds in the north
and southwest grow gradually darker as the sun goes down,
since we now see the side opposite to the sun, but those
high overhead, whose under sides we see reflecting the
day, are light. The small clouds low in the western sky were
at first dark also, but, as the sun descends, they are lit up
and aglow all but their cores. Those in the east, though we
see their sunward sides, are a dark blue, presaging night,
only the highest faintly glowing. A roseate redness, clear as
amber, suffuses the low western sky about the sun, in which
the small clouds are mostly melted, only their golden edges
still revealed. The atmosphere there is like some kinds of
wine, perchance, or molten cinnabar, if that is red, in
which also all kinds of pearls and precious stones are melted.
Clouds generally near the horizon, except near the sun, are
now a dark blue. (The sun sets.) It is half past seven. . . .
The roseate glow deepens to purple. The low western sky is
now, and has been for some minutes, a splendid map, where
the fancy can trace islands, continents, and cities beyond
compare. The glow forsakes the high eastern clouds; the

uppermost clouds in the west now darken, the glow having forsaken them too; they become a dark blue, and anon their under sides reflect a deep red, like heavy damask curtains, after they had already been dark. The general redness gradually fades into a pale reddish tinge in the horizon, with a clear white light above it, in which the clouds grow more conspicuous and darker and darker blue, appearing to follow in the wake of the sun, and it is now a quarter to eight, or fifteen minutes after sunset, twenty-five minutes from the first. A quarter of an hour later, or half an hour after sunset, the white light grows cream-colored above the increasing horizon redness, passing through white into blue above. The western clouds, high and low, are now dark fuscous, not dark blue, but the eastern clouds are not so dark as the western. Now, about twenty minutes after the first glow left the clouds above the sun's place, there is a second faint fuscous or warm brown glow on the edges of the dark clouds there, sudden and distinct, and it fades again, and it is early starlight, but the tops of the eastern clouds still are white, reflecting the day. The cream-color grows more yellowish or amber. About three quarters of an hour after sunset the evening red is deepest, i.e. a general atmospheric redness close to the west horizon. There is more of it, after all, than I expected, for the day has been clear and rather cool, and the evening red is what was the blue haze by day. The moon, now in her first quarter, now begins to preside—her light to prevail—though for the most part eclipsed by clouds. As the light in the west fades, the sky there, seen between the clouds, has a singular clarity and serenity.

July 27. . . . It is pleasing to behold at this season contrasted shade and sunshine on the side of neighboring hills. They are not so attractive to the eye when all in the shadow of a cloud or wholly open to the sunshine. Each must enhance the other.

Aug. 3. . . . 12 M. At the east window. A temperate noon. I hear a cricket creak in the shade; also the sound of a distant piano. The music reminds me of imagined heroic ages; it suggests such ideas of human life and the field which the earth affords as the few noblest passages of poetry. Those few interrupted strains which reach me through the trees suggest the same thoughts and aspirations that all melody, by whatever sense appreciated, has ever done. I am affected.

What coloring variously fair and intense our life admits of! How a thought will mould and paint it! Impressed by some vague vision, as it were, elevated into a more glorious sphere of life, we no longer know this, we can deny its existence. We say we are enchanted, perhaps. But what I am impressed by is the fact that this enchantment is no delusion. So far as truth is concerned, it is a fact such as what we *call* our actual existence, but it is a far higher and more glorious fact. It is evidence of such a sphere, of such possibilities. It is its truth and reality that affect me. A thrumming of piano-strings beyond the gardens and through the elms. At length the melody steals into my being. I know not when it began to occupy me. By some fortunate coincidence of thought or circumstance I am attuned to the universe, I am fitted to hear, my being moves in a sphere of melody, my fancy and imagination are excited to an inconceivable degree. This is no longer the dull earth on which I stood. It is possible to live a grander life here; already the steed is stamping, the knights are prancing; already our thoughts bid a proud farewell to the so-called actual life and its humble glories. Now this is the verdict of a soul in health. But the soul diseased says that its own vision and life alone is true and sane. What a different aspect will courage put upon the face of things! This suggests what a perpetual flow of spirit would produce.

Aug. 6. . . . As I always notice the tone of the bell when I go into a new town, so surely, methinks, I notice some peculiarity in the accent and manners of the inhabitants.

Aug. 7. When I think of the thorough drilling to which young men are subjected in the English universities, acquiring a minute knowledge of Latin prosody and of Greek particles and accents, so that they can not only turn a passage of Homer into English prose or verse, but readily a passage of Shakespeare into Latin hexameters or elegiacs— that this and the like of this is to be liberally educated—I am reminded how different was the education of the actual Homer and Shakespeare. The worthies of the world and liberally educated have always, in this sense, got along with little Latin and less Greek.

Aug. 8. . . . The entertaining a single thought of a certain elevation makes all men of one religion. It is always some base alloy that creates the distinction of sects. Thought greets thought over the widest gulfs of time with unerring freemasonry. I know, for instance, that Sadi [the medieval Persian poet] entertained once identically the same thought that I do, and thereafter I can find no essential difference between Sadi and myself. He is not Persian, he is not ancient, he is not strange to me. By the identity of his thoughts with mine he still survives. It makes no odds what atoms serve us. Sadi possessed no greater privacy or individuality than is thrown open to me. He had no more interior and essential and sacred self than can come naked into my thought this moment. Truth and a true man is something essentially public, not private. If Sadi were to come back to claim a *personal* identity with the historical Sadi, he would find there were too many of us; he could not get a skin that would contain us all. The symbol of a personal identity preserved in this sense is a mummy from the catacombs—a whole skin, it may [be], but no life within it. By living the life of a man is made common property. By sympathy with Sadi I have embowelled him. In his thought I have a sample of *him,* a slice from his core, which makes it unimportant where certain bones which the thinker once employed may lie; but I could not have got this without being equally entitled to it with himself. The difference between any man and that posterity amid whom he is famous is too insignificant to sanction that he should be set up again in any world as distinct from them. Methinks I can be as intimate with the essence of an ancient worthy as, so to speak, he was himself.

Aug. 29. . . . We boast that we belong to the nineteenth century, and are making the most rapid strides of any nation. But consider how little this village does for its own culture. We have a comparatively decent system of common schools, schools for infants only, as it were, but, excepting the half-starved Lyceum in the winter, no school for ourselves. It is time that we had uncommon schools, that we did not leave off our education when we begin to be men. Comparatively few of my townsmen evince any interest in their own culture, however much they may boast of the school tax they pay. It is time that villages were universities, and their elder inhabitants the fellows, with leisure—if they are indeed so well off—to pursue liberal studies as long as they live. In this country the village should in many respects take the place of the nobleman who has gone by the board. It should be the patron of the fine arts. It is rich enough; it only wants the refinement. It can spend money enough on such things as farmers value, but it is thought utopian to propose spending money for things which more intelligent men know to be of far more worth. If we live in the nineteenth century, why should we not enjoy the advantages which the nineteenth century has to offer? Why should our life be in any respect provincial? As the nobleman of cultivated taste surrounds himself with whatever conduces to his culture—books, paintings, statuary, etc.—so let the village do. This town—how much has it ever spent directly on its own culture? To act collectively is according to the spirit of our institutions, and I am confident that, as our circumstances are more flourishing, our means are greater. New England can hire all the wise men in the world to come and teach her, and board them round the while, and not be provincial at all. That is the uncommon school we want. The one hundred and twenty-five dollars which is subscribed in this town every winter for a Lyceum is better spent than any other equal sum.

Aug. 31. . . . It is worth the while to have had a cloudy, even a stormy, day for an excursion, if only that you are out at the clearing up. The beauty of the landscape is the greater, not only by reason of the contrast with its recent lowering aspect, but because of the greater freshness and purity of the air and of vegetation, and of the repressed and so recruited spirits of the beholder. Sunshine is nothing to be observed or described, but when it is seen in patches on the hillsides, or suddenly bursts forth with splendor at the end of a storm. I derive pleasure now from the shadows of the clouds diversifying the sunshine on the hills, where lately all was shadow. The spirits of the cows at pasture on this very hillside appear excited. They are restless from a kind of joy, and are not content with feeding. The weedy shore is suddenly blotted out by this rise of waters.

Sept. 9. There are enough who will flatter me with sweet words, and anon use bitter ones to balance them, but they are not my friends. Simple sincerity and truth are rare indeed. One acquaintance criticises me to my face, expecting every moment that I will become his friend to pay for it. I hear my acquaintance thinking his criticism aloud.

We love to talk with those who can make a good guess at us, not with those who talk to us as if we were somebody else all the while. Our neighbors invite us to be amiable toward their vices. How simple is the law of love! One who loves us acts accordingly, and anon we come together and succeed together without let or hindrance.

Sept. 11. Genius is, like the snapping-turtle, born with a great developed head. They say our brain at birth is one sixth the weight of the body.

Oct. 16. Saturday. The sidewalks are covered with the impressions of leaves which fell yesterday and were pressed into the soil by the feet of the passers, leaving a myriad dark spots—like bird-tracks or hieroglyphics to a casual observer.

Oct. 20. . . . Many a man, when I tell him that I have been on to a mountain, asks if I took a glass with me. No doubt, I could have seen further with a glass, and particular objects more distinctly—could have counted more meeting-houses; but this has nothing to do with the peculiar beauty and grandeur of the view which an elevated position affords. It was not to see a few particular objects, as if they were near at hand, as I had been accustomed to see them, that I ascended the mountain, but to see an infinite variety far and near in their relation to each other, thus reduced to a single picture. The facts of science, in comparison with poetry, are wont to be as vulgar as looking from the mountain with a telescope. It is a counting of meeting-houses. At the public house, the mountain-house, they keep a glass to let, and think the journey to the mountain-top is lost, that you have got but half the view, if you have not taken a glass with you.

Oct. 28. . . . I heard one boy say to another in the street today, "You don't know much more than a piece of putty."

Nov. 23. . . . I had a thought in a dream last night which surprised me by its strangeness, as if it were based on an experience in a previous state of existence, and could not be entertained by my waking self. Both the thought and the language were equally novel to me, but I at once perceived it to be true and to coincide with my experience in this state.

1853

Through the good offices of Greeley, Putnam's Monthly Magazine *ran three extracts from Thoreau's writing about his visit to Canada. The Boston publisher Munroe sent to the author 706 unsold copies of the* Week. *The author announced firmly in his journal that he was the better for this experience. Thoreau made another trip into the Maine woods. His journal during 1853 has a generous amplitude to it. But science, symbolized by the Latin names for things, plays an increasing role and philosophy grows the less.*

Jan. 7. . . . About ten minutes before 10 A.M., I heard a very loud sound, and felt a violent jar, which made the house rock and the loose articles on my table rattle, which I knew must be either a powder mill blown up or an earthquake. Not knowing but another and more violent might take place, I immediately ran downstairs, but I saw from the door a vast expanding column of whitish smoke rising in the west directly over the powder mills four miles distant. It was unfolding its volumes above, which made it widest there. In three or four minutes it had all risen and spread itself into a lengthening, somewhat copper-colored cloud parallel with the horizon from north to south, and about ten minutes after the explosion it passed over my head, being several miles long from north to south and distinctly dark and smoky toward the north, not nearly so high as the few cirrhi in the sky. I jumped into a man's wagon and rode toward the mills. In a few minutes more, I saw behind me, far in the east, a faint salmon-colored cloud carrying the news of the explosion to the sea, and perchance over [the] head of the absent proprietor.

Arrived probably before half past ten. There were perhaps thirty or forty wagons there. The kernel mill had blown up first, and killed three men who were in it, said to be turning a roller with a chisel. In three seconds after, one of the mixing-houses exploded. The kernel-house was swept away, and fragments, mostly but a foot or two in length, were strewn over the hills and meadows, as if sown, for thirty rods, and the slight snow then on the ground was for the most part melted around. The mixing-house, about ten rods west, was not so completely dispersed, for most of the machinery remained, a total wreck. The press-house, about twelve rods east, had two thirds [of] its boards off, and a mixing-house next westward from that which blew up had lost some boards on the east side. The boards fell out (i.e. of these buildings which did not blow up), the air within apparently rushing out to fill up the vacuum occasioned by the explosions, and so, the powder being bared to the fiery particles in the air, another building explodes. The powder on the floor of the bared press-house was six inches deep in some places, and the crowd were thoughtlessly going into it. A few windows were broken thirty or forty rods off. Timber six inches square and eighteen feet long was thrown over a hill eighty feet high at least—a dozen rods; thirty rods was about the limit of fragments. The drying-house, in which was a fire, was perhaps twenty-five rods distant and escaped. Every timber and piece of wood which was blown up was as black as if it had been dyed, except where it had broken on falling; other breakages were completely concealed by the color. I mistook what had been iron hoops in the woods for leather straps. Some of the clothes of the men were in the tops of the trees, where undoubtedly their bodies had been and left them. The bodies were naked and black, some limbs and bowels here and there, and a head at a distance from its trunk. The feet were bare; the hair singed to a crisp. I smelt the powder half a mile before I got there. Put the different buildings thirty rods apart, and then but one will blow up at a time.

March 5. . . . The secretary of the Association for the Advancement of Science requests me, as he probably has thousands of others, by a printed circular letter from Washington the other day, to fill the blank against certain questions, among which the most important one was what branch of science I was specially interested in, using the term science in the most comprehensive sense possible. Now, though I could state to a select few that department of human inquiry which engages me, and should be rejoiced at an opportunity to do so, I felt that it would be to make myself the laughing-stock of the scientific community to describe or attempt to describe to them that branch of science which specially interests me, inasmuch as they do not believe in a science which deals with the higher law. So I was obliged to speak to their condition and describe to them that poor part of me which alone they can understand. The fact is I am a mystic, a transcendentalist, and a natural philosopher to boot. Now I think of it, I should have told them at once that I was a transcendentalist. That would have been the shortest way of telling them that they would not understand my explanations.

How absurd that, though I probably stand as near to nature as any of them, and am by constitution as good an observer as most, yet a true account of my relation to nature should excite their ridicule only! If it had been the secretary of an association of which Plato or Aristotle was the president, I should not have hesitated to describe my studies at once and particularly.

March 10. This is the first really spring day. The sun is brightly reflected from all surfaces, and the north side of the street begins to be a little more passable to foot-travellers. You do not think it necessary to button up your coat.

March 12. . . . It is essential that a man confine himself to pursuits—a scholar, for instance, to studies—which lie next to and conduce to his life, which do not go against the grain, either of his will or his imagination. The scholar finds in his experience some studies to be most fertile and radiant with light, others dry, barren, and dark. If he is wise, he will not persevere in the last, as a plant in a cellar will strive toward the light. He will confine the observations of his mind as closely as possible to the experience or life of his senses. His thought must live with and be inspired with the life of the body. The deathbed scenes and observations even of the best and wisest afford but a sorry picture of our humanity. Some men endeavor to live a constrained life, to subject their whole lives to their wills, as he who said he would give a sign if he were conscious after his head was cut off—but he gave no sign. Dwell as near as possible to the channel in which your life flows. A man may associate with such companions, he may pursue such employments, as will darken the day for him. Men choose darkness rather than light.

March 15. There were few colder nights last winter than the last. The water in the flower-stand containing my pet tortoise froze solid—completely enveloping him, though I had a fire in my chamber all the evening—also that in my pail pretty thick. But the tortoise, having been thawed out on the stove, leaving the impression of his back shell in the ice, was even more lively than ever. His efforts at first had been to get under his chip, as if to go into the mud. Today the weather is severely and remarkably cold. It is not easy to keep warm in my chamber. I have not taken a more blustering walk the past winter than this afternoon.

March 21. . . . It is a genial and reassuring day; the mere warmth of the west wind amounts almost to balminess. The softness of the air mollifies our own dry and congealed substance. I sit down by a wall to see if I can muse again. We become, as it were, pliant and ductile again to strange but memorable influences; we are led a little way by our genius. We are affected like the earth, and yield to the elemental tenderness; winter breaks up within us; the frost is coming out of me, and I am heaved like the road; accumulated masses of ice and snow dissolve, and thoughts like a freshet pour down unwonted channels. A strain of music comes to solace the traveller over earth's downs and dignify his chagrins, the petty men whom he meets are the shadows of grander to come. Roads lead elsewhither than to Carlisle and Sudbury. The earth is uninhabited but fair to inhabit, like the old Carlisle road. Is then the road so rough that it should be neglected? Not only narrow but rough is the way that leadeth to life everlasting. Our experience does not wear upon us. It is seen to be fabulous or symbolical, and the future is worth expecting. Encouraged, I set out once more to climb the mountain of the earth, for my steps are symbolical steps, and in all my walking I have not reached the top of the earth yet.

March 22. . . . That is an interesting morning when one first uses the warmth of the sun instead of fire; bathes in the sun, as anon in the river; eschewing fire, draws up to a garret window and warms his thoughts at nature's great central fire, as does the buzzing fly by his side. Like it, too, our muse, wiping the dust off her long-unused wings, goes blundering through the cobweb of criticism, more dusty still—what venerable cobweb is that, which has hitherto escaped the broom, whose spider is invisible, but the *North American Review?*—and carries away the half of it.

March 29. . . . Walking along near the edge of the meadow under Lupine Hill, I slumped through the sod into a muskrat's nest, for the sod was only two inches thick over it, which was enough when it was frozen. I laid it open with my hands. There were three or four channels or hollowed paths, a rod or more in length, not merely worn but made in the meadow, and centring at the mouth of this burrow. They were three or four inches deep, and finally became indistinct and were lost amid the cranberry vines and grass toward the river. The entrance to the burrow was just at the edge of the upland, here a gently sloping bank, and was probably just beneath the surface of the water six weeks ago. It was about twenty-five rods distant from the true bank of the river. From this a straight gallery, about six inches in diameter every way, sloped upward about eight feet into the bank just beneath the turf, so that the end was about a foot higher than the entrance. There was a somewhat circular enlargement about one foot in horizontal diameter and the same depth with the gallery; and [in] it was nearly a peck of coarse meadow stubble, showing the marks of the scythe, with which was mixed accidentally a very little of the moss which grew with it. Three short galleries, only two feet long, were continued from this centre somewhat like rays toward the high land, as if they had been prepared in order to be ready for a sudden rise of the water, or had been actually made so far under such an emergency. The nest was of course thoroughly wet and, humanly speaking, uncomfortable, though the creature could breathe in it. But it is plain that the muskrat cannot be subject to the toothache. I have no doubt this was made and used last winter, for the grass was as fresh as that in the meadow (except that it was pulled up), and the sand which had been taken out lay partly in a flattened heap in the meadow, and no grass had sprung up through it.

April 1. . . . Hear ducks, disturbed, make a quacking or loud croaking. Now, at night, the scent of muskrats is very strong in particular localities. Next to the skunk it is perceived further than that of any of our animals that I think of. I perceive no difference between this and the musk with which ladies scent themselves, though here I pronounce it a strong, rank odor. In the faint reflected twilight, I distinguish one rapidly swimming away from me, leaving a widening ripple behind, and now hear one plunge from some willow or rock. A faint croaking from over the meadow up the Assabet, exactly like frogs. Can it be ducks? They stop when I walk toward them. How happens it that I never found them on the water when spearing? Now and then, when I pass an opening in the trees which line the shore, I am startled by the reflection of some brighter star from a bay.

April 3. . . . No fields are so barren to me as the men of whom I expect everything but get nothing. In their neighborhood I experience a painful yearning for society, which cannot be satisfied, for the hate is greater than the love.

April 30. . . . Moses Emerson, the kind and gentlemanly man who assisted and looked after me in Haverhill, said that a good horse was worth seventy-five dollars, and all above was fancy, and that when he saw a man driving a fast horse he expected he would fail soon.

May 10. . . . Saw, quite near, a skunk, in a cloud of long, coarse black and white hair, within a rod and a half, sharply staring at me with head to the ground, with its black, shining, bead-like eyes. It was at the edge of its hole. Its head is so narrow, and snout long and pointed, that it can make those deep holes in the spring. By the way, what makes these innumerable little punctures just through the grass in woodland paths, as with a stick? Is this, too, by the skunk?

From the hill, I look westward over the landscape. The deciduous woods are in their hoary youth, every expanding bud swaddled with downy webs. From this more eastern hill, with the whole breadth of the river valley on the west, the mountains appear higher still, the width of the blue border is greater—not mere peaks, or a short and shallow sierra, but a high blue table-land with broad foundations, a deep and solid base or tablet, in proportion to the peaks that rest on it. As you ascend, the near and low hills sink and flatten into the earth; no sky is seen behind them; the distant mountains rise. The truly great are distinguished. Vergers, crests of the waves of earth, which in the highest break at the summit into granitic rocks over which the air beats. A part of their hitherto concealed base is seen blue. You see, not the domes only, but the body, the façade, of these terrene temples. You see that the foundation answers to the superstructure. Moral structures. (The sweet-fern leaves among odors now.) The successive lines of haze which divide the western landscape, deeper and more misty over each intervening valley, are not yet very dense; yet there is a light atmospheric line along the base of the mountains for their whole length, formed by this denser and grosser atmosphere through which we look next the earth, which almost melts them into the atmosphere, like the contact of molten metal with that which is unfused; but their pure, sublimed tops and main body rise, palpable skyland above it, like the waving signal of the departing who have already left these shores. It will be worth the while to observe carefully the direction and altitude of the mountains from the Cliffs. The value of the mountains in the horizon—would not that be a good theme for a lecture? The text for a discourse on real values, and permanent; a sermon on the mount. They are stepping-stones to heaven—as the rider has a horse-block at his gate—by which to mount when we would commence our pilgrimage to heaven; by which we gradually take our departure from earth, from the time when our youthful eyes first rested on them—from this bare actual earth, which has so little of the hue of heaven. They make it easier to die and easier to live. They let us off.

(With Alcott [Bronson Alcott, the Transcendentalist] almost alone is it possible to put all institutions behind us. Every other man owns some stock in this or that one, and will not forget it.)

May 14. . . . E. Wood has added a pair of ugly wings to his house, bare of trees and painted white, particularly conspicuous from the river. You might speak of the alar extent of this house, monopolizing so much of our horizon; but alas! it is not formed for flight, after all.

May 15. . . . The first cricket's chirrup which I have chanced to hear now falls on my ear and makes me forget all else; all else is a thin and movable crust down to that depth where he resides eternally. He already foretells autumn. Deep under the dry border of some rock in this hillside he sits, and makes the finest singing of birds outward and insignificant, his own song is so much deeper and more significant. His voice has set me thinking, philosophizing, moralizing at once. It is not so wildly melodious, but it is wiser and more mature than that of the wood thrush. With this elixir I see clear through the summer now to autumn, and any summer work seems frivolous. I am disposed to ask this humblebee that hurries humming past so busily if he knows what he is about. At one leap I go from the just opened buttercup to the life everlasting. This singer has antedated autumn. His strain is superior (inferior?) to seasons. It annihilates time and space; the summer is for time-servers.

May 17. . . . Returning toward Fair Haven, I perceive at Potter's fence the first whiff of that ineffable fragrance from the Wheeler meadow—as it were the promise of strawberries, pineapples, etc., in the aroma of their flowers, so blandly sweet—aroma that fitly foreruns the summer and the autumn's most delicious fruits. It would certainly restore all such sick as could be conscious of it. The odors of no garden are to be named with it. It is wafted from the garden of gardens. It appears to blow from the river meadow from the west or southwest, here about forty rods wide or more. If the air here always possessed this bland sweetness, this spot would become famous and be visited by sick and well from all parts of the earth. It would be carried off in bottles and become an article of traffic which kings would strive to monopolize. The air of Elysium cannot be more sweet.

May 28. . . . Mayhew in his "London Labour and London Poor," treating of the costermongers, or those who get their living in the streets of London, speaks of "the muscular irritability begotten by continued wandering," making one "unable to rest for any time on one place." Mentions the instance of a girl who had been accustomed to sell sprats in the streets, who having been taken into a gentleman's house out of charity, "the pressure of shoes was intolerable to her." "But no sooner did she hear from her friends, that sprats were again in the market, than as if there were some magical influence in the fish, she at once requested to be freed from the confinement, and permitted to return to her old calling." I am perhaps equally accustomed to a roaming field-life, experience a good deal of that muscular irritability, and have a good many friends who let me know when sprats are in the market.

May 31. Some incidents in my life have seemed far more

allegorical than actual; they were so significant that they plainly served no other use. That is, I have been more impressed by their allegorical significance and fitness; they have been like myths or passages in a myth, rather than mere incidents or history which have to wait to become significant. Quite in harmony with my subjective philosophy. This, for instance: that, when I thought I knew the flowers so well, the beautiful purple azalea or pinxter-flower should be shown me by the hunter who found it. Such facts are lifted quite above the level of the actual. They are all just such events as my imagination prepares me for, no matter how incredible. Perfectly in keeping with my life and characteristic. Ever and anon something will occur which my philosophy has not dreamed of. The limits of the actual are set some thoughts further off. That which had seemed a rigid wall of vast thickness unexpectedly proves a thin and undulating drapery. The boundaries of the actual are no more fixed and rigid than the elasticity of our imaginations. The fact that a rare and beautiful flower which we never saw, perhaps never heard [of], for which therefore there was no place in our thoughts, may at length be found in our immediate neighborhood, is very suggestive.

June 9. . . . I was amused by the account which Mary, the Irish girl who left us the other day, gave of her experience at——— ———, the milkman's, in the north part of the town. She said that twenty-two lodged in the house the first night, including two pig men, that Mr. ——— kept ten men, had six children and a deaf wife, and one of the men had his wife with him, who helped sew, beside taking care of her own child. Also all the cooking and washing for his father and mother, who live in another house and whom he is bound to carry through, is done in his house, and she, Mary, was the only girl they hired; and the workmen were called up at four by an alarm clock which was set a quarter of an hour ahead of the clock downstairs and that more than as much ahead of the town clock—and she was on her feet from that hour till nine at night. Each man had two pairs of overalls in the wash, and the cans to be scalded were countless. Having got through washing the breakfast dishes by a quarter before twelve, Sunday noon, by———'s time, she left, no more to return. He had told her that the work was easy, that girls had lived with him to recover their health, and then went away to be married.

June 13, 9 A.M. To Orchis Swamp.

Find that there are two young hawks; one has left the nest and is perched on a small maple seven or eight rods distant. This one appears much smaller than the former one. I am struck by its large, naked head, so vulture-like, and large eyes, as if the vulture's were an inferior stage through which the hawk passed. Its feet, too, are large, remarkably developed, by which it holds to its perch securely like an old bird, before its wings can perform their office. It has a buff breast, striped with dark brown. Pratt, when I told him of this nest, said he would like to carry one of his rifles down there. But I told him that I should be sorry to have them killed. I would rather save one of these hawks than have a hundred hens and chickens. It was worth more to see them soar, especially now that they are so rare in the landscape. It is easy to buy eggs, but not to buy hen-hawks. My neighbors would not hesitate to shoot the last pair of hen-hawks in the town to save a few of their chickens! But such economy is narrow and grovelling. It is unnecessarily to sacrifice the greater value to the less. I would rather never taste chickens' meat nor hens' eggs than never to see a hawk sailing through the upper air again. This sight is worth incomparably more than a chicken soup or a boiled egg. So we exterminate the deer and substitute the hog. It was amusing to observe the swaying to and fro of the young hawk's head to counterbalance the gentle motion of the bough in the wind.

June 14. . . . C. [Ellery Channing] says he saw a "lurker" yesterday in the woods on the Marlborough road. He heard a distressing noise like a man sneezing but long continued, but at length found it was a man wheezing. He was oldish and grizzled, the stumps of his grizzled beard about an inch long, and his clothes in the worst possible condition—a wretched-looking creature, an escaped convict hiding in the woods, perhaps. He appeared holding on to his paunch, and wheezing as if it would kill him. He appeared to have come straight through the swamp, and—what was most interesting about him, and proved him to be a lurker of the first class—one of our party, as C. said—he kept straight through a field of rye which was fully grown, not regarding it in the least; and, though C. tried to conceal himself on the edge of the rye, fearing to hurt his feelings if the man should mistake him for the proprietor, yet they met, and the lurker, giving him a short bow, disappeared in the woods on the opposite side of the road. He went through everything.

June 20. . . . Up North River to Nawshawtuct.

The moon full. Perhaps there is no more beautiful scene than that on the North River seen from the rock this side the hemlocks. As we look up-stream, we see a crescent-shaped lake completely embosomed in the forest. There is nothing to be seen but the smooth black mirror of the water, on which there is now the slightest discernible bluish mist, a foot high, and thick-set alders and willows and the green woods without an interstice sloping upward from its very surface, like the sides of a bowl. The river is here for half a mile completely shut in by the forest. One hemlock, which the current has undermined, has fallen over till it lies parallel with the water, a foot or two above it and reaching two thirds across the stream, its extremity curving upward to the light, now dead. Here it has been a year or two, and it has only taken the place of others which have successively fallen in and been carried away by the stream. One lies now cast up on the shore. Some wild roses, so pale now in the twilight that they look exactly like great blackberry blossoms. I think *these* would look so at midday.

Saw a little skunk coming up the river-bank in the woods at the White Oak, a funny little fellow, about six inches long and nearly as broad. It faced me and actually compelled me to retreat before it for five minutes. Perhaps I was between it and its hole. Its broad black tail, tipped with white, was erect like a kitten's. It had what looked like a broad white band drawn tight across its forehead or tophead, from which two lines of white ran down, one on each side of its back, and there was a narrow white line down its snout. It raised its back, sometimes ran a few feet forward, sometimes backward, and repeatedly turned its tail to me, prepared to discharge its fluid like the old. Such was its instinct. And all the while it kept up a fine grunting like a little pig or a squirrel. It reminded me that the red squirrel, the woodchuck, and the skunk all make a similar sound. Now there are young rabbits, skunks, and probably woodchucks.

Walking amid the bushes and the ferns just after moonrise, I am refreshed with many sweet scents which I cannot trace to their source. How the trees shoot! The tops of young pines toward the moon are covered with fine shoots some eighteen inches long. Will they grow much more this year? There is a peculiarly soft, creamy light round the moon, now it is low in the sky. The bullfrogs begin about 8:30. They lie at their length on the surface amid the pads. I touched one's nose with my finger, and he only gave a sudden froggish belch and moved a foot or two off. How hard to imitate their note exactly—its sonorousness. Here, close by, it is like *er er ough, er er er ough,* with a sonorous trump which these letters do not suggest. On our return, having reached the reach by Merrick's pasture, we got the best view of the moon in the southeast, reflected in the water, on account of the length of the reach. The creamy light about it is also perfectly reflected; the path of insects on the surface between us and the moon is lit up like fire. The leafy-columned elms, planted by the river at foot of Prichard's field, are exceedingly beautiful, the moon being behind them, and I see that they are not too near together, though sometimes hardly a rod apart, their branches crossing and interlacing. Their trunks look like columns of a portico wreathed with evergreens on the evening of an illumination for some great festival. They are the more rich, because in this creamy light you cannot distinguish the trunk from the verdure that drapes it.

This is the most sultry night we have had. All windows and doors are open in the village and scarcely a lamp is lit. I pass many families sitting in their yards. The shadows of the trees and houses are too extended, now that the moon is low in the heavens, to show the richest tracery.

June 22. . . . I find my clothes covered with young caterpillars these days.

June 23. . . . The other day I saw what I took to be a scarecrow in a cultivated field, and noticing how unnaturally it was stuffed out here and there and how ungainly its arms and legs were, I thought to myself, "Well, it is thus they make these things; they do not stand much about it;" but looking round again after I had gone by, I saw my scarecrow walking off with a real live man in it.

July 1. I am surveying the Bedford road these days, and have no time for my Journal. . . .

July 21. 2 P.M. Went, in pursuit of boys who had stolen my boat-seat, to Fair Haven.

July 30. . . . . Many go to Europe *to finish their education,* and when they have returned their friends remark that the most they have acquired is a correct pronunciation of English. It is a premature hardening but hollowing of the shell. They become valuable utensils of the gourd kind, but have no palatable and nutritious inside. Instead of acquiring nutritious and palatable qualities to their pulp, it is all absorbed into a prematurely hardened shell. They went away squashes, and they return gourds. They are all expressed, or squeezed out; their essential oil is gone. They are pronounced for you; they are good to stand before or for a noun or man as handles; not even hollow gourds always, but the handle without the mug. They pronounce with the sharp precise report of a rifle, but the likeness is in the sound only, for they have no bullets to fire.

Aug. 7. . . . Here is the barber sailing up the still, dark, cloud-reflecting river in the long boat which he built so elaborately himself, with two large sails set. He is quite alone thus far from town, and so quiet and so sensibly employed—bound to Fair Haven Bay, instead of meeting comrades in a shop on the Mill-Dam or sleeping away his Sabbath in a chamber—that I think of him as having experienced religion. I know so much good of him, at least, that one dark, still Sunday he sailed alone from the village to Fair Haven Bay. What chance was there to serve the devil by that excursion? If he had had a companion I should have had some doubts—but being alone, it seemed communion day with him.

Aug. 10. . . . [Bronson] Alcott spent the day with me yesterday. He spent the day before with Emerson. He observed that he had got his wine and now he had come after his venison. Such was the compliment he paid me. The question of a livelihood was troubling him. He knew of nothing which he could do for which men would pay him. He could not compete with the Irish in cradling grain. His early education had not fitted him for a clerkship. He had offered his services to the Abolition Society, to go about the country and speak for freedom as their agent, but they declined him. This is very much to their discredit; they should have been forward to secure him. Such a connection with him would confer unexpected dignity on their enterprise. But they cannot tolerate a man who stands by a head above them. They are as bad—Garrison and Phillips, etc.—as the overseers and faculty of Harvard College. They require a man who will train well *under* them. Consequently they have not in their employ any but small men—trainers.

Aug. 11. . . . Found———rather garrulous (his breath smelled of rum). Was complaining that his sons did not get married. He told me his age when he married (thirty-odd years ago), how his wife bore him eight children and then died, and in what respect she proved herself a true woman, etc., etc. I saw that it was as impossible to speak of marriage to such a man—to the mass of men—as of poetry. Its advantages and disadvantages are not such as they have dreamed of. Their marriage is prose or worse. To be married at least should be the one poetical act of a man's life. If you fail in this respect, in what respect will you succeed? The marriage which the mass of men comprehend is but little better than the marriage of the beasts. It would be just as fit for such a man to discourse to you on the love of flowers, thinking of them as hay for his oxen.

What shall we name this season?—this very late afternoon, or very early evening, this severe and placid season of the day, most favorable for reflection, after the insufferable heats and the bustle of the day are over and before the dampness and twilight of evening! The serene hour, the Muses' hour, the season of reflection! It is commonly desecrated by being made teatime. It begins perhaps with the very earliest condensation of moisture in the air, when the shadows of hills are first observed, and the breeze begins to go down, and birds begin again to sing. The pensive season. It is earlier than the "chaste eve" of the poet. Bats have not come forth. It is not twilight. There is no dew yet on the grass, and still less any early star in the heavens. It is the turning point between afternoon and evening. The few sounds now heard, far or near, are delicious. It is not more dusky and obscure, but clearer than before. The clearing of the air by condensation of mists more than balances the increase of shadows. Chaste eve is merely *preparing* with "dewy finger" to draw o'er all "the gradual dusky veil." Not yet "the ploughman homeward plods his weary way," nor owls nor beetles are abroad. It is a season somewhat earlier than is celebrated by the poets. There is not such a sense of lateness and approaching night as they describe. I mean when the first emissaries of Evening come to smooth the lakes and streams. The poet arouses himself and collects his thoughts. He postpones tea indefinitely. Thought has taken her siesta. Each sound has a broad and deep relief of silence.

Aug. 19. Friday. 9 A.M. To Sudbury by boat with W. E. C. [Ellery Channing].

Cooler weather. Last Sunday we were sweltering here and one hundred died of the heat in New York; today they have fires in this village. After more rain, with wind in the night, it is now clearing up cool. There is a broad, clear crescent of blue in the west, slowly increasing, and an agreeable autumnal coolness, both under the high, withdrawn clouds and the edges of the woods, and a considerable wind wafts us along with our one sail and two umbrellas, sitting in thick coats. I was going to sit and write or mope all day in the house, but it seems wise to cultivate animal spirits, to embark in enterprises which employ and recreate the whole body. Let the divine spirits like the huntsman with his bugle accompany the animal spirit that would fain range the forest and meadow. Even the gods and goddesses, Apollo and Diana, are found in the field, though they are superior to the dog and the deer.

It is a glorious and ever-memorable day. We observe attentively the first beautiful days in the spring, but not so much in the autumn. We might expect that the first fair days after so much rain would be remarkable. It is a day affecting the spirits of men, but there is nobody to enjoy it but ourselves. What do the laborer ox and the laborer man care for the beautiful days? Will the haymaker when he comes home tonight know that this has been such a beautiful day? This day itself has been the great phenomenon, but will it be reported in any journal, as the storm is, and the heat? It is like a great and beautiful flower unnamed. I see a man trimming willows on the Sudbury causeway and others raking hay out of the water in the midst of all this clarity and brightness, but are they aware of the splendor of this day? The mass of mankind, who live in houses or shops, or are *bent* upon their labor out of doors, know nothing of the beautiful days which are passing about and around them. Is not such a day worthy of a hymn? It is such a day as mankind might spend in

praising and glorifying nature. It might be spent as a natural
Sabbath, if only all men would accept the hint, devoted to
unworldly thoughts. The first bright day of the fall, the earth
reflector. The dog-day mists are gone; the washed earth
shines; the cooler air braces man. No summer day is so beautiful as the fairest spring and fall days.

Aug. 23. . . . Live in each season as it passes; breathe the
air, drink the drink, taste the fruit, and resign yourself
to the influences of each. Let them be your only diet drink
and botanical medicines. In August live on berries, not dried
meats and pemmican, as if you were on shipboard making
your way through a waste ocean, or in a northern desert. Be
blown on by all the winds. Open all your pores and bathe in
all the tides of Nature, in all her streams and oceans, at all
seasons. Miasma and infection are from within, not without.
The invalid, brought to the brink of the grave by an unnatural life, instead of imbibing only the great influence that Nature is, drinks only the tea made of a particular herb, while
he still continues his unnatural life—saves at the spile and
wastes at the bung. He does not love Nature or his life, and
so sickens and dies, and no doctor can cure him. Grow green
with spring, yellow and ripe with autumn. Drink of each
season's influence as a vial, a true panacea of all remedies
mixed for your especial use. The vials of summer never
made a man sick, but those which he stored in his cellar.
Drink the wines, not of your bottling, but Nature's bottling;
not kept in goatskins or pigskins, but the skins of a myriad
fair berries. Let Nature do your bottling and your pickling
and preserving. For all Nature is doing her best each moment
to make us well. She exists for no other end. Do not resist
her. With the least inclination to be well, we should not be
sick. Men have discovered—or think they have discovered
—the salutariness of a few wild things only, and not of all
nature. Why, "nature" is but another name for health, and
the seasons are but different states of health. Some men think
that they are not well in spring, or summer, or autumn,
or winter; it is only because they are not *well in* them.
    . . . Most poems, like the fruits, are sweetest toward
the blossom end.

Sept. 1. . . . There are two kinds of simplicity—one that
is akin to foolishness, the other to wisdom. The philosopher's style of living is only outwardly simple, but inwardly

complex. The savage's style is both outwardly and inwardly simple. A simpleton can perform many mechanical labors, but is not capable of profound thought. It was their limited view, not in respect to *style,* but to the *object* of living. A man who has equally limited views with respect to the end of living will not be helped by the most complex and refined style of living. It is not the tub that makes Diogenes, the Jove-born, but Diogenes the tub.

Sept. 11. . . . Checkerberries are full-grown, but green. They must have been new mitchella berries, then, that I saw some time ago. River cornel berries have begun to disappear. In a stubble field, I go through a very fine, diffusely branching grass now going to seed, which is like a reddish mist to my eyes, two feet deep, and trembling around me.

Sept. 12. . . . It occurred to me when I awoke this morning, feeling regret for intemperance of the day before in eating fruit, which had dulled my sensibilities, that man was to be treated as a musical instrument, and if any viol was to be made of sound timber and kept well tuned always, it was he, so that when the bow of events is drawn across him he may vibrate and resound in perfect harmony. A sensitive soul will be continually trying its strings to see if they are in tune. A man's body must be rasped down exactly to a shaving. It is of far more importance than the wood of a Cremona violin.

Oct. 24. Early on Nawshawtuct.
Black willows bare. Golden willow with yellow leaves. Larch yellow. Most alders by river bare except at top. Waxwork shows red. Celtis almost bare, with greenish-yellow leaves at top. Some hickories bare, some with rich goldenbrown leaves. Locusts half bare, with greenish-yellow leaves. Catnip fresh and green and in bloom. Barberries green, reddish, or scarlet. Cranberry beds at distance in meadows (from hill) are red, for a week or more. Lombardy poplar yellow. Red maples and elms alone very conspicuously bare in our landscape. White thorns bare, and berries mostly fallen, reddening the ground. Hedge-mustard still fresh and in bloom. Buttonwoods half bare. The rock maple leaves a clear yellow; now and then [one] shows some blood in its veins, and blushes. People are busy raking the leaves before their houses; some put them over their strawberries.

Oct. 26. . . . When, after feeling dissatisfied with my life, I aspire to something better, am more scrupulous, more reserved and continent, as if expecting somewhat, suddenly I find myself full of life as a nut of meat—am overflowing with a quiet, genial mirthfulness. I think to myself, I must attend to my diet; I must get up earlier and take a morning walk; I must have done with luxuries and devote myself to my muse. So I dam up my stream, and my waters gather to a head. I am freighted with thought.

Nov. 8. . . . At evening the snow turned to rain, and the sugaring soon disappeared.

Nov. 12. I cannot but regard it as a kindness in those who have the steering of me that, by the want of pecuniary wealth, I have been nailed down to this my native region so long and steadily, and made to study and love this spot of earth more and more. What would signify in comparison a thin and diffused love and knowledge of the whole earth instead, got by wandering? . . .

Nov. 15. . . . After having some business dealings with men, I am occasionally chagrined, and feel as if I had done some wrong, and it is hard to forget the ugly circumstance. I see that such intercourse long continued would make one thoroughly prosaic, hard, and coarse. But the longest intercourse with Nature, though in her rudest moods, does not thus harden and make coarse. A hard, insensible man whom we liken to a rock is indeed much harder than a rock. From hard, coarse, insensible men with whom I have no sympathy, I go to commune with the rocks, whose hearts are comparatively soft.

Dec. 2. . . . The skeleton which at first sight excites only a shudder in all mortals becomes at last not only a pure but suggestive and pleasing object to science. The more we know of it, the less we associate it with any goblin of our imaginations. The longer we keep it, the less likely it is that any such will come to claim it. We discover that the only spirit which haunts it is a universal intelligence which has created it in harmony with all nature. Science never saw a ghost, nor does it look for any, but it sees everywhere the traces, and it is itself the agent, of a Universal Intelligence.

Dec. 22. . . . . Surveying the last three days. They have not yielded much that I am aware of. All I find is old bound-marks, and the slowness and dullness of farmers recon-firmed. They even complain that I walk too fast for them. Their legs have become stiff from toil. This coarse and hurried outdoor work compels me to live grossly or be in-attentive to my diet; that is the worst of it. Like work, like diet; that, I find, is the rule. Left to my chosen pursuits, I should never drink tea nor coffee, nor eat meat. The diet of any class or generation is the natural result of its employ-ment and locality. It is remarkable how unprofitable it is for the most part to talk with farmers. They commonly stand on their good behavior and attempt to moralize or philoso-phize in a serious conversation. Sportsmen and loafers are better company. For society a man must not be too *good* or well-disposed, to spoil his natural disposition. The bad are frequently good enough to let you see how bad they are, but the good as frequently endeavor [to] get be-tween you and themselves.

I have dined out five times and tea'd once within a week. Four times there was tea on the dinner table, always meat, but once baked beans, always pie, but no puddings. I suspect tea has taken the place of cider with farmers. I am reminded of Haydon the painter's experience when he went about painting the nobility. I go about to the houses of the farmers and squires in like manner. This is my portrait-painting— when I would fain be employed on higher subjects. I have offered myself much more earnestly as a lecturer than a sur-veyor. Yet I do not get any employment as a lecturer; was not invited to lecture once last winter, and only once (with-out pay) this winter. But I can get surveying enough, which a hundred others in this county can do as well as I, though it is not boasting much to say that a hundred others in New England cannot lecture as well as I on my themes. But they who do not make the highest demand on you shall rue it. It is because they make a low demand on themselves. All the while that they use only your humbler faculties, your higher unemployed faculties, like an invisible cimetar, are cutting them in twain. Woe be to the generation that lets any higher faculty in its midst go unemployed! That is to deny God and know him not, and he, accordingly, will know not of them.

Dec. 26. . . . . Was overtaken by an Irishman seeking work.

I asked him if he could chop wood. He said he was not long in this country; that he could cut one side of a tree well enough, but he had not learned to change hands and cut the other without going around it—what we call crossing the carf. . . .

Dec. 29. . . . All day a driving snow-storm, imprisoning most, stopping the cars, blocking up the roads. No school today. I cannot see a house fifty rods off from my window through [it]; yet in midst of all I see a bird, probably a tree sparrow, partly blown, partly flying, over the house to alight in a field. The snow penetrates through the smallest crevices under doors and side of windows.

P.M. Tried my snow-shoes. They sink deeper than I expected, and I throw the snow upon my back. When I returned, twenty minutes after, my great tracks were not to be seen. It is the worst snow-storm to bear that I remember. The strong wind from the north blows the snow almost horizontally, and, beside freezing you, almost takes your breath away. The driving snow blinds you, and where you are protected, you can see but little way, it is so thick. Yet in spite, or on account, of all, I see the first flock of arctic snowbirds (*Emberiza nivalis*) near the depot, white and black, with a sharp, whistle-like note. An hour after I discovered half a pint of snow in each pocket of my greatcoat.

What a contrast between the village street now and last summer! The leafy elms then resounding with the warbling vireo, robins, bluebirds, and the fiery hangbird, etc., to which the villagers, kept indoors by the heat, listen through open lattices. Now it is like a street in Nova Zembla—if they were to have any there. I wade to the post-office as solitary a traveller as ordinarily in a wood-path in winter. The snow is mid-leg deep, while drifts as high as one's head are heaped against the houses and fences, and here and there range across the street like snowy mountains. You descend from this, relieved, into capacious valleys with a harder bottom, or more fordable. The track of one large sleigh alone is visible, nearly snowed up. There is not a track leading from any door to indicate that the inhabitants have been forth today, any more than there is track of any quadruped by the wood-paths. It is all pure untrodden snow, banked up against the houses now at 4 P.M., and no evidence that a villager has been abroad today. In one place the drift covers the front-yard fence and stretches thence upward to the top of the front door, shutting all in, and frequently the snow lies banked up three or four feet high against the front doors, and the windows are all snowed up, and there is a drift over each window, and the clapboards are all hoary with it. It is as if the inhabitants were all frozen to death, and now you threaded the desolate streets weeks after that calamity. There is not a sleigh or vehicle of any kind on the Mill-Dam, but one saddled horse on which a farmer has come into town. The cars are nowhere. Yet they are warmer, merrier than ever there within. At the post-office they ask each traveller news of the cars—"Is there any train up or down?" —or how deep the snow is on a level.

1854

The major event was one of unsuspected magnitude:
Ticknor & Fields, at their own risk, published Walden on
August 9. Other events included Thoreau's increasing in-
volvement in the struggle against slavery. On July 4 he delivered the address "Slavery in Massachusetts," which the
Liberator and Horace Greeley's New York paper then reprinted.
This was a banner year for him among the lyceums, for he
delivered five public lectures. On the private side this was
the year that Thoreau made two new and thereafter devoted friends, the Quaker Daniel Ricketson of New Bedford
and the English gentleman-traveler Thomas Cholmondeley.
For the journal it is one of the best years, with its varying tendencies judiciously balanced against one another. The
journal is as full of good things—we hope Thoreau would
forgive the comparison—as a fruitcake. Here, as an indication, are the subject headings given by the editor Bradford
Torrey for the items Thoreau writes about in April: "Dry
Weather—The Flicker's Cackle—The River falling—Hawks
and Farmers—Butterflies and Frogs—The Lecturer's Theme—
The Croaking Frogs—Criticising a Composition—Sundry Birds
and Flowers—Man and Music—An Injury to the River—A
Wood Fungus—A Sparrow in the House—Politeness and Sim-
plicity—Statistics and the American Mind—Snipes on the
Meadow—April Snow—Early Vegetation—Bees and Willow
Blossoms—Wisdom and Living—Vegetation and Birds—Some
April Birds—A White-headed Eagle—Two Mergansers—Shep-
herd's Purse—The Ruby-crowned Wren—Snoring Frogs—
Myrtle-Birds—An Unprofaned Hour—Faithfulness to One's
Genius—The Rise and Fall of Walden—Supply and Demand
—A Blue Heron."

Jan. 13. . . . In the deep hollow this side of Britton's
Camp, I heard a singular buzzing sound from the ground,
exactly like that of a large fly or bee in a spider's web. I
kneeled down, and with pains traced it to a small bare spot
as big as my hand, amid the snow, and searched there amid
the grass stubble for several minutes, putting the grass aside

with my fingers, till, when I got nearest to the spot, not knowing but I might be stung, I used a stick. The sound was incessant, like that of a large fly in agony, but though it made my ears ache, and I had my stick directly on the spot, I could find neither prey nor oppressor. At length I found that I interrupted or changed the tone with my stick, and so traced it to a few spires of dead grass occupying about a quarter of an inch in diameter and standing in the melted snow water. When I bent these one side it produced a duller and baser tone. It was a sound issuing from the earth, and as I stooped over it, the thought came over me that it might be the first puling infantine cry of an earthquake, which would ere long ingulf me. There was no bubble in the water. Perhaps it was air confined under the frozen ground, now expanded by the thaw, and escaping upward through the water by a hollow grass stem. I left it after ten minutes, buzzing as loudly as at first. Could hear it more than a rod.

Jan. 14. . . . I just had a coat come home from the tailor's. Ah me! Who am I that should wear this coat? It was fitted upon one of the devil's angels about my size. Of what use that measuring of me if he did not measure my character, but only the breadth of my shoulders, as it were a peg to hang it on. This is not the figure that I cut. This is the figure the tailor cuts. That presumptuous and impertinent fashion whispered in his ear, so that he heard no word of mine. As if I had said, "Not my will, O Fashion, but thine be done." We worship not the Parcae, nor the Graces, but Fashion, offspring of Proteus and Vanessa, of Whim and Vanity. She spins and weaves and cuts with the authority of the Fates. Oh, with what delight I could thrust a spear through her vitals or squash her under my heel! Every village might well keep constantly employed a score of knights to rid it of this monster. It changes men into bears or monkeys with a single wave of its wand. The head monkey at Paris, Count D'Orsay, put on the traveller's cap, and now all the monkeys in the world do the same thing. He merely takes the breadth of my shoulders and proceeds to fit the garment to Puck, or some other grotesque devil of his acquaintance to whom he has sold himself.

Jan. 27. . . . The greatest compliment that was ever paid me was when one asked me what I *thought,* and attended to my answer.

Feb. 12. . . . P.M. Skate to Pantry Brook.

Put on skates at mouth of Swamp Bridge Brook. The ice appears to be nearly two inches thick. There are many rough places where the crystals are very coarse, and the old ice on the river (for I spoke of a new ice since the freshet) is uneven and covered, more or less, with the scales of a thin ice whose water is dried up. In some places, where the wind has been strong, the foam is frozen into great concentric ridges, over which with an impetus I dash. It is hobbling and tearing work.

Just beyond the bathing place, I see the wreck of an ice-fleet, which yesterday morning must have been very handsome. It reminds me of a vast and crowded fleet of sloops with large slanting sails all standing to the north. These sails are, some of them, the largest specimens of the leaf-structure in ice that I have seen, eight or nine inches long. Perhaps this structure is more apparent now they have wasted so much. Their bases can be seen continuing quite through the level ice which has formed about them, as if the wind and waves, breaking up a thin ice, had held it in that position while it froze in.

One accustomed to glide over a boundless and variegated ice floor like this cannot be much attracted by tessellated floors and mosaic work. I skate over a thin ice all tessellated, so to speak, or in which you see the forms of the crystals as they shot. This is separated by two or three feet of water from the old ice resting on the meadow. The water, consequently, is not dark, as when seen against a muddy bottom, but a clear yellow, against which the white air-bubbles in and under the ice are very conspicuous.

Landed at Fair Haven Hill. I was not aware till I came out how pleasant a day it was. It was very cold this morning, and I have been putting [on] wood in vain to warm my chamber, and lo! I come forth, and am surprised to find it warm and pleasant. There is very little wind, here under Fair Haven especially. I begin to dream of summer even. I take off my mittens.

Here is a little hollow which, for a short time every spring, gives passage to the melting snow, and it was consequently wet there late into the spring. I remember well when a few little alder bushes, encouraged by the moisture, first sprang up in it. They now make a perfect little grove, fifteen feet high, and maybe half a dozen rods long, with a rounded outline, as if they were one mass of moss, with the wrecks of ferns in their midst and the sweet-fern about its edge. And so, perchance, a swamp is beginning to be formed. The shade and the decaying vegetation may at last produce a spongy soil, which will supply a constant rill. Has not something like this been the history of the alder swamp and brook a little further along? True, the first is on a small scale and rather elevated, part way up the hill; and ere long trout begin to glance in the brook, where first was merely a course for melted snow which turned the dead grass-blades all one way—which combed the grassy tresses down the hill.

This is a glorious winter afternoon. The clearness of a winter day is not impaired, while the air is still and you feel a direct heat from the sun. It is not like the relenting of a thaw with a southerly wind. There is a bright sheen from the snow, and the ice booms a little from time to time. On those parts of the hill which are bare, I see the radical leaves of the buttercup, mouse-ear, and the thistle.

Especially do gray rocks or cliffs with a southwest exposure attract us now, where there is warmth and dryness. The gray color is nowhere else so agreeable to us as in these rocks in the sun at this season, where I hear the trickling of water under great ice organ-pipes.

What a floor it is I glide thus swiftly over! It is a study for the slowest walker. See the shells of countless air-bubbles within and beneath it, some a yard or two in diameter. Beneath they are crowded together from the size of a dollar downward. They give the ice a white-spotted or freckled appearance. Specimens of every coin (*numismata*) from the first minting downward. I hear the pond faintly boom or mutter in a low voice, promising another spring to the fishes. I saw yesterday deeply scalloped oak leaves which had sunk nearly an inch into the ice of Walden, making a perfect impression of their forms, on account of the heat they absorbed. Their route is thus downward to dust again, through water and snow and ice and every obstacle. This thin meadow ice with yellow water under it yields a remarkable hollow sound, like a drum, as I rip over it, as if it were about to give way under me—some of that gong-like roar which I have described elsewhere—the ice being tense. I crossed the road at Bidens Brook. Here the smooth ice was dusty (from the road) a great distance, and I thought it would dull my skates.

Feb. 18. . . . I read some of the speeches in Congress about the Nebraska Bill—a thing the like of which I have not done for a year. What trifling upon a serious subject! while honest men are sawing wood for them outside. Your Congress halls have an ale-house odor—a place for stale jokes and vulgar wit. It compels me to think of my fellow-creatures as apes and baboons.

Feb. 19. Many college textbooks which were a weariness and a stumbling block when *studied,* I have since read a little in with pleasure and profit. . . .

March 15. . . . Painted my boat.

March 31. . . . In criticising your writing, trust your fine instinct. There are many things which we come very near questioning, but do not question. When I have sent off my manuscripts to the printer, certain objectionable sentences or expressions are sure to obtrude themselves on my attention with force, though I had not consciously suspected them before. My critical instinct then at once breaks the ice and comes to the surface.

April 8. . . . At the Lyceum the other night I felt that the lecturer had chosen a theme too foreign to himself and so failed to interest me as much as formerly. He described things not in or near to his heart, but toward his extremities and superficies. The poet deals with his privatest experience. There was no *central* nor centralizing thought in the lecture.

Some poets mature early and die young. Their fruits have a delicious flavor like strawberries, but do not keep till fall or winter. Others are slower in coming to their growth. Their fruits may be less delicious, but are a more lasting food and are so hardened by the sun of summer and the coolness of autumn that they keep sound over winter. The first are June-eatings, early but soon withering; the last are russets, which last till June again.

April 12. . . . Waited at Lincoln depot an hour and a half. Heard the telegraph harp. I perceived distinctly that man melts at the sound of music, just like a rock exposed to a furnace heat. They need not have fabled that Orpheus moved the rocks and trees, for there is nothing more insensible than man; he sets the fashion to the rocks, and it is as surprising to see him melted, as when children see the lead begin to flow in a crucible. I observe that it is when I have been intently, and it may be laboriously, at work, and am somewhat listless or abandoned after it, reposing, that the muse visits me, and I see or hear beauty. It is from out the shadow of my toil that I look into the light. The music of the spheres is but another name for the Vulcanic force. May not such a record as this be kept on one page of the Book of Life: "A man was melted today."

April 17. . . . It is remarkable how the American mind runs to statistics. Consider the number of meteorological observers and other annual phenomena. The Smithsonian Institution is a truly national institution. Every shopkeeper makes a record of the arrival of the first martin or bluebird to his box. Dodd, the broker, told me last spring that he knew when the first bluebird came to his boxes, he made a memorandum of it: John Brown, merchant, tells me this morning that the martins first came to his box on the thirteenth, he "made a minute of it." Beside so many entries in their day-books and ledgers, they record these things.

April 29. The ideal of a market is a place where all things are bought and sold. At an agricultural meeting in New York the other day, one said that he had lately heard a man inquiring for spurry seed; he wanted it to sow on drifting sand. His presumption had been that if he wanted it, i.e., if there was a demand, there was a supply to satisfy that demand. He went simply to the shop instead of going to the weed itself. But the supply does not anticipate the demand.

May 1. . . . Early starlight by riverside.

May 10. . . . In Boston yesterday an ornithologist said significantly, "If you held the bird in your hand——"; but I would rather hold it in my affections.

May 17. 5:30 A.M. To Island.
The water is now tepid in the morning to the hands (may have been a day or two), as I slip my hands down the paddle. Hear the wood pewee, the warm-weather sound. As I was returning over the meadow this side of the Island, I saw the snout of a mud turtle above the surface—little more than an

inch of the point—and paddled toward it. Then, as he moved slowly on the surface, different parts of his shell and head just appearing looked just like the scalloped edges of some pads which had just reached the surface. I pushed up and found a large snapping-turtle on the bottom. He appeared of a dirty brown there, very nearly the color of the bottom at present. With his great head, as big as an infant's, and his vigilant eyes as he paddled about on the bottom in his attempts to escape, he looked not merely repulsive, but to some extent terrible even as a crocodile. At length, after thrusting my arm in up to the shoulder two or three times, I succeeded in getting him into the boat, where I secured him with a lever under a seat. I could get him from the landing to the house only by turning him over and drawing him by the tail, the hard crests of which afforded a good hold; for he was so heavy that I could not hold him off so far as to prevent his snapping at my legs. He weighed thirty and a half pounds.

May 28. . . . The inhumanity of science concerns me, as when I am tempted to kill a rare snake that I may ascertain its species. I feel that this is not the means of acquiring true knowledge.

June 1. . . . Within little more than a fortnight the woods, from bare twigs, have become a sea of verdure, and young *shoots* have contended with one another in the race. The leaves have unfurled all over the country like a parasol. Shade is produced, and the birds are concealed and their economies go forward uninterruptedly, and a covert is afforded to the animals generally. But thousands of worms and insects are preying on the leaves while they are young and tender. Myriads of little parasols are suddenly spread all the country over, to shield the earth and the roots of the trees from parching heat, and they begin to flutter and rustle in the breeze. Checkerberry shoots in forward places are now just fit to eat, they are so young and tender. In a long walk I have found these somewhat refreshing. From Bare Hill there is a bluish mist on the landscape, giving it a glaucous appearance.

Now I see gentlemen and ladies sitting at anchor in boats on the lakes in the calm afternoons, under parasols, making use of nature, not always accumulating money. The farmer hoeing is wont to look with scorn and pride on a man sitting

in a motionless boat a whole half-day, but he does not
realize that the object of his own labor is perhaps merely
to add another dollar to his heap, nor through what coarseness and inhumanity to his family and servants he often ac-
complishes this. He has an Irishman or a Canadian working
for him by the month; and what, probably, is the lesson
that he is teaching him by precept and example? Will it make
that laborer more of a man? this earth more like heaven?
The veiny-leaved hawkweed tomorrow. I see the sand cherry
in puffs like the Canada plum in some places.

June 13. . . . It is surprising how thickly strewn our soil
is with arrowheads. I never see the surface broken in sandy
places but I think of them. I find them on all sides, not only
in corn and grain and potato and bean fields, but in pastures
and woods, by woodchucks' holes and pigeon beds, and, as
tonight, in a pasture where a restless cow has pawed the
ground. . . .

June 16. . . . Again I scent the white water-lily, and a
season I had waited for is arrived. How indispensable all
these experiences to make up the summer! It is the emblem
of purity, and its scent suggests it. Growing in stagnant
and muddy [water], it bursts up so pure and fair to the
eye and so sweet to the scent, as if to show us what purity
and sweetness reside in, and can be extracted from, the
slime and muck of the earth. I think I have plucked the
first one that has opened for a mile at least. What confirma-
tion of our hopes is in the fragrance of the water-lily! I
shall not so soon despair of the world for it, notwithstanding slavery, and the cowardice and want of principle of the
North. It suggests that the time may come when man's
deeds will smell as sweet. Such, then, is the odor our planet
emits. Who can doubt, then, that Nature is young and
sound? If Nature can compound this fragrance still annually, I shall believe her still full of vigor, and that there
is virtue in man, too, who perceives and loves it. It is as
if all the pure and sweet and virtuous was extracted from
the slime and decay of earth and presented thus in a flower.
The resurrection of virtue! It reminds me that Nature has
been partner to no Missouri compromise. I scent no compromise in the fragrance of the white water-lily. In it, the
sweet, and pure, and innocent are wholly sundered from
the obscene and baleful. I do not scent in this the time-

serving irresolution of a Massachusetts Governor, nor of a Boston Mayor. All good actions have contributed to this fragrance. So behave that the odor of your actions may enhance the general sweetness of the atmosphere, that, when I behold or scent a flower, I may not be reminded how inconsistent are your actions with it; for all odor is but one form of advertisement of a moral quality. If fair actions had not been performed, the lily would not smell sweet. The foul slime stands for the sloth and vice of man; the fragrant flower that springs from it, for the purity and courage which springs from its midst. It is these sights and sounds and fragrances put together that convince us of our immortality. No man believes against all evidence. Our external senses consent with our internal. This fragrance assures me that, though all other men fall, one shall stand fast; though a pestilence sweep over the earth, it shall at least spare one man. The genius of Nature is unimpaired. Her flowers are as fair and as fragrant as ever.

June 18. . . . It is not any such free-soil party as I have seen, but a free-man party—i.e. a party of free men—that is wanted. It is not any politicians, even the truest and soundest, but, strange as it may sound, even godly men, as Cromwell discovered, who are wanted to fight this battle—men not of policy but of probity. Politicians! I have looked into the eyes of two or three of them, but I saw nothing there to satisfy me. They will vote for my man tomorrow if I will vote for theirs today. They will whirl round and round, not only horizontally like weathercocks, but vertically also.

My advice to the State is simply this: to dissolve her union with the slaveholder instantly. She can find no respectable law or precedent which sanctions its continuance. And to each inhabitant of Massachusetts, to dissolve his union with the State, as long as she hesitates to do her duty.

Aug. 2. . . . My attic chamber has compelled me to sit below with the family at evening for a month. I feel the necessity of deepening the stream of my life; I must cultivate privacy. It is very dissipating to be with people too much. As C. [Ellery Channing] says, it takes the edge off a man's thoughts to have been much in society. I cannot spare my moonlight and my mountains for the best of man I am likely to get in exchange.

The surface of the forest on the east of the river presents

a singularly cool and wild appearance—cool as a pot of green paint—stretches of green light and shade, reminding me of some lonely mountainside. The nighthawk flies low, skimming over the ground now. How handsome lie the oats which have been cradled in long rows in the field, a quarter of a mile uninterruptedly! The thick stub ends, so evenly laid, are almost as rich a sight to me as the graceful tops. A few fireflies in the meadows. I am uncertain whether that so large and bright and high was a firefly or a shooting star. Shooting stars are but fireflies of the firmament. The crickets on the causeway make a *steady* creak, on the dry pasture-tops an *interrupted* one. I was compelled to stand to write when a soft, faint light from the western sky came in between two willows.

Fields today sends me a specimen copy of my "Walden." It is to be published on the twelfth *inst.*

Aug. 7. It is inspiriting at last to hear the wind whistle and moan about my attic, after so much trivial summer weather, and to feel cool in my thin pants.

Sept. 6. . . . 9 P.M. There is now approaching from the west one of the heaviest thunder-showers (apparently) and with the most incessant flashes that I remember to have seen. It must be twenty miles off, at least, for I can hardly hear the thunder at all. The almost incessant flashes reveal the form of the cloud, at least the upper and lower edge of it, but it stretches north and south along the horizon further than we see. Every minute I see the crinkled lightning, intensely bright, dart to earth or forkedly along the cloud. It does not always dart *direct* to earth, but sometimes very crookedly, like the bough of a tree, or along the cloud forkedly. The forked thunderbolt of the poets. It seems like a tremendous dark battery bearing down on us, with an incessant fire kept up behind it. And each time, apparently, it strikes the earth or something on it with terrific violence. We feel the rush of the cool wind while the thunder is yet scarcely audible. The flashes are, in fact, incessant for an hour or more, though lighting up different parts of the horizon—now the edges of the cloud, now far along the horizon—showing a clearer golden space beneath the cloud where rain is falling, through which stream tortuously to earth the brilliant bolts. It is a visible striking or launching of bolts on the devoted villages. It crinkles through the clear yellow portion beneath the cloud where it rains, like fiery snakes or worms, like veins in the eye. At first it was a small and very distant cloud in the southwestern horizon, revealed by its own flashes—its rugged upper outline and its whole form revealed by the flashes—and no thunder heard. It seemed like a ship firing broadsides, but it gradually advanced and extended itself, and united with others north and south along the horizon, and the thunder began to be heard, and wind came, etc. At last came the rain, but not heavy, nor the thunder loud, but the flashes were visible all around us.

Sept. 8. . . . The grapes would no doubt be riper a week hence, but I am compelled to go now before the vines are stripped. I partly smell them out. I pluck splendid great bunches of the purple ones, with a rich bloom on them and the purple glowing through it like a fire; large red ones, also, with light dots, and some clear green. Sometimes I crawl under low and thick bowers, where they have run over the alders only four or five feet high, and see the grapes hanging from a hollow hemisphere of leaves over my head. At other times I see them dark-purple or black against the silvery undersides of the leaves, high overhead where they have run over birches or maples, and either climb or pull them down to pluck them. The witchhazel on Dwarf Sumach Hill looks as if it would begin to blossom in a day or two.

I have brought home a half-bushel of grapes to scent my chamber with. It is impossible to get them home in a basket with all their rich bloom on them, which, no less than the form of the clusters, makes their beauty. As I paddled home with my basket of grapes in the bow, every now and then their perfume was wafted to me in the stern, and I thought that I was passing a richly laden vine on shore. Some goldfinches twitter over, while I am pulling down the vines from the birch-tops. The ripest rattle off and strew the ground before I reach the clusters, or, while I am standing on tiptoe and endeavoring gently to break the tough peduncle, the petiole of a leaf gets entangled in the bunch and I am compelled to strip them all off loosely.

Sept. 12. . . . A sprinkling drove me back for an umbrella.

Sept. 24. . . . Man identifies himself with earth or the material, just as he who has the least tinge of African blood in his veins regards himself as a Negro and is identified with that race. Spirit is strange to him; he is afraid of ghosts.

P.M. By boat to Grape Cliff.

These are the stages in the river fall: first, the two varieties of yellow lily pads begin to decay and blacken (long ago); second, the first fall rains come after dog-days and raise and cool the river, and winds wash the decaying sparganium, etc., etc., to the shores and clear the channel more or less; third, when the first harder frosts come (as this year the twenty-first and twenty-second *inst.*), the button-bushes, which before had attained only a dull mixed yellow, are suddenly bitten, wither, and turn brown, all but the protected parts.

The *first* fall is so gradual as not to make much impression, but the last suddenly and conspicuously gives a fall aspect to the scenery of the river. The button-bushes thus withered, covered still with the gray, already withered mikania, suddenly paint with a rich brown the river's brim. It is like the crust, the edging, of a boy's turnover done brown. And the black willows, slightly faded and crisped with age or heat, enhance my sense of the year's maturity. There, where the land appears to lap over the water by a mere edging, these thinner portions are first done brown. I float over the still liquid middle.

Oct. 7. Went to Plymouth to lecture and survey Watson's [Marston Watson, a friend of Thoreau] grounds. Returned the fifteenth.

Nov. 20. . . . . Started for Philadelphia from foot of Liberty Street at 6 P.M., via Newark, etc., etc., Bordentown, etc., etc., Camden Ferry, to Philadelphia, all in the dark. Saw only the glossy panelling of the cars reflected out into the dark, like the magnificent lit façade of a row of edifices reaching all the way to Philadelphia, except when we stopped and a lanthorn or two showed us a ragged boy and the dark buildings of some New Jersey town. Arrive at 10 P.M.; time, four hours from New York, thirteen from Boston, fifteen from Concord. Put up at Jones's Exchange Hotel, 77 Dock Street; lodgings thirty-seven and a half cents per night, meals separate; not to be named with French's in New York; next door to the fair of the Franklin Institute, then open, and over against the Exchange, in the neighborhood of the printing offices.

Nov. 21. Looked from the cupola of the State House, where the Declaration of Independence was declared. The best view of the city I got. Was interested in the squirrels, gray and black, in Independence and Washington Squares. Heard that they have, or have had, deer in Logan Square. The squirrels are fed, and live in boxes in the trees in the winter. Fine view from Fairmount water-works. The line of the hypotenuse of the gable end of Girard College was apparently deflected in the middle six inches or more, reminding me of the anecdote of the church of the Madeleine in Paris.

Dec. 8. . . . Winter has come unnoticed by me, I have been so busy writing. This is the life most lead in respect to Nature. How different from my habitual one! It is hasty, coarse, and trivial, as if you were a spindle in a factory. The other is leisurely, fine, and glorious, like a flower. In the first case you are merely getting your living; in the second you live as you go along. You travel only on roads of the proper grade without jar or running off the track, and sweep round the hills by beautiful curves.

Dec. 14. . . . Good sleighing still, with but little snow. A warm, thawing day. The river is open almost its whole length. It is a beautifully smooth mirror within an icy frame. It is well to improve such a time to walk by it. This strip of water of irregular width over the channel, between broad fields of ice, looks like a polished silver mirror, or like another surface of polished ice, and often is distinguished from the surrounding ice only by its reflections. I have rarely seen any reflections—of weeds, willows, and elms, and the houses of the village—so distinct, the stems so black and distinct; for they contrast not with a green meadow but clear white ice, to say nothing of the silvery surface of the water. Your eye slides first over a plane surface of smooth ice of one color to a water surface of silvery smoothness, like a gem set in ice, and reflecting the weeds and trees and houses and clouds with singular beauty. The reflections are particularly simple and distinct. These twigs are not referred to and confounded with a broad green meadow from which they spring, as in summer, but, instead of that dark-green ground, absorbing the light, is this abrupt white field of ice. We see so little open and smooth water at this season that I am inclined to improve such an opportunity to walk along the river, and moreover the meadows, being more or less frozen, make it more feasible than in summer.

Dec. 21. . . . . What a grovelling appetite for profitless jest and amusement our countrymen have! Next to a good dinner, at least, they love a good joke—to have their sides tickled, to laugh sociably, as in the East they bathe and are shampooed. Curators of lyceums write to me:

DEAR SIR—I hear that you have a lecture of some humor. Will you do us the favor to read it before the Bungtown Institute?

1855

Putnam's Monthly Magazine *printed four selections from Thoreau's report on visiting Cape Cod. The publishers of* Walden *told him that over the first year they had sold 344 copies and they sent him a check for $51.60. For two or three months near the middle of the year he lay on his back, exasperatingly ill. He was slow in recuperating; in fact he never again was as well as he had been before this illness. But his autumn was brightened by a magnificent gift from Thomas Cholmondeley of forty-four volumes "relating to ancient Hindu literature and scarcely one of them to be bought in America." The journal shows that he managed to write extensively despite his illness, though the writing lacks a certain verve that it had when he was really well. It is not dry and factual but it is not first-rate Thoreau either.*

Jan. 12. P.M. To Flint's Pond via Minott's meadow.

After a spitting of snow in the forenoon, I see the blue sky here and there, and the sun is coming out. It is still and warm. The earth is two thirds bare. I walk along the Mill Brook below Emerson's, looking into it for some life.

Perhaps what most moves us in winter is some reminiscence of far-off summer. How we leap by the side of the open brooks! What beauty in the running brooks! What life! What society! The cold is merely superficial; it is summer still at the core, far, far within. It is in the cawing of the crow, the crowing of the cock, the warmth of the sun on our backs. I hear faintly the cawing of a crow far, far away, echoing from some unseen wood-side, as if deadened by the spring-like vapor which the sun is drawing from the ground. It mingles with the slight murmur of the village, the sound of children at play, as one stream empties gently into another, and the wild and tame are one. What a delicious sound! It is not merely crow calling to crow, for it speaks to me too. I am part of one great creature with him; if he has voice, I have ears. I can hear when he calls, and have engaged not to shoot nor stone him if he will caw to me each spring. On the one hand, it may be, is the sound of children at school saying their a, b, ab's, on the other, far in the wood-fringed horizon, the cawing of crows from their blessed eternal vacation, out at their long recess, children who have got dismissed! While the vaporous incense goes up from all the fields of the spring—if it were spring. Ah, bless the Lord, O my soul! bless him for wildness, for crows that will not alight within gunshot! and bless him for hens, too, that croak and cackle in the yard!

Where are the shiners now, and the trout? I see none in the brook. Have the former descended to the deep water of the river? Ah, may I be there to see when they go down! Why can they not tell me? Or gone into the mud? There are few or no insects for them now.

Jan. 20. . . . In many instances the snow had lodged on trees yesterday in just such forms as a white napkin or counterpane dropped on them would take—protuberant in the middle, with many folds and dimples. An ordinary leaf-less bush supported so much snow on its twigs—a perfect maze like a whirligig, though not in one solid mass—that you could not see through it. We heard only a few *chic-a-dees.* Sometimes the snow on the bent pitch pines made me think of rams' or elephants' heads, ready to butt you. In particular places, standing on their snowiest side, the woods were incredibly fair, white as alabaster. Indeed the young pines reminded you of the purest statuary, and the stately full-grown ones towering around affected you as if you stood in a titanic sculptor's studio, so purely and delicately white, transmitting the light, their dark trunks all concealed. And in many places, where the snow lay on withered oak leaves between you and the light, various delicate fawn-colored and cinnamon tints, blending with the white, still enhanced the beauty.

Feb. 16. . . . I find in the leavings of the partridges numerous ends of twigs. They are white with them, some half an inch long and stout in proportion. Perhaps they are apple twigs. The bark (and bud, if there was any) has been entirely digested, leaving the bare, white, hard wood of the twig. Some of the ends of apple twigs looked as if they had been bitten off. It is surprising what a quantity of this wood they swallow with their buds. What a hardy bird, born amid the dry leaves, of the same color with them, that, grown up, lodges in the snow and lives on buds and twigs! Where apple buds are just freshly bitten off they do not seem to have taken so much twig with them.

Feb. 18. . . . Why do laborers so commonly turn out their feet more than the class still called gentlemen, apparently pushing themselves along by the sides of their feet? I think you can tell the track of a clown from that of a gentleman, though he should wear a gentleman's boots.

Feb. 21. . . . How plain, wholesome, and earthy are the colors of quadrupeds generally! The commonest I should say is the tawny or various shades of brown, answering to the russet which is the prevailing color of the earth's surface, perhaps, and to the yellow of the sands beneath. The darker brown mingled with this answers to the darker-colored soil of the surface. The white of the polar bear, ermine weasel, etc., answers to the snow; the spots of the pards, perchance, to the earth spotted with flowers or tinted leaves of autumn; the black, perhaps, to night, and muddy bottoms and dark waters. There are few or no bluish animals.

March 20. . . . Trying the other day to imitate the honking of geese, I found myself flapping my sides with my elbows, as with wings, and uttering something like the syllables *mow-ack* with a nasal twang and twist in my head; and I produced their note so perfectly in the opinion of the hearers that I thought I might possibly draw a flock down.

March 22. . . . Going along [the] steep side-hill on the south of the pond about 4 P.M., on the edge of the little patch of wood which the choppers have not yet levelled— though they have felled many an acre around it this winter —I observed a rotten and hollow hemlock stump about two feet high and six inches in diameter, and instinctively approached with my right hand ready to cover it. I found a flying squirrel in it, which, as my left hand had covered a small hole at the bottom, ran directly into my right hand. It struggled and bit not a little, but my cotton glove protected me, and I felt its teeth only once or twice. It also uttered three or four dry shrieks at first, something like *cr-r-rack cr-r-r-ack cr-r-r-rack*. I rolled it up in my handkerchief and, holding the ends tight, carried it home in my hand, some three miles. It struggled more or less all the way, especially when my feet made any unusual or louder noise going through leaves or bushes. I could count its claws as they appeared through the handkerchief, and once it got its head out a hole. It even bit through the handkerchief.

Color, as I remember, above a chestnut ash, inclining to fawn or cream color (?), slightly browned; beneath white, the under edge of its wings (?) tinged yellow, the upper dark, perhaps black, making a dark stripe. Audubon and Bachman do not speak of any such stripe! It was a very cunning little animal, reminding me of a mouse in the room. Its very large and prominent black eyes gave it an interesting innocent look. Its very neat flat, fawn-colored, distichous tail was a great ornament. Its "sails" were not very obvious when it was at rest, merely giving it a flat appearance beneath. It would leap off and upward into the air two or three feet from a table, spreading its "sails," and fall to the floor in vain; perhaps strike the side of the room in its upward spring and endeavor to cling to it. It would run up the window by the sash, but evidently found the furniture and walls and floor too hard and smooth for it and after some falls became quiet. In a few moments it allowed me to stroke it, though far from confident.

I put it in a barrel and covered it for the night. It was quite busy all the evening gnawing out, clinging for this purpose and gnawing at the upper edge of a sound oak barrel, and then dropping to rest from time to time. It had defaced the barrel considerably by morning, and would probably have escaped if I had not placed a piece of iron against the gnawed part. I had left in the barrel some bread, apple, shagbarks, and cheese. It ate some of the apple and one shagbark, cutting it quite in two transversely.

In the morning it was quiet, and *squatted* somewhat curled up amid the straw, with its tail passing under it and the end curled over its head very prettily, as if to shield it from the light and keep it warm. I always found it in this position by day when I raised the lid.

March 23. P.M. To Fair Haven Pond.

Carried my flying squirrel back to the woods in my handkerchief. I placed it, about 3:30 P.M., on the very stump I had taken it from. It immediately ran about a rod over the leaves and up a slender maple sapling about ten feet, then after a moment's pause sprang off and skimmed downward toward a large maple nine feet distant, whose trunk it struck three or four feet from the ground. This it rapidly ascended, on the opposite side from me, nearly thirty feet, and there clung to the main stem with its head downward, eying me. After two or three minutes' pause I saw that it was preparing for another spring by raising its head and looking off, and away it went in admirable style, more like a bird than any quadruped I had dreamed of and far surpassing the impression I had received from naturalists' accounts. I marked the spot it started from and the place where it struck, and measured the height and distance carefully. It sprang off from the maple at the height of twenty-eight and a half feet, and struck the ground at the foot of a tree fifty and a half feet distant, measured horizontally. Its flight was not a *regular* descent; it varied from a direct line both horizontally and vertically. Indeed it skimmed much like a hawk and part of its flight was nearly horizontal, and it diverged from a right line eight or ten feet to the right, making a curve in that direction. There were six trees from six inches to a foot in diameter, one a hemlock, in a direct line between the two termini, and these it skimmed partly round, and passed through their thinner limbs; did not as I could perceive touch a twig. It skimmed its way like a hawk between and around the trees. Though it was a windy day, this was on a steep hillside away from the wind and covered with wood, so it was not aided by that. As the ground rose about two feet, the distance was to the absolute height as fifty and a half to twenty-six and a half, or it advanced about two feet for every one foot of descent. After its vain attempts in the house, I was not prepared for this exhibition. It did not fall heavily as in the house, but struck the ground gently enough, and I cannot believe that the mere extension of the skin enabled it to skim so far. It must be still further aided by its organization. Perhaps it fills itself with air first. . . .

March 24. . . . I am not sure that the osiers are decidedly brighter yet.

March 29. . . . As I stand on Heywood's Peak, looking over Walden, more than half its surface already sparkling blue water, I inhale with pleasure the cold but wholesome air like a draught of cold water, contrasting it in my memory with the wind of summer, which I do not thus eagerly swallow. This, which is a chilling wind to my fellow, is decidedly refreshing to me, and I swallow it with eagerness as a panacea. I feel an impulse, also, already, to jump into the half-melted pond. This cold wind is refreshing to my palate, as the warm air of summer is not, methinks. I love to stand there and be blown on as much as a horse in July. A field of ice nearly half as big as the pond has drifted against the eastern shore and crumbled up against it, forming a shining white wall of its fragments.

April 19. . . . From Heywood's Peak I thought I saw the head of a loon in the pond, thirty-five or forty rods distant. Bringing my glass to bear, it seemed sunk very low in the water—all the neck concealed—but I could not tell which end was the bill. At length I discovered that it was the whole body of a little duck, asleep with its head in its back, exactly in the middle of the pond. It had a moderate-sized black head and neck, a white breast, and *seemed* dark-brown above, with a white spot on the side of the head, not reaching to the outside, from base of mandibles, and another, perhaps, on the end of the wing, with some black there. It sat drifting round a little, but with ever its breast toward the wind, and from time to time it raised its head and looked round to see if it were safe. I think it was the smallest duck I ever saw. Floating buoyantly asleep on the middle of Walden Pond. Was it not a female of the buffle-headed or spirit duck? I believed the wings looked blacker when it flew, with some white beneath. It floated like a little casket, and at first I doubted a good while if it possessed life, until I saw it raise its head and look around. It had chosen a place for its nap exactly equidistant between the two shores there, and, with its breast to the wind, swung round only as much as a vessel held by its anchors in the stream. At length the cars scared it.

May 5. . . . Looking over my book, I found I had done my errands, and said to myself I would find a crow's nest. (I had heard a crow scold at a passing hawk a quarter of an hour before.) I had hardly taken this resolution when, looking up, I saw a crow wending his way across an interval in the woods toward the highest pines in the swamp, on which he alighted. I directed my steps to them and was soon greeted with an angry *caw*, and, within five minutes from my resolve, I detected a new nest close to the top of the tallest white pine in the swamp. A crow circled cawing about it within gunshot, then over me surveying, and, perching on an oak directly over my head within thirty-five feet, cawed angrily. But suddenly, as if having taken a new resolution, it flitted away, and was joined by its mate and two more, and they went off silently a quarter of a mile or more and lit in a pasture, as if they had nothing to concern them in the wood.

May 7. . . . A short distance beyond this and the hawk's-nest pine, I observed a middling-sized red oak standing a little aslant on the side-hill over the swamp, with a pretty large hole in one side about fifteen feet from the ground, where apparently a limb on which a felled tree lodged had been cut some years before and so broke out a cavity. I thought that such a hole was too good a one not to be improved by some inhabitant of the wood. Perhaps the gray squirrels I had just seen had their nest there. Or was not the entrance big enough to admit a screech owl? So I thought I would tap on it and put my ear to the trunk and see if I could hear anything stirring within it, but I heard nothing. Then I concluded to look into it. So I shinned up, and when I reached up one hand to the hole to pull myself up by it, the thought passed through my mind perhaps something may take hold my fingers, but nothing did. The first limb was nearly opposite to the hole, and, resting on this, I looked in, and, to my great surprise, there squatted, filling the hole, which was about six inches deep and five to six wide, a sal-mon-brown bird not so big as a partridge, seemingly asleep within three inches of the top and close to my face. It was a minute or two before I made it out to be an owl. It was a salmon-brown or fawn (?) above, the feathers shafted with small blackish-brown somewhat hastate (?) marks, *grayish* toward the ends of the wings and tail, as far as I could see. A large white circular space about or behind eye, banded in rear by a pretty broad (one third of an inch) and quite conspicuous perpendicular *dark*-brown stripe. Egret, say one and a quarter inches long, sharp, triangular, reddish-brown without mainly. It lay crowded in that small space, with its tail somewhat bent up and one side of its head turned up with one egret, and its large dark eye open only by a long slit about a sixteenth of an inch wide; visible breathing. After a little while I put in one hand and stroked it repeatedly, whereupon it reclined its head a little lower and closed its eye entirely. Though curious to know what was under it, I disturbed it no farther at that time.

June 2. Still windier than before, and yet no rain. It is now very dry indeed, and the grass is suffering. Some springs commonly full at this season are dried up. The wind shakes the house night and day. From that cocoon of the *Attacus cecropia* which I found—I think it was on the twenty-fourth of May—on a red maple shrub, three or four feet from the ground, on the edge of the meadow by the new Bedford road just this side of Beck Stow's, came out this forenoon a splendid moth. I had pinned the cocoon to the sash at the upper part of my window and quite forgotten it. About the middle of the forenoon Sophia came in and exclaimed that there was a moth on my window. At first I supposed that she meant a cloth-eating moth, but it turned out that my *A. cecropia* had come out and dropped down to the windowsill, where it hung on the *side* of a slipper (which was inserted into another) to let its wings hang down and develop themselves. At first the wings were not only not unfolded laterally, but not longitudinally, the thinner ends of the forward ones for perhaps three quarters of an inch being very feeble and occupying very little space. It was surprising to see the creature unfold and expand before our eyes, the wings gradually elongating, as it were by their own gravity; and from time to time the insect assisted this operation by a slight shake. It was wonderful how it waxed and grew, revealing some new beauty every fifteen minutes, which I called Sophia to see, but never losing its hold on the shoe. It looked like a young emperor just donning the most splendid ermine robes that ever emperor wore, the wings every moment acquiring greater expansion and their at first wrinkled edge becoming more tense. At first its wings appeared double, one within the other. At last it advanced so far as to spread its wings completely but feebly when we approached. This occupied several hours. It continued to hang to the shoe, with its wings ordinarily closed erect behind its back, the rest of the day; and at dusk, when apparently it was waving its wings preparatory to its evening flight, I gave it ether and so saved it in a perfect state. As it lies, not spread to the utmost, it is five and nine tenths inches by two and a quarter.

June 18. . . . At 3 P.M., as I walked up the bank by the Hemlocks, I saw a painted tortoise just beginning its hole; then another a dozen rods from the river on the bare barren field near some pitch pines, where the earth was covered with cladonias, cinquefoil, sorrel, etc. Its hole was about two thirds done. I stooped down over it, and, to my surprise, after a slight pause it proceeded in its work, directly under and within eighteen inches of my face. I retained a constrained position for three quarters of an hour or more for fear of alarming it. It rested on its fore legs, the front part of its shell about one inch higher than the rear, and this position was not changed essentially to the last. The hole was oval, broadest behind, about one inch wide and one and three quarters long, and the dirt already removed was quite wet or moistened. It made the hole and removed the dirt with its hind legs only, not using its tail or shell, which last of course could not enter the hole, though there was some dirt on it. It first scratched two or three times with one hind foot; then took up a pinch of the loose sand and deposited it directly behind that leg, pushing it backward to its full length and then deliberately opening it and letting the dirt fall; then the same with the other hind foot. This it did rapidly, using each leg alternately with perfect regularity, standing on the other one the while, and thus tilting up its shell each time, now to this side, then to that. There was half a minute or a minute between each change. The hole was made as deep as the feet could reach, or about two inches. It was very neat about its work, not scattering the dirt about any more than was necessary. The completing of the hole occupied perhaps five minutes.

It then without any pause drew its head completely into its shell, raised the rear a little, and protruded and dropped a wet flesh-colored egg into the hole, one end foremost, the red skin of its body being considerably protruded with it. Then it put out its head again a little, slowly, and placed the egg at one side with one hind foot. After a delay of about two minutes it again drew in its head and dropped another, and so on to the fifth—drawing in its head each time, and pausing somewhat longer between the last. The eggs were placed in the hole without any *particular* care— only well down flat and [each] out of the way of the next—and I could plainly see them from above.

After these ten minutes or more, it without pause or turning began to scrape the moist earth into the hole with its hind legs, and, when it had half filled it, it carefully pressed it down with the edges of its hind feet, dancing on them alternately, for some time, as on its knees, tilting from side to side, pressing by the whole weight of the rear of its shell. When it had drawn in thus all the earth that had been moistened, it stretched its hind legs further back and to each side, and drew in the dry and lichen-clad crust, and then danced upon and pressed that down, still not moving the rear of its shell more than one inch to right or left all the while, or changing the position of the forward part at all. The thoroughness with which the covering was done was remarkable. It persevered in drawing in and dancing on the dry surface which had never been disturbed, long after you thought it had done its duty, but it never moved its fore feet, nor once looked round, nor saw the eggs it had laid. There were frequent pauses throughout the whole, when it rested, or ran out its head and looked about circumspectly, at any noise or motion. These pauses were especially long during the covering of its eggs, which occupied more than half an hour. Perhaps it was hard work.

When it had done, it immediately started for the river at a pretty rapid rate (the suddenness with which it made these transitions was amusing), pausing from time to time, and I judged that it would reach it in fifteen minutes. It was not easy to detect that the ground had been disturbed there. An Indian could not have made his cache more skillfully. In a few minutes all traces of it would be lost to the eye.

The object of moistening the earth was perhaps to enable it to take it up in its hands (?), and also to prevent its falling back into the hole. Perhaps it also helped to make the ground more compact and harder when it was pressed down.

Aug. 10. . . . Middle of huckleberrying.

Oct. 2. . . . Returning along the shore, we saw a man and woman putting off in a small boat, the first we had seen. The man was black. He rowed, and the woman steered. R. [Daniel Ricketson] called to them. They approached within a couple of rods in the shallow water. "Come nearer," said R. "Don't be afraid; I ain't a-going to hurt you." The woman answered, "I never saw the man yet that I was afraid of." The man's name was Thomas Smith, and, in answer to R.'s very direct questions as to how much he was of the native stock, said that he was one-fourth Indian. He then asked the woman, who sat unmoved in the stern with a brown dirt-colored dress on, a regular countrywoman with half an acre of face (squaw-like), having first inquired of Tom if she was his woman, how much Indian blood she had in her. She did not answer directly so home a question, yet at length as good as acknowledged to one-half Indian, and said that she came from Carver, where she had a sister; the only half-breeds about here. Said her name was Sepit, but could not spell it. R. said, "Your nose looks rather Indiany." Where will you find a Yankee and his wife going a-fishing thus? They lived on the shore. Tom said he had seen turtles in the pond that weighed between fifty and sixty; had caught a pickerel that morning that weighed four or five pounds; had also seen them washed up with another in their mouths.

Oct. 12. . . . . Carried home a couple of rails which I fished out of the bottom of the river and left on the bank to dry about three weeks ago. One was a chestnut which I have noticed for some years on the bottom of the Assabet, just above the spring on the east side, in a deep hole. It looked as if it had been there a hundred years. It was so heavy that C. and I had as much as we could do to lift it, covered with mud, on to the high bank. It was scarcely lighter today, and I amused myself with asking several to lift one half of it after I had sawed it in two. They failed at first, not being prepared to find it so heavy, though they could easily lift it afterward. It was a regular segment of a log, and though the thin edge was comparatively firm and solid, the sap-wood on the broad and rounded side, now that it had been lying in the air, was quite spongy and had opened into numerous great chinks, five eighths of an inch wide by an inch deep. The whole was of a rusty brown externally, having imbibed some iron from the water. When split up it was of a dark blue black, if split parallel with the layers, or alternately black and light brown, if split across them. There were concentric circles of black, as you looked at the end, coinciding nearly with the circles of pores, perhaps one sixteenth of an inch wide. When you looked at these on the side of a stick split across the circles, they reminded you of a striped waistcoat or sheepskin. But after being exposed to the air a little while, the whole turned to an almost uniform pale slate color, the light brown turning slate and the dark stripes also paling into slate. It had a strong dye-stuff-like scent, etc.

The other was a round oak stick, and, though it looked almost as old as the first, was quite sound even to the bark, and evidently quite recent comparatively, though full as heavy. The wood had acquired no peculiar color. Some farmers load their wood with gunpowder to punish thieves. There's no danger that mine will be loaded.

Pieces of both of these sank at once in a pail of water.

Oct. 18. . . . How much beauty in decay! I pick up a white oak leaf, dry and stiff, but yet mingled red and green, October-like, whose pulpy part some insect has eaten beneath, exposing the delicate network of its veins. It is very beautiful held up to the light—such work as only an insect eye could perform. Yet, perchance, to the vegetable kingdom such a revelation of ribs is as repulsive as the skeleton in the animal kingdom. In each case it is some little gourmand, working for another end, that reveals the wonders of nature. There are countless oak leaves in this condition now, and also with a submarginal line of network exposed.

Oct. 23. . . . Now is the time for chestnuts. A stone cast against the trees shakes them down in showers upon one's head and shoulders. But I cannot excuse myself for using the stone. It is not innocent, it is not just, so to maltreat the tree that feeds us. I am not disturbed by considering that if I thus shorten its life I shall not enjoy its fruit so long, but am prompted to a more innocent course by motives purely of humanity. I sympathize with the tree, yet I heaved a big stone against the trunks like a robber—not too good to commit murder. I trust that I shall never do it again. These gifts should be accepted, not merely with gentleness, but with a certain humble gratitude. The tree whose fruit we would obtain should not be too rudely shaken even. It is not a time of distress, when a little haste and violence even might be pardoned. It is worse than boorish, it is criminal, to inflict an unnecessary injury on the tree that feeds or shadows us. Old trees are our parents, and our parents'

parents, perchance. If you would learn the secrets of Nature, you must practice more humanity than others. The thought that I was robbing myself by injuring the tree did not occur to me, but I was affected as if I had cast a rock at a sentient being—with a duller sense than my own, it is true, but yet a distant relation. Behold a man cutting down a tree to come at the fruit! What is the moral of such an act?

Nov. 5. . . . I know many children to whom I would fain make a present on some one of their birthdays, but they are so far gone in the luxury of presents—have such perfect museums of costly ones—that it would absorb my entire earnings for a year to buy them something which would not be beneath their notice.

Nov. 7. . . . I find it good to be out this still, dark, mizzling afternoon; my walk or voyage is more suggestive and profitable than in bright weather. The view is contracted by the misty rain, the water is perfectly smooth, and the stillness is favorable to reflection. I am more open to impressions, more sensitive (not calloused or indurated by sun and wind), as if in a chamber still. My thoughts are concentrated; I am all compact. The solitude is real, too, for the weather keeps other men at home. This mist is like a roof and walls over and around, and I walk with a domestic feeling. The sound of a wagon going over an unseen bridge is louder than ever, and so of other sounds. I am *compelled* to look at near objects. All things have a soothing effect; the very clouds and mists brood over me. My power of observation and contemplation is much increased. My attention does not wander. The world and my life are simplified. What now of Europe and Asia?

Nov. 9. . . . I deal so much with my fuel—what with finding it, loading it, conveying it home, sawing and splitting it—get so many values out of it, am warmed in so many ways by it, that the heat it will yield when in the stove is of a lower temperature and a lesser value in my eyes—though when I feel it I am reminded of all my adventures. I just turned to put on a stick. I had my choice in the box of gray chestnut rail, black and brown snag of an oak stump, dead white pine top, gray and round, with stubs of limbs, or else old bridge plank, and chose the last. Yes, I lose sight of the ultimate uses of this wood and work, the immediate ones are so great, and yet most of mankind, those called most successful in obtaining the necessaries of life—getting their living—obtain none of this, except a mere vulgar and per-haps stupefying warmth. I feel disposed, to this extent, to do the getting a living and the living for any three or four of my neighbors who really want the fuel and will appreciate the act, now that I have supplied myself.

Nov. 11. . . . . The bricks of which the muskrat builds his house are little masses or wads of the dead weedy rubbish on the muddy bottom, which it probably takes up with its mouth. It consists of various kinds of weeds, now aggluti-nated together by the slime and dried conferva threads, utricularia, hornwort, etc.—a streaming, tuft-like wad. The building of these cabins appears to be coincident with the commencement of their clam diet, for now their vegetable food, excepting roots, is cut off. I see many small collections of shells already left along the river's brink. Thither they resort with their clam to open and eat it. But if it is the edge of a meadow which is being overflowed, they must raise it and make a permanent dry stool there, for they cannot afford to swim far with each clam. I see where one has left half a peck of shells on perhaps the foundation of an old stool or a harder clod, which the water is just about to cover, and he has begun his stool by laying two or three *fresh* wads upon the shells, the foundation of his house. Thus their cabin is first apparently intended merely for a stool, and afterward, when it is large, is perforated as if it were the bank! There is no cabin for a long way above the Hemlocks, where there is no low meadow bordering the stream.

Nov. 17. . . . . It is interesting to me to talk with [Reuben] Rice, he lives so thoroughly and satisfactorily to himself. He has learned that rare art of living, the very elements of which most professors do not know. His life has been not a failure but a success. Seeing me going to sharpen some plane-irons, and hearing me complain of the want of tools, he said that I ought to have a chest of tools. But I said it was not worth the while. I should not use them enough to pay for them. "You would use them more, if you had them," said he. "When I came to do a piece of work I used to find commonly that I wanted a certain tool, and I made it a rule first always to make that tool. I have spent as much as three thousand dollars thus on my tools." Comparatively speaking, his life is a success; not such a failure as most men's. He gets more out of any enterprise than his neighbors, for he helps himself more and hires less. Whatever pleasure there is in it he enjoys. By good sense and calculation he has become rich and has invested his property well, yet practices a fair and neat economy, dwells not in untidy luxury. It costs him less to live, and he gets more out of life, than others. To get his living, or keep it, is not a hasty or disagreeable toil. He works slowly but surely, enjoying the sweet of it. He buys a piece of meadow at a profitable rate, works at it in pleasant weather, he and his son, when they are inclined, goes a-fishing or a-bee-hunting or a-rifle-shooting quite as often, and thus the meadow gets redeemed, and potatoes get planted, perchance, and he is very sure to have a good crop stored in his cellar in the fall, and some to sell. He always has the best of potatoes there. In the same spirit in which he and his son tackle up their Dobbin (he never keeps a fast horse) and go a-spearing or a-fishing through the ice, they also tackle up and go to their Sudbury farm to hoe or harvest a little, and when they return they bring home a load of stumps in their hay-rigging, which impeded their labors, but, perchance, supply them with their winter wood. All the woodchucks they shoot or trap in the bean field are brought home also. And thus their life is a long sport and they know not what hard times are.

Nov. 18. . . . It is fouler and uglier to have too much than not to have enough.

Dec. 11. P.M. To Holden Swamp, Conantum.

For the first time I wear gloves, but I have not walked *early* this season.

I see no birds, but hear, methinks, one or two tree sparrows. No snow; scarcely any ice to be detected. It is only an aggravated November. I thread the tangle of the spruce swamp, admiring the leafets of the swamp pyrus which had put forth again, now frostbitten, the great yellow buds of the swamp-pink, the round red buds of the high blueberry, and the fine sharp red ones of the panicled andromeda. Slowly I worm my way amid the snarl, the thicket of black alders and blueberry, etc.; see the forms, apparently, of rabbits at the foot of maples, and catbirds' nests now exposed in the leafless thicket.

Standing there, though in this *bare* November landscape, I am reminded of the incredible phenomenon of small birds in winter—that ere long, amid the cold powdery snow, as it were a fruit of the season, will come twittering a flock of delicate crimson-tinged birds, lesser redpolls, to sport and feed on the seeds and buds now just ripe for them on the sunny side of a wood, shaking down the powdery snow there in their cheerful social feeding, as if it were high midsummer to them. These crimson aerial creatures have wings which would bear them quickly to the regions of summer, but here is all the summer they want. What a rich contrast! tropical colors, crimson breasts, on cold white snow! Such etherealness, such delicacy in their forms, such ripeness in their colors, in this stern and barren season! It is as surprising as if you were to find a brilliant crimson flower which flourished amid snows. They greet the chopper and the hunter in their furs. Their Maker gave them the last touch and launched them forth the day of the Great Snow. He made this bitter imprisoning cold before which man quails, but He made at the same time these warm and glowing creatures to twitter and be at home in it. He said not only, Let there be linnets in winter, but linnets of rich plumage and pleasing twitter, bearing summer in their natures. The snow will be three feet deep, the ice will be two feet thick, and last night, perchance, the mercury sank to thirty degrees below zero. All the fountains of nature seem to be sealed up. The traveller is frozen on his way. But under the edge of yonder birch wood will be a little flock of crimson-breasted lesser redpolls, busily feeding on the seeds of the birch and shaking down the powdery snow! As if a flower were created to be now in bloom, a peach to be now first fully ripe on its stem. I am struck by the perfect confidence and success of nature. There is no question about the existence of these delicate creatures, their adaptedness to their circumstances. There is superadded superfluous paintings and adornments, a crystalline, jewel-like health and soundness, like the colors reflected from ice-crystals.

When some rare northern bird like the pine grosbeak is seen thus far south in the winter, he does not suggest poverty, but dazzles us with his beauty. There is in them a warmth akin to the warmth that melts the icicle. Think of these brilliant, warm-colored, and richly warbling birds, birds of paradise, dainty-footed, downy-clad, in the midst of a New England, a Canadian winter. The woods and fields, now somewhat solitary, being deserted by their more tender summer residents, are now frequented by these rich but delicately tinted and hardy northern immigrants of the air. Here is no imperfection to be suggested. The winter, with its snow and ice, is not an evil to be corrected. It is as it was designed and made to be, for the artist has had leisure to add beauty to use. My acquaintances, angels from the north. I had a vision thus prospectively of these birds as I stood in the swamps. I saw this familiar—too *familiar*—fact at a different angle, and I was charmed and haunted by it. But I could only attain to be thrilled and enchanted, as by the sound of a strain of music dying away. I had seen into paradisaic regions, with their air and sky, and I was no longer wholly or merely a denizen of this vulgar earth. Yet had I hardly a foothold there. I was only sure that I was charmed, and no mistake. It is only necessary to behold thus the least fact or phenomenon, however familiar, from a point a hair's breadth aside from our habitual path or routine, to be overcome, enchanted by its beauty and significance. Only what we have touched and worn is trivial—our scurf, repetition, tradition, conformity. To perceive freshly, with fresh senses, is to be inspired. Great winter itself looked like a precious gem, reflecting rainbow colors from one angle.

My body is all sentient. As I go here or there, I am tickled by this or that I come in contact with, as if I touched the wires of a battery. I can generally recall—have fresh in my mind—several scratches last received. These I continually recall to mind, reimpress, and harp upon. The age of miracles is each moment thus returned. Now it is wild apples, now river reflections, now a flock of lesser redpolls. In winter, too, resides immortal youth and perennial summer. Its head is not silvered; its cheek is not blanched but has a ruby tinge to it.

If any part of nature excites our pity, it is for ourselves we grieve, for there is eternal health and beauty. We get only transient and partial glimpses of the beauty of the world. Standing at the right angle, we are dazzled by the colors of the rainbow in colorless ice. From the right point of view, every storm and every drop in it is a rainbow. Beauty and music are not mere traits and exceptions. They

are the rule and character. It is the exception that we see
and hear. Then I try to discover what it was in the vision
that charmed and translated me. What if we could daguer-
reotype our thoughts and feelings! For I am surprised and
enchanted often by some quality which I cannot detect. I
have seen an attribute of another world and condition of
things. It is a wonderful fact that I should be affected, and
thus deeply and powerfully, more than by aught else in all
my experience—that this fruit should be borne in me, sprung
from a seed finer than the spores of fungi, floated from other
atmospheres! finer than the dust caught in the sails of
vessels a thousand miles from land! Here the invisible seeds
settle, and spring, and bear flowers and fruits of immortal
beauty.

Dec. 23. . . . I admire those old root fences which have
almost entirely disappeared from tidy fields—white pine
roots got out when the neighboring meadow was a swamp
—the monuments of many a revolution. These roots have
not penetrated into the ground, but spread over the surface,
and, having been cut off four or five feet from the stump,
were hauled off and set up on their edges for a fence. The
roots are not merely interwoven, but grown together into
solid frames, full of loopholes like Gothic windows of
various sizes and all shapes, triangular and oval and harp-
like, and the slenderer parts are dry and resonant like harp-
strings. They are rough and unapproachable, with a hundred
snags and horns which bewilder and balk the calculation of
the walker who would surmount them. The part of the
trees above ground presents no such fantastic forms. Here is
one seven paces, or more than a rod, long, six feet high in
the middle, and yet only one foot thick, and two men could
turn it up, and in this case the roots were six or nine inches
thick at the extremities. The roots of pines growing in
swamps grow thus in the form of solid frames or rackets,
and those of different trees are interwoven with all so that
they stand on a very broad foot and stand or fall together
to some extent before the blasts, as herds meet the assault
of beasts of prey with serried front. You have thus only to
dig into the swamp a little way to find your fence—post,
rails, and slats already solidly grown together and of material more durable than any timber. How pleasing a thought
that a field should be fenced with the roots of the trees got

out in clearing the land a century before! I regret them as momentoes of the primitive forest. The tops of the same trees made into fencing stuff would have decayed generations ago. These roots are singularly unobnoxious to the effects of moisture.

1856

To all appearances Thoreau recovered his health by spring. He again became active. He walked and surveyed, lectured and wrote. He had his picture taken with his new throat beard. His leading disciples, H. G. O. Blake and Daniel Ricketson, continued to look to him for inspiration and intellectual sustenance. In fall he went to a utopian community, Eagleswood in New Jersey, where he surveyed the extensive grounds. While visiting there he took time out to see Walt Whitman in Brooklyn. The two writers dealt uneasily with one another but after the meeting both felt impressed. Thoreau announced, "He is a great fellow." The journal recovers some of the ground it had lost through Thoreau's malaise of the previous year. Once again the pages are crowded with paragraphs that give an appearance of professional ease. The range of subjects is still wide. Yet the facts seem smaller and more exact—and there seem to be more of them.

Jan. 1. . . . On the ice at Walden are very beautiful great leaf crystals in great profusion. The ice is frequently thickly covered with them for many rods. They seem to be connected with the rosettes—a running together of them. They look like a loose web of small white feathers springing from a tuft of down, for their shafts are lost in a tuft of fine snow like the down about the shaft of a feather, as if a feather bed had been shaken over the ice. They are, on a close examination, surprisingly perfect leaves, like ferns, only very broad for their length and commonly more on one side the midrib than the other. They are from an inch to an inch and a half long and three quarters wide, and slanted, where I look, from the southwest. They have, first, a very distinct midrib, though so thin that they cannot be taken up; then, distinct ribs branching from this, commonly opposite, and minute ribs springing again from these last, as in many ferns, the last running to each crenation in the border. How much further they are subdivided, the naked

229

eye cannot discern. They are so thin and fragile that they melt under your breath while looking closely at them. A fisherman says they were much finer in the morning. In other places the ice is strewn with a different kind of frostwork in little patches, as if oats had been spilled, like fibres of asbestos rolled, a half or three quarters of an inch long and an eighth or more wide. Here and there patches of them a foot or two over. Like some boreal grain spilled.

Jan. 6. . . . I am come forth to observe the drifts.

Jan. 10. . . . I love to wade and flounder through the swamp now, these bitter cold days when the snow lies deep on the ground, and I need travel but little way from the town to get to a Nova Zembla solitude—to wade through the swamps, all snowed up, untracked by man, into which the fine dry snow is still drifting till it is even with the tops of the water andromeda and halfway up the high blueberry bushes. I penetrate to islets inaccessible in summer, my feet slumping to the sphagnum far out of sight beneath, where the alder berry glows yet and the azalea buds, and perchance a single tree sparrow or a chickadee lisps by my side, where there are few tracks even of wild animals; perhaps only a mouse or two have burrowed up by the side of some twig, and hopped away in straight lines on the surface of the light, deep snow, as if too timid to delay, to another hole by the side of another bush; and a few rabbits have run in a path amid the blueberries and alders about the edge of the swamp. This is instead of a Polar Sea expedition and going after Franklin. There is but little life and but few objects, it is true. We are reduced to admire buds, even like the partridges, and bark, like the rabbits and mice—the great yellow and red forward-looking buds of the azalea, the plump red ones of the blueberry, and the fine sharp red ones of the panicled andromeda, sleeping along its stem, the speckled black alder, the rapid-growing dogwood, the pale-brown and cracked blueberry, etc. Even a little shining bud which lies sleeping behind its twig and dreaming of spring, perhaps half concealed by ice, is object enough. I feel myself upborne on the andromeda bushes beneath the snow, as on a springy basketwork, then down I go up to my middle in the deep but silent snow, which has no sympathy with my mishap. Beneath the level of this snow how many sweet berries will be hanging next August!

Jan. 18. . . . P.M. To Walden to learn the temperature of the water.

Jan. 20. In my experience I have found nothing so truly impoverishing as what is called wealth, i.e. the command of greater means than you had before possessed, though comparatively few and slight still, for you thus inevitably acquire a more expensive habit of living, and even the very same necessaries and comforts cost you more than they once did. Instead of gaining, you have lost some independence, and if your income should be suddenly lessened, you would find yourself poor, though possessed of the same means which once made you rich. Within the last five years I have had the command of a little more money than in the previous five years, for I have sold some books and some lectures; yet I have not been a whit better fed or clothed or warmed or sheltered, not a whit richer, except that I have been less concerned about my living, but perhaps my life has been the less serious for it, and, to balance it, I feel now that there is a possibility of failure. Who knows but I *may* come upon the town, if, as is likely, the public want no more of my books, or lectures (which last is already the case)? Before, I was much likelier to take the town upon my shoulders. That is, I have lost some of my independence on them, when they would say that I had gained an independence. If you wish to give a man a sense of poverty, give him a thousand dollars. The next hundred dollars he gets will not be worth more than ten that he used to get. Have pity on him; withhold your gifts.

Jan. 24. . . . I have seen many a collection of stately elms which better deserved to be represented at the General Court than the manikins beneath—than the barroom and victualling cellar and groceries they overshadowed. When I see their magnificent domes, miles away in the horizon, over intervening valleys and forests, they suggest a village, a community, there. But, after all, it is a secondary consideration whether there are human dwellings beneath them; these may have long since passed away. I find that into my idea of the village has entered more of the elm than of the human being. They are worth many a political borough. They constitute a borough. The poor human representative of his party sent out from beneath their shade will not suggest a tithe of the dignity, the true nobleness and comprehensiveness of view, the sturdiness and independence, and the serene beneficence that they do. They look from township to township. A fragment of their bark is worth the backs of all the politicians in the union. They are free-soilers in their own broad sense. They send their roots north and south and east and west into many a conservative's Kansas and Carolina, who does not suspect such underground railroads— they improve the subsoil he has never disturbed—and many times their length, if the support of their principles requires it. They battle with the tempests of a century. See what scars they bear, what limbs they lost before we were born! Yet they never adjourn; they steadily vote for their principles, and send their roots further and wider from the *same centre*. They die at their posts, and they leave a tough butt for the choppers to exercise themselves about, and a stump which serves for their monument. They attend no caucus, they make no compromise, they use no policy. Their one principle is growth. They combine a true radicalism with a true conservatism. Their radicalism is not cutting away of roots, but an infinite multiplication and extension of them under all surrounding institutions. They take a firmer hold on the earth that they may rise higher into the heavens. Their conservative heart-wood, in which no sap longer flows, does not impoverish their growth, but is a firm column to support it; and when their expanding trunks no longer require it, it utterly decays. Their conservatism is a dead but solid heart-wood, which is the pivot and firm column of support to all this growth, appropriating nothing to itself, but forever by its support assisting to extend the area of their radicalism. Half a century after they are dead at the core, they are preserved by radical reforms. They do not, like men, from radicals turn conservative. Their conservative part dies out first; their radical and growing part survives. They acquire new States and Territories, while the old dominions decay, and become the habitation of bears and owls and coons.

Jan. 26. When I took the ether [at the dentist's] my consciousness amounted to this: I put my finger on myself in order to keep the place, otherwise I should never have returned to this world.

. . . Talking with Miss Mary Emerson [R. W. Emerson's aunt] this evening, she said, "It was not the fashion to be so original when I was young." She is readier to take my view—look through my eyes for the time—than any young person that I know in the town.

March 4. To Carlisle, surveying.

I had two friends [the first, Emerson; the second, unknown]. The one offered me friendship on such terms that I could not accept it, without a sense of degradation. He would not meet me on equal terms, but only be to some extent my patron. He would not come to see me, but was hurt if I did not visit him. He would not readily accept a favor, but would gladly confer one. He treated me with ceremony occasionally, though he could be simple and downright sometimes; and from time to time acted a part, treating me as if I were a distinguished stranger; was on stilts, using made words. Our relation was one long tragedy, yet I did not directly speak of it. I do not believe in complaint, nor in explanation. The whole is but too plain, alas, already. We grieve that we do not love each other, that we cannot confide in each other. I could not bring myself to speak, and so recognize an obstacle to our affection.

I had another friend, who, through a slight obtuseness, perchance, did not recognize a fact which the dignity of friendship would by no means allow me to descend so far as to speak of, and yet the inevitable effect of that ignorance was to hold us apart forever.

March 10. . . . Think of the art of printing, what miracles it has accomplished! Covered the very waste paper which flutters under our feet like leaves and is almost as cheap, a stuff now commonly put to the most trivial uses, with thought and poetry! The woodchopper reads the wisdom of ages recorded on the paper that holds his dinner, then lights his pipe with it. When we ask for a scrap of paper for the most trivial use, it may have the confessions of Augustine or the sonnets of Shakespeare, and we not observe it. The student kindles his fire, the editor packs his trunk, the sportsman loads his gun, the traveller wraps his dinner, the Irishman papers his shanty, the schoolboy peppers the plastering, the belle pins up her hair, with the printed thoughts of men. Surely he who can see so large a portion of earth's surface thus darkened with the record of human thought and experience, and feel no desire to learn to read it, is without curiosity. He who cannot read is worse than deaf and blind, is yet but half alive, is still-born.

Still there is little or no chopping, for it will not pay to shovel the snow away from the trees; unless they are quite large, and then you must work standing in it two feet deep. There is an eddy about the large trees beside, which produces a hollow in the snow about them, but it lies close up to the small ones on every side.

March 19. P.M. To Walden.

Measured the snow again. West of railroad, 15; east of railroad, 11 4/5; average, 13 2/5; Trillium Woods, 16 3/4. The last measurement was on the seventh, when it averaged about sixteen inches in the open land. This depth it must have preserved, owing to the remarkably cold weather, till the thirteenth at least. So it chances that the snow was constantly sixteen inches deep, at least, on a level in open land, from January thirteenth to March thirteenth. It is remarkable how rapidly it has settled on the east of the railroad as compared with the west since the seventh (or I may say rather the thirteenth). The whole average settling, in open land, since say the thirteenth, is a little less than three inches.

WHAT BEFELL AT MRS. BROOKS'S

On the morning of the seventeenth, Mrs. Brooks's Irish girl Joan fell down the cellar stairs, and was found by her mistress lying at the bottom, apparently lifeless. Mrs. Brooks ran to the street-door for aid to get her up, and asked a Miss Farmer, who was passing, to call the blacksmith near by. The latter lady turned instantly, and, making haste across the road on this errand, fell flat in a puddle of melted snow, and came back to Mrs. Brooks's, bruised and dripping and asking for opodeldoc. Mrs. Brooks again ran to the door and called to George Bigelow to complete the unfinished errand. He ran nimbly about it and fell flat in another puddle near the former, but, his joints being limber, got along without opodeldoc and raised the blacksmith. He also notified James Burke, who was passing, and he, rushing in to render aid, fell off one side of the cellar stairs in the dark. They no sooner got the girl upstairs than she came to and went raving, then had a fit.

March 21. . . . 10 A.M. To my red maple sugar camp.

Found that, after a pint and a half had run from a single tube after 3 P.M. yesterday, it had frozen about half an inch thick, and this morning a quarter of a pint more had run. Between 10:30 and 11:30 A.M. this forenoon, I caught two and three quarters pints more, from six tubes, at the same tree, though it is completely overcast and threatening rain. Four and one half pints in all. This sap is an agreeable drink, like iced water (by chance), with a pleasant but slight sweetish taste. I boiled it down in the afternoon, and it made an ounce and a half of sugar, without any molasses, which appears to be the average amount yielded by the sugar maple in similar situations, *viz.* south edge of a wood, a tree partly decayed, two feet [in] diameter.

It is worth the while to know that there is all this sugar in our woods, much of which might be obtained by using the refuse wood lying about, without damage to the proprietors, who use neither the sugar nor the wood.

I left home at ten and got back before twelve with two and three quarters pints of sap, in addition to the one and three quarters I found collected.

I put in saleratus and a little milk while boiling, the former to neutralize the acid, and the latter to collect the impurities in a skum. After boiling it till I burned it a little, and my small quantity would not flow when cool, but was as hard as half-done candy, I put it on again, and in a minute it was softened and turned to sugar.

While collecting sap, the little of yesterday's lodging snow that was left, dropping from the high pines in Trillium Wood and striking the brittle twigs in its descent, makes me think that the squirrels are running there.

I noticed that my fingers were purpled, evidently from the sap on my auger.

Had a dispute with Father about the *use* of my making this sugar when I knew it could be done and might have bought sugar cheaper at Holden's. He said it took me from my studies. I said I made it my study; I felt as if I had been to a university.

It dropped from each tube about as fast as my pulse beat, and, as there were three tubes directed to each vessel, it flowed at the rate of about one hundred and eighty drops in a minute into it. One maple, standing immediately north of a thick white pine, scarcely flowed at all, while a smaller, farther in the wood, ran pretty well. The south side of a tree bleeds first in spring. I hung my pails on the tubes or a nail. Had two tin pails and a pitcher. Had a three-quarters-inch auger. Made a dozen spouts, five or six inches long, hole as large as a pencil, smoothed with a pencil.

March 23. I spend a considerable portion of my time observing the habits of the wild animals, my brute neighbors. By their various movements and migrations they fetch the year about to me. Very significant are the flight of geese and the migration of suckers, etc., etc. But when I consider that the nobler animals have been exterminated here—the cougar, panther, lynx, wolverene, wolf, bear, moose, deer, the beaver, the turkey, etc., etc.—I cannot but feel as if I lived in a tamed, and, as it were, emasculated country. Would not the motions of those larger and wilder animals have been more significant still? Is it not a maimed and imperfect nature that I am conversant with? As if I were to study a tribe of Indians that had lost all its warriors. Do not the forest and the meadow now lack expression, now that I never see nor think of the moose with a lesser forest on his head in the one, nor of the beaver in the other? When I think what were the various sounds and notes, the migrations and works, and changes of fur and plumage which ushered in the spring and marked the other seasons of the year, I am reminded that this my life in nature, this particular round of natural phenomena which I call a year, is lamentably incomplete. I listen to [a] concert in which so many parts are wanting. The whole civilized country is to some extent turned into a city, and I am that citizen whom I pity. Many of those animal migrations and other phenomena by which the Indians marked the season are no longer to be observed. I seek acquaintance with Nature—to know her moods and manners. Primitive Nature is the most interesting to me. I take infinite pains to know all the phenomena of the spring, for instance, thinking that I have here the entire poem, and then, to my chagrin, I hear that it is but an imperfect copy that I possess and have read, that my ancestors have torn out many of the first leaves and grandest passages, and mutilated it in many places. I should not like to think that some demigod had come before me and picked out some of the best of the stars. I wish to know an entire heaven and an entire earth. All the great trees and beasts, fishes and fowl are gone. The streams, perchance, are somewhat shrunk.

March 28. . . . Farewell, my friends, my path inclines to this side the mountain, yours to that. For a long time you have appeared further and further off to me. I see that you will at length disappear altogether. For a season my path seems lonely without you. The meadows are like barren ground. The memory of me is steadily passing away from you. My path grows narrower and steeper, and the night is approaching. Yet I have faith that, in the definite future, new suns will rise, and new plains expand before me, and I trust that I shall therein encounter pilgrims who bear that same virtue that I recognized in you, who will be that very virtue that was you. I accept the everlasting and salutary law, which was promulgated as much that spring that I first knew you, as this that I seem to lose you.

April 6. . . . As I am going along the Corner road by the meadow mouse brook, hear and see, a quarter of a mile northwest, on those conspicuous white oaks near the river in Hubbard's second grove, the crows buffeting some intruder. The crows had betrayed to me some large bird of the hawk kind which they were buffeting. I suspected it before I looked carefully. I saw several crows on the oaks, and also what looked to my naked eye like a cluster of the palest and most withered oak leaves with a black base about as big as a crow. Looking with my glass, I saw that it was a great bird. The crows sat about a rod off, higher up, while another crow was occasionally diving at him, and all were cawing. The great bird was just starting. It was chiefly a dirty white with great broad wings with black tips and black on other parts, giving it the appearance of dirty white, barred with black. I am not sure whether it was a white-headed eagle or a fish hawk. There appeared much more white than belongs to either, and more black than the fish hawk has. It rose and wheeled, flapping several times, till it got under way; then, with its rear to me, presenting the least surface, it moved off steadily in its orbit over the woods northwest, with the slightest possible undulation of its wings—a noble planetary motion, like Saturn with its ring seen edgewise. It is so rare that we see a large body self-sustained in the air. While crows sat still and silent and confessed their lord. Through my glass I saw the outlines of this sphere against the sky, trembling with life and power as it skimmed the topmost twigs of the wood toward some more solitary oak amid the meadows. To my naked eye it showed only so much black as a crow in its talons might. Was it not the white-headed eagle in the state when it is called the sea eagle? Perhaps its neck-feathers were erected.

I went to the oaks. Heard there a nuthatch's faint vibrating *tut-tut,* somewhat even like croaking of frogs, as it made its way up the oak bark and turned head down to peck. Anon it answered its mate with a *gnah gnah.* Smelt a skunk on my return, at Hubbard's blueberry swamp, which some dogs that had been barking there for half an hour had probably worried, for I did not smell it when I went along first. I smelt this all the way thence home, the wind being south-west, and it was quite as perceptible in our yard as at the swamp. The family had already noticed it, and you might have supposed that there was a skunk in the yard, yet it was three quarters of a mile off, at least.

April 10. Thursday. Fast-Day. Some fields are dried sufficiently for the games of ball with which this season is commonly ushered in. I associate this day, when I can remember it, with games of baseball played over behind the hills in the russet fields toward Sleepy Hollow, where the snow was just melted and dried up, and also with the uncertainty I always experienced whether the shops would be shut, whether we should have an ordinary dinner, an extraordinary one, or none at all, and whether there would be more than one service at the meeting-house. This last uncertainty old folks share with me. This is a windy day, drying up the fields; the first we have had for a long time.

May 15. . . . Cleared out the Beech Spring, which is a copious one. So I have done some service, though it was a wet and muddy job. Cleared out a spring while you have been to the wars. Now that warmer days make the traveller thirsty, this becomes an important work. This spring was filled and covered with a great mass of beech leaves, amid and beneath which, damp and wet as they were, were myriads of snow-fleas and also their white exuviae; the latter often whitening a whole leaf, mixed with live ones. It looks as if for coolness and moisture—which the snow had afforded—they were compelled to take refuge here.

May 25. . . . I found five arrowheads at Clamshell Hill.

June 10. . . . A painted tortoise laying her eggs ten feet from the wheel-track on the Marlborough road. She paused at first, but I sat down within two feet, and she soon resumed her work. Had excavated a hollow about five inches wide and six long in the moistened sand, and cautiously, with long intervals, she continued her work, resting always on the same spot her fore feet, and never looking round, her eye shut all but a narrow slit. Whenever I moved, perhaps to brush off a mosquito, she paused. A wagon approached, rumbling afar off, and then there was a pause, till it had passed and long, long after, a tedious, *naturlangsam* pause of the slow-blooded creature, a sacrifice of time such as those animals are up to which slumber half a year and live for centuries. It was twenty minutes before I discovered that she was not making the hole but filling it up slowly, having laid her eggs. She drew the moistened sand under herself, scraping it along from behind with both feet brought together, the claws turned inward. In the long pauses the ants troubled her (as mosquitoes me) by running over her eyes, which made her snap or dart out her head suddenly, striking the shell. She did not dance on the sand, nor finish covering the hollow quite so carefully as the one observed last year. She went off suddenly (and quickly at first), with a slow but sure instinct through the wood toward the swamp.

Aug. 1. . . . Since July thirtieth, inclusive, we have had perfect dog-days without interruption. The earth has suddenly [become] invested with a thick musty mist. The sky has become a mere fungus. A thick blue musty veil of mist is drawn before the sun. The sun has not been visible, except for a moment or two once or twice a day, all this time, nor the stars by night. Moisture reigns. You cannot dry a napkin at the window, nor press flowers without their mildewing. You imbibe so much moisture from the atmosphere that you are not so thirsty, nor is bathing so grateful as a week ago. The burning heat is tempered, but as you lose sight of the sky and imbibe the musty, misty air, you exist as a vegetable, a fungus. Unfortunate those who have not got their hay. I see them wading in overflowed meadows and pitching the black and mouldy swaths about in vain that they may dry. In the meanwhile, vegetation is becoming rank, vines of all kinds are rampant. Squashes and melons *are said* to grow a foot in a night. But weeds grow as fast. The corn unrolls. Berries abound and attain their full size. Once or twice in the day there is an imperfect gleam of yellow sunlight for a moment through some thinner part of the veil, reminding us that we have not seen the sun so long, but no blue sky is revealed. The earth is completely invested with cloud-like wreaths of vapor (yet fear no rain and need no veil), beneath which flies buzz hollowly and torment, and mosquitoes hum and sting as if they were born of such an air. The drooping spirits of mosquitoes revive, and they whet their stings anew. Legions of buzzing flies blacken the furniture. (For a week *at least* have heard that snapping sound under pads.) We have a dense fog every night, which lifts itself but a short distance during the day. At sundown I see it curling up from the river and meadows. However, I love this moisture in its season. I believe it is good to breathe, wholesome as a vapor bath. Toadstools shoot up in the yards and paths.

Aug. 7. . . . Heard this forenoon what I thought at first to be children playing on pumpkin stems in the next yard, but it turned out to be the new steam-whistle music, what they call the Calliope (!) in the next town. It sounded still more like the pumpkin stem near at hand, only a good deal louder. Again I mistook it for an instrument in the house or at the door, when it was a quarter of a mile off, from habit locating it by its loudness. At Acton, six miles off, it sounded like some new seraphim in the next house with the blinds closed. All the milkmen and their horses stood still to hear it. The horses stood it remarkably well. It was not so musical as the ordinary whistle.

Aug. 16. . . . Ambrosia pollen now begins to yellow my clothes.

Aug. 19. . . . When huckleberries are getting stale on dry hillsides, amid the huckleberry bushes and in sprout-lands and by paths you may observe them. The broad meshes of their panicles rarely catch the eye. There is something witchlike about them; though so rare and remote, yet evidently, from those bur-like pods, expecting to come in contact with some travelling man or beast without their knowledge, to be transported to new hillsides; lying in wait, as it were, to catch by the hem of the berry-pickers' garments and so get a lift to new quarters. They occupy a great deal of room, but are the less obvious for it. They put their chains about you, and they cling like savage children to their mother's back or breast. They escape your observation, as it were under bare poles. You only notice as far up as their green sails are set, perchance, or to the cross-trees, not the tall, tapering, raking spars, whence are looped the lifelines and halyards. Or it is like that slanting mast and rigging in navy yards where masts are inserted.

Aug. 25. P.M. To Hill by boat.

Silvery cinquefoil now begins to show itself commonly again. Perhaps it is owing to the rain, spring-like, which we have in August.

I paddle directly across the meadow, the river is so high, and land east of the elm on the third or fourth row of potatoes. The water makes more show on the meadows than yesterday, though hardly so high, because the grass is more flatted down. I easily make my way amid the thin spires. Almost every stem which rises above the surface has a grasshopper or caterpillar upon it. Some have seven or eight grasshoppers, clinging to their masts, one close and directly above another, like shipwrecked sailors, now the third or fourth day exposed. Whither shall they jump? It is a quarter of a mile to shore, and countless sharks lie in wait for them. They are so thick that they are like a crop which the grass bears; some stems are bent down by their weight. This flood affects other inhabitants of these fields than men; not only the owners of the grass, but its inhabitants much more. It drives them to their upper stories—to take refuge in the rigging. Many that have taken an imprudent leap are seen struggling in the water. How much life is drowned out that inhabits about the roots of the meadow-grass! How many a family, perchance, of short-tailed meadow mice has had to scamper or swim!

The river-meadow cranberries are covered deep. I can count them as they lie in dense beds a foot under water, so distinct and white, or just beginning to have a red cheek. They will probably be spoiled, and this crop will fail. Potatoes, too, in the low land on which water has stood so long, will rot.

The farmers commonly say that the spring floods, being of cold water, do not injure the grass like later ones when the water is warm, but I suspect it is not so much owing to the warmth of the water as to the age and condition of the grass and whatever else is exposed to them. They say that if you let the water rise and stand some time over the roots of trees in warm weather it will kill them. This, then, may be the value of these occasional freshets in August: they steam and kill the shrubs and trees which had crept into the river meadows, and so keep them open perpetually, which, perchance, the spring floods alone might not do. It is commonly supposed that our river meadows were much drier than now originally, or when the town was settled. They were probably drier before the dam was built at Billerica, but if they were much or at all drier than now originally, I ask what prevented their being converted into maple swamps? Maples, alders, birches, etc., are creeping into them quite fast on many sides at present. If they had been so dry as is supposed they would not have been open meadows. It seems to be true that high water in midsummer, when perchance the trees and shrubs are in a more tender state, kills them. It "steams" them, as it does the grass; and maybe the river thus asserts its rights, and possibly it would still to great extent, though the meadows should be considerably raised. Yet, I ask, why do maples, alders, etc., at present border the stream, though they do not spring up to any extent in the open meadow? Is it because the immediate bank is commonly more firm as well as higher (their seeds also are more liable to be caught there), and where it is low they are protected by willows and button-bushes, which can bear the flood? Not even willows and button-bushes prevail in the Great Meadows—though many of the former, at least, spring up there—except on the most elevated parts or hummocks. The reason for this cannot be solely in the fact that the water stands over them there a part of the year, because they are still more exposed to the water in many places on the shore of the river where yet they thrive. Is it then owing to the soft character of the ground in the meadow and the ice tearing up the meadow so extensively? On the immediate bank of the river that kind of sod and soil is not commonly formed which the ice lifts up. Why is the black willow so strictly confined to the bank of the river? What is the use, in Nature's economy, of these occasional floods in August? Is it not partly to preserve the meadows open?

Aug. 30. . . . If you would really take a position outside the street and daily life of men, you must have deliberately planned your course, you must have business which is not your neighbors' business, which they cannot understand. For only absorbing employment prevails, succeeds, takes up space, occupies territory, determines the future of individuals and states, drives Kansas out of your head, and actually and permanently occupies the only desirable and free Kansas against all border ruffians. . . .

. . . I enjoyed this cranberrying very much, notwithstanding the wet and cold, and the swamp seemed to be yielding its crop to me alone, for there are none else to pluck it or to value it. I told the proprietor once that they grew here, but he, learning that they were not abundant enough to be gathered for the market, has probably never thought of them since. I am the only person in the township who regards them or knows of them, and I do not regard them in the light of their pecuniary value. I have no doubt I felt richer wading there with my two pockets full, treading on wonders at every step, than any farmer going to market with a hundred bushels which he has raked, or hired to be raked. I got further and further away from the town every moment, and my good genius seemed [to] have smiled on me, leading me hither, and then the sun suddenly came out clear and bright, but it did not warm my feet. I would gladly share my gains, take one, or twenty, into partnership and get this swamp with them, but I do not know an individual whom this berry cheers and nourishes as it does me. When I exhibit it to them I perceive that they take but a momentary interest in it and commonly dismiss it from their thoughts with the consideration that it cannot be profitably cultivated. . . .

. . . I see that all is not garden and cultivated field and crops, that there are square rods in Middlesex County as purely primitive and wild as they were a thousand years ago, which have escaped the plow and the axe and the scythe and the cranberry-rake, little oases of wildness in the desert of our civilization, wild as a square rod on the moon, supposing it to be uninhabited. I believe almost in the personality of such planetary matter, feel something akin to reverence for it, can even worship it as terrene, titanic matter extant in my day. We are so different we admire each other, we healthily attract one another. I love it as a maiden. . . .

Aug. 31. . . . Some are so inconsiderate as to ask to walk or sail with me regularly every day—I have known such—and think that, because there will be six inches or a foot between our bodies, we shall not interfere! These things are settled by fate. The good ship sails—when she is ready. For freight or passage apply to————?? Ask my friend where. What is getting into a man's carriage when it is full, compared with putting your foot in his mouth and popping right into his mind without considering whether it is occupied or not? If I remember aright, it was only on condition *that you were asked,* that you were to go with a man one mile or twain. Suppose a man asks, not you to go with him, but to go with you! Often, I would rather undertake to shoulder a barrel of pork and carry it a mile than take into my company a man. It would not be so heavy a weight upon my mind. I could put it down and only feel my *back* ache for it.

Sept. 1. . . . We go admiring the pure and delicate tints of fungi on the surface of the damp swamp there, following up along the north side of the brook past the right of the old camp. There are many very beautiful lemon-yellow ones of various forms, some shaped like buttons, some becoming finely scalloped on the edge, some club-shaped and hollow, of the most delicate and rare but decided tints, contrasting well with the decaying leaves about them. There are others also pure white, others a wholesome red, others brown, and some even a light indigo-blue above and beneath and throughout. When colors come to be taught in the schools, as they should be, both the prism (or the rainbow) and these fungi should be used by way of illustration, and if the pupil does not learn colors, he may learn fungi, which perhaps is better. You almost envy the wood frogs and toads that hop amid such gems—some pure and bright enough for a breastpin. Out of every crevice between the dead leaves oozes some vehicle of color, the unspent wealth of the year, which Nature is now casting forth, as if it were only to empty herself.

Sept. 2. . . . It commonly chances that I make my most interesting botanical discoveries when I [am] in a thrilled and expectant mood, perhaps wading in some remote swamp where I have just found something novel and feel more than usually remote from the town. Or some rare plant which for some reason has occupied a strangely prominent place in my thoughts for some time will present itself. My expectation ripens to discovery. I am prepared for strange things.

Sept. 8. Brattleboro. Rains.

Sept. 10. . . . Ascended the Fall Mountain with a heavy valise on my back, against the advice of the toll-man. But when I got up so soon and easily I was amused to remember his anxiety. . . .

Oct. 1. . . . It is cooler and windier, and I wear two thin coats.

Oct. 19. . . . I have often noticed the inquisitiveness of birds, as the other day of a sparrow, whose motions I should not have supposed to have any reference to me, if I had not watched it from first to last. I stood on the edge of a pine and birch wood. It flitted from seven or eight rods distant to a pine within a rod of me, where it hopped about stealthily and chirped awhile, then flew as many rods the other side and hopped about there a spell, then back to the pine again, as near me as it dared, and again to its first position, very restless all the while. Generally I should have supposed that there was more than one bird, or that it was altogether accidental—that the chirping of this sparrow eight or ten rods [away] had no reference to me—for I could see nothing peculiar about it. But when I brought my glass to bear on it, I found that it was almost steadily eying me and was all alive with excitement.

Oct. 21. . . . Father told me about his father the other night—that he remembers his father used to breakfast before the family at one time, on account of his business, and he with him. His father used to eat the under crusts of biscuits, and he the upper. His father died in 1801, aged forty-seven. When the war came on, he was apprentice or journeyman to a cooper who employed many hands. He called them together, and told them that on account of the war his business was ruined and he had no more work for them. So, my father thinks, his father went privateering. Yet he remembers his telling him of his being employed digging at some defenses, when a cannon-ball came and sprinkled the sand all over them.

Dec. 1. . . . I see the old pale-faced farmer out again on his sled now for the five-thousandth time—Cyrus Hubbard, a man of a certain New England probity and worth, immortal and natural, like a natural product, like the sweetness of a nut, like the toughness of hickory. He, too, is a redeemer for me. How superior actually to the faith he professes! He is not an office-seeker. What an institution, what a revelation is a man! We are wont foolishly to think that the creed which a man professes is more significant than the fact he is. It matters not how hard the conditions seemed, how mean the world, for a man is a prevalent force and a new law himself. He is a system whose law is to be observed. The old farmer condescends to countenance still this nature and order of things. It is a great encouragement that an honest man makes this world his abode. He rides on the sled drawn by oxen, world-wise, yet comparatively so young, as if they had seen scores of winters. The farmer spoke to me, I can swear, clean, cold, moderate as the snow. He does not melt the snow where he treads. Yet what a faint impression that encounter may make on me after all! Moderate, natural, true, as if he were made of earth, stone, wood, snow. I thus meet in this universe kindred of mine, composed of these elements. I see men like frogs; their peeping I partially understand.

Dec. 3. . . . For years my appetite was so strong that I fed—I browsed—on the pine forest's edge seen against the winter horizon. How cheap my diet still! Dry sand that has fallen in railroad cuts and slid on the snow beneath is a condiment to my walk. I ranged about like a gray moose, looking at the spiring tops of the trees, and fed my imagination on them—far-away, ideal trees not disturbed by the axe of the woodcutter, nearer and nearer fringes and eyelashes of my eye. Where was the sap, the fruit, the value of the forest for me, but in that line where it was relieved against the sky? That was my wood-lot; that was my lot in the woods. The silvery needles of the pine straining the light.

Dec. 4. . . . When I bought my boots yesterday, Hastings ran over his usual rigmarole. Had he any stout old-fashioned cowhide boots? Yes, he thought he could suit me. "There's something that'll turn water about as well as anything. Billings had a pair just like them the other [day], and he said they kept his feet as dry as a bone. But what's more than that, they were made above a year ago upon honor. They are just the thing, you may depend on it. I had an eye to you when I was making them." "But they are too soft and thin for me. I want them to be thick and stand out from my foot." "Well, there is another pair, maybe a little thicker. I'll tell you what it is, these were made of dry hide."

Both were warranted single leather and not split. I took the last. But after wearing them round this cold day I found that the little snow which rested on them and melted wet the upper leather through like paper and wet my feet, and I told H. of it, that he might have an offset to Billings's experience. "Well, you can't expect a new pair of boots to turn water at first. I tell the farmers that the time to buy boots is at midsummer, or when they are hoeing their potatoes, and the pores have a chance to get filled with dirt."

Dec. 10. . . . Yesterday I walked under the murderous Lincoln Bridge, where at least ten men have been swept dead from the cars within as many years. I looked to see if their heads had indented the bridge, if there were sturdy blows given as well as received, and if their brains lay about. But I could see neither the one nor the other. The bridge is quite uninjured, even, and straight, not even the paint worn off or discolored. The ground is clean, the snow spotless, and the place looks as innocent as a bank whereon the wild thyme grows. It does its work in an artistic manner. We have another bridge of exactly the same character on the other side of the town, which has killed one, at least, to my knowledge. Surely the approaches to our town are well guarded. These are our modern Dragons of Wantley. Boucaniers of the Fitchburg Railroad, they lie in wait at the narrow passes and decimate the employees. The Company has signed a bond to give up one employee at this pass annually. The Vermont mother commits her son to their charge, and when she asks for him, again the Directors say: "I am not your son's keeper. Go look beneath the ribs of the Lincoln Bridge." It is a monster which would not have minded Perseus with his Medusa's head. If he could be held back only four feet from where he now crouches, all travellers might pass in safety and laugh him to scorn. This would require but a little resolution in our legislature, but it is preferred to pay tribute still. I felt a curiosity to see this famous bridge, naturally far greater than my curiosity to see the gallows on which Smith was hung, which was burned in the old courthouse, for the exploits of this bridge are ten times as memorable. Here they are killed without priest, and the bridge, unlike the gallows, is a fixture. Besides, the gallows bears an ill name, and I think deservedly. No doubt it has hung many an innocent man, but this Lincoln Bridge, long as it has been in our midst and busy as it has been, no legislature, nobody, indeed, has ever seriously complained of, unless it was some bereaved mother, who was naturally prejudiced against it. To my surprise, I found no difficulty in getting a sight of it. It stands right out in broad daylight in the midst of the fields. No sentinels, no spiked fence, no crowd about it, and you have to pay no fee for looking at it. It is perfectly simple and easy to construct, and does its work silently. The days of the gallows are numbered. The next time this county has a Smith to dispose of, they have only to hire him out to the Fitchburg Railroad Company. Let the priest accompany him to the freight train, pray with him, and take leave of him there. Another advantage I have hinted at, an advantage to the morals of the community, that, strange as it may seem, no crowd ever assembles at this spot; there are no morbidly curious persons, no hardened reprobates, no masculine women, no anatomists there.

Dec. 12. . . . I saw Lynch's dog stealthily feeding at a half of his master's pig, which lay dressed on a wheelbarrow at the door. A little yellow-brown dog, with fore feet braced on the ice and outstretched neck, he eagerly browsed along the edge of the meat, half a foot to right and left, with incessant short and rapid snatches, which brought it away as readily as if it had been pudding. He evidently knew very well that he was stealing, but made the most of his time. The little brown dog weighed a pound or two more afterward than before.

Dec. 18. . . . At my lecture [on "Walking" in Amherst, New Hampshire], the audience attended to me closely, and I was satisfied; that is all I ask or expect generally. Not one spoke to me afterward, nor needed they. I have no doubt that they liked it, in the main, though few of them would have dared to say so, provided they were conscious of it. Generally, if I can only get the ears of an audience, I do not care whether they say they like my lecture or not. I think I know as well as they can tell. At any rate, it is none of my business, and it would be impertinent for me to inquire. The stupidity of most of these country towns, not to include the cities, is in its innocence infantile. Lectured in basement (vestry) of the orthodox church, and I trust helped to undermine it.

Dec. 29. . . . We must go out and re-ally ourselves to Nature every day. We must make root, send out some little fibre at least, even every winter day. I am sensible that I am imbibing health when I open my mouth to the wind. Staying in the house breeds a sort of insanity always. Every house is in this sense a hospital. A night and a forenoon is as much confinement to those wards as I can stand. I am aware that I recover some sanity which I had lost the instant that I come abroad.

Dec. 30. . . . Consider that Iroquois, torturing his captive, roasting him before a slow fire, biting off the fingers of him alive, and finally eating the heart of him dead, betraying not the slightest evidence of humanity; and now behold him in the council chamber, where he meets the representatives of the hostile nation to treat of peace, conducting with such perfect dignity and decorum, betraying such a sense of justness. These savages are equal to us civilized men in their treaties, and, I fear, not essentially worse in their wars.

1857

The most portentous event was Thoreau's meeting with John Brown of Kansas. He was introduced to him by a zealous young Harvard graduate, F. B. Sanborn, who later devoted much of his life to Thoreau's literary remains. Sanborn was a paying dinner guest in the Thoreau household and when Brown visited Concord looking for support, Sanborn brought Brown with him. Thoreau was not much impressed at the beginning but later he watched Brown's fiery career with rising interest and admiration. Thoreau again visited Cape Cod and the Maine wilderness. The journal is extensive and exact.

Jan. 7. . . . I should not be ashamed to have a shrub oak for my coat-of-arms.

Jan. 11. . . . The other day a man came "just to get me to run a line in the woods." This is the usual request. "Do you know where one end of it is?" I asked. (It was the Stratton lot.) "No," said he, "I don't know either end; that is what I want to find." "Do you know either of the next sides of the lot?" Thinking a moment, he answered, "No." "Well, do you know any one side of the whole lot, or any corner?" After a little hesitation he said that he did not. Here, then, was a wood-lot of half a dozen acres, well enough described in a deed dated 1777, courses and distances given, but he could not tell exactly in what part of the universe any particular part of it was, but he expected me to find out. This was what he understood by "running." On the strength of this deed he had forbidden a man to chop wood somewhere.

For some years past I have partially offered myself as a lecturer; have been advertised as such several years. Yet I have had but two or three invitations to lecture in a year, and some years none at all. I congratulate myself on having been permitted to stay at home thus, I am so much richer for it. . . .

Jan. 13. I hear one thrumming a guitar below stairs. It

reminds me of moments that I have lived. What a comment on our life is the least strain of music! It lifts me up
above all the dust and mire of the universe. I soar or hover
with clean skirts over the field of my life. It is ever life within life, in concentric spheres. The field wherein I toil or
rust at any time is at the same time the field for such different kinds of life! The farmer's boy or hired man has an instinct which tells him as much indistinctly, and hence his
dreams and his restlessness; hence, even, it is that he wants
money to realize his dreams with. The identical field where I
am leading my humdrum life, let but a strain of music be
heard there, is seen to be the field of some unrecorded crusade or tournament the thought of which excites in us an
ecstasy of joy. The way in which I am affected by this faint
thrumming advertises me that there is still some health and
immortality in the springs of me. What an elixir is this
sound! I, who but lately came and went and lived under
a dish cover, live now under the heavens. It releases me;
it bursts my bonds. Almost all, perhaps all, our life is, speaking comparatively, a stereotyped despair; i.e., we never at
any time realize the full grandeur of our destiny. We forever and ever and habitually underrate our fate. Talk of
infidels! Why, all of the race of man, except in the rarest
moments when they are lifted above themselves by an ecstasy,
are infidels. With the very best disposition, what does my
belief amount to? This poor, timid, unenlightened, thick-
skinned creature, what *can* it believe? I am, of course,
hopelessly ignorant and unbelieving until some divinity stirs
within me. Ninety-nine one-hundredths of our lives we
are mere hedgers and ditchers, but from time to time we
meet with reminders of our destiny.

Jan. 27. . . . The most poetic and truest account of objects is generally by those who first observe them, or the
discoverers of them, whether a sharper perception and curiosity in them led to the discovery or the greater novelty
more inspired their report. Accordingly I love most to read
the accounts of a country, its natural productions and curi-
osities, by those who first settled it, and also the earliest,
though often unscientific, writers on natural science.

Feb. 8. . . . Again and again I congratulate myself on
my so-called poverty. I was almost disappointed yesterday to find thirty dollars in my desk which I did not know

that I possessed, though now I should be sorry to lose it. The week that I go away to lecture, however much I may get for it, is unspeakably cheapened. The preceding and succeeding days are a mere sloping down and up from it.

In the society of many men, or in the midst of what is called success, I find my life of no account, and my spirits rapidly fall. I would rather be the barrenest pasture lying fallow than cursed with the compliments of kings, than be the sulphurous and accursed desert where Babylon once stood. But when I have only a rustling oak leaf, or the faint metallic cheep of a tree sparrow, for variety in my winter walk, my life becomes continent and sweet as the kernel of a nut. I would rather hear a single shrub oak leaf at the end of a wintry glade rustle of its own accord at my approach, than receive a shipload of stars and garters from the strange kings and peoples of the earth.

. . . And now another friendship is ended. I do not know what has made my friend [probably Lidian Emerson] doubt me, but I know that in love there is no mistake, and that every estrangement is well founded. But my destiny is not narrowed, but if possible the broader for it. The heavens withdraw and arch themselves higher. I am sensible not only of a moral, but even a grand physical pain, such as gods may feel, about my head and breast, a certain ache and fullness. This rending of a tie, it is not my work nor thine. It is no accident that we mind; it is only the awards of fate that are affecting. I know of no eons, or periods, no life and death, but these meetings and separations. My life is like a stream that is suddenly dammed and has no outlet; but it rises the higher up the hills that shut it in, and will become a deep and silent lake. Certainly there is no event comparable for grandeur with the eternal separation—if we may conceive it so—from a being that we have known. I become in a degree sensible of the meaning of finite and infinite. What a grand significance the word "never" acquires! With one with whom we have walked on high ground we cannot deal on any lower ground ever after. We have tried for so many years to put each other to this immortal use, and have failed. Undoubtedly our good genii have mutually found the material unsuitable. We have hitherto paid each other the highest possible compliment; we have recognized each other constantly as divine, have afforded each other that opportunity to live that no other wealth or kindness can afford. And now, for some reason inappreciable by us, it has become necessary for us to withhold this mutual aid. Perchance there is none beside who knows us for a god, and none whom we know for such. Each man and woman is a veritable god or goddess, but to the mass of their fellows disguised. There is only one in each case who sees through the disguise. That one who does not stand so near to any man as to see the divinity in him is truly alone. I am perfectly sad at parting from you. I could better have the earth taken away from under my feet, than the thought of you from my mind. One while I think that some great injury has been done, with which you are implicated, again that you are no party to it. I fear that there may be incessant tragedies, that one may treat his fellow as a god but receive somewhat less regard from him. I now almost for the first time *fear* this. Yet I believe that in the long run there is no such inequality.

Feb. 20. . . . I wish that there was in every town, in some place accessible to the traveller, instead [of] or beside the common directories, etc., a list of the worthies of the town, i.e. of those who are *worth* seeing.

Feb. 28. . . . It is a singular infatuation that leads men to become clergymen in regular, or even irregular, standing. I pray to be introduced to new men, at whom I may stop short and taste their peculiar sweetness. But in the clergyman of the most liberal sort I see no perfectly independent human nucleus, but I seem to see some indistinct scheme hovering about, to which he has lent himself, to which he belongs. It is a very fine cobweb in the lower stratum of the air, which stronger wings do not even discover. Whatever he may say, he does not know that one day is as good as another. Whatever he may say, he does not know that a man's creed can never be written, that there are no particular expressions of belief that deserve to be prominent. He dreams of a certain sphere to be filled by him, something less in diameter than a great circle, maybe not greater than a hogshead. All the staves are got out, and his sphere is already hooped. . . .

March 26. . . . You take your walk some pretty cold and windy, but sunny March day, through rustling woods, perhaps, glad to take shelter in the hollows or on the south side of the hills or woods. When ensconced in some sunny and sheltered hollow, with some just melted pool at its bottom, as you recline on the fine withered sedge, in which the mice have had their galleries, leaving it pierced with countless holes, and are, perchance, dreaming of spring there, a single dry, hard croak, like a grating twig, comes up from the pool. Such is the earliest voice of the pools, where there is a small smooth surface of melted ice bathing the bare button-bushes or water andromeda or tufts of sedge; such is the earliest voice of the liquid pools, hard and dry and grating. Unless you watch long and closely, not a ripple nor a bubble will be seen, and a marsh hawk will have to look sharp to find one. The notes of the croaking frog and the hylodes are not only contemporary with, but analogous to, the blossoms of the skunk-cabbage and white maple.

Are not March and November *gray* months?

March 28. . . . Often I can give the truest and most interesting account of any adventure I have had after years have elapsed, for then I am not confused, only the most significant facts surviving in my memory. Indeed, all that continues to interest me after such a lapse of time is sure to be pertinent, and I may safely record all that I remember.

April 7. . . . At sundown I went out to gather bayberries to make tallow of. Holding a basket beneath, I rubbed them off into it between my hands, and so got about a quart, to which were added enough to make about three pints. They are interesting little gray berries clustered close about the short bare twigs, just below the last year's growth. The berries have little prominences, like those of an orange, encased with tallow, the tallow also filling the interstices, down to the nut.

They require a great deal of boiling to get out all the tallow. The outmost case soon melted off, but the inmost part I did not get even after many hours of boiling. The oily part rose to the top, making it look like a savory black broth, which smelled just like balm or other herb tea. I got about a quarter of a pound by weight from these say three pints of berries, and more yet remained. Boil a great while, let it cool, then skim off the tallow from the surface; melt again and strain it. What I got was more yellow than what I have seen in the shops. A small portion cooled in the form of small corns (nuggets I called them when I picked them out from amid the berries), flat hemispherical, of a very pure lemon yellow, and these needed no straining. The berries were left black and massed together by the remaining tallow.

April 23. I saw at [Daniel] Ricketson's a young woman, Miss Kate Brady, twenty years old, her father an Irishman, a worthless fellow, her mother a smart Yankee. The daughter formerly did sewing, but now keeps school for a livelihood. She was born at the Brady house, I think in Freetown, where she lived till twelve years old and helped her father in the field. There she rode horse to plow and was knocked off the horse by apple tree boughs, kept sheep, caught fish, etc., etc. I never heard a girl or woman express so strong a love for nature. She purposes to return to that lonely ruin, and dwell there alone, since her mother and sister will not accompany her; says that she knows all about farming and keeping sheep and spinning and weaving, though it would puzzle her to shingle the old house. There she thinks she can "live free." I was pleased to hear of her plans, because they were quite cheerful and original, not professedly reformatory, but growing out of her love for "Squire's Brook and the Middleborough ponds." A strong love for outward nature is singularly rare among both men and women. The scenery immediately about her homestead is quite ordinary, yet she appreciates and can use that part of the universe as no other being can. Her own sex, so tamely bred, only jeer at her for entertaining such an idea, but she has a strong head and a love for good reading, which may carry her through. I would by no means discourage, nor yet particularly encourage her, for I would have her so strong as to succeed in spite of all ordinary discouragements.

April 26. . . . A great part of our troubles are literally domestic or originate in the house and from living indoors. I could write an essay to be entitled "Out of Doors"—undertake a crusade against houses. What a different thing Christianity preached to the house-bred and to a party who lived out of doors! Also a sermon is needed on economy of fuel. What right has my neighbor to burn ten cords of wood, when I burn only one? Thus robbing our half-naked town of this precious covering. Is he so much colder than I? It is expensive to maintain him in our midst. If some earn the salt of their porridge, are we certain that they earn the fuel of their kitchen and parlor? One man makes a little of the driftwood of the river or of the dead and refuse (unmarketable!) [wood] of the forest suffice, and Nature rejoices in him. Another, Herod-like, requires ten cords of the best of young white oak or hickory, and he is commonly esteemed a virtuous man. He who burns the most wood on his hearth is the least warmed by the sight of it growing. Leave the trim wood-lots to widows and orphan girls. Let men tread gently through nature. Let us religiously burn stumps and worship in groves, while Christian vandals lay waste the forest temples to build miles of meeting-houses and horse-sheds and feed their box stoves.

May 3. . . . Up and down the town, men and boys that are under subjection are polishing their shoes and brushing their go-to-meeting clothes. I, a descendant of Northmen who worshipped Thor, spend my time worshipping neither Thor nor Christ; a descendant of Northmen who sacrificed men and horses, sacrifice neither men nor horses. I care not for Thor nor for the Jews. I sympathize not today with those who go to church in newest clothes and sit quietly in straight-backed pews. I sympathize rather with the boy who has none to look after him, who borrows a boat and paddle and in common clothes sets out to explore these temporary vernal lakes. I meet such a boy paddling along under a sunny bank, with bare feet and his pants rolled up above his knees, ready to leap into the water at a moment's warning. . . .

May 8. . . . Within a week I have had made a pair of corduroy pants, which cost when done $1.60. They are of that peculiar clay color, reflecting the light from portions of their surface. They have this advantage, that, beside being very strong, they will look about as well three months hence as now—or as ill, some would say. Most of my friends are disturbed by my wearing them. I can get four or five pairs for what one ordinary pair would cost in Boston, and each of the former will last two or three times as long under the same circumstances. The tailor said that the stuff was not made in this country; that it was worn by the Irish at home, and now they would not look at it, but others would not wear it, durable and cheap as it is, because it is worn by the Irish. Moreover, I like the color on other accounts. Anything but black clothes.

May 27. P.M. To Hill.
I hear the sound of fife and drum the other side of the village, and am reminded that it is May Training. Some thirty young men are marching in the streets in two straight sections, with each a very heavy and warm cap for the season

on his head and a bright red stripe down the legs of his pantaloons, and at their head march two with white stripes down their pants, one beating a drum, the other blowing a fife. I see them all standing in a row by the side of the street in front of their captain's residence, with a dozen or more ragged boys looking on, but presently they all remove to the opposite side, as it were with one consent, not being satisfied with their former position, which probably had its disadvantages. Thus they march and strut the better part of the day, going into the tavern two or three times, to abandon themselves to unconstrained positions out of sight, and at night they may be seen going home singly with swelling breasts.

June 3. . . . I have several friends and acquaintances who are very good companions in the house or for an afternoon walk, but whom I cannot make up my mind to make a longer excursion with; for I discover, all at once, that they are too gentlemanly in manners, dress, and all their habits. I see in my mind's eye that they wear black coats, considerable starched linen, glossy hats and shoes, and it is out of the question. It is a great disadvantage for a traveller to be a gentleman of this kind; he is so ill-treated, only a prey to landlords. It would be too much of a circumstance to enter a strange town or house with such a companion. You could not travel incognito; you might get into the papers. You should travel as a common man. If such a one were to set out to make a walking journey, he would betray himself at every step. Every one would see that he was trying an experiment, as plainly as they see that a lame man is lame by his limping. The natives would bow to him, other gentlemen would invite him to ride, conductors would warn him that this was the second-class car, and many would take him for a clergyman; and so he would be continually pestered and balked and run upon. You would not see the natives at all. Instead of going in quietly at the back door and sitting by the kitchen fire, you would be shown into a cold parlor, there to confront a fireboard, and excite a commotion in a whole family. The women would scatter at your approach, and their husbands and sons would go right up to hunt up their black coats—for they all have them; they are as cheap as dirt. You would go trailing your limbs along the highways, mere bait for corpulent innholders, as a pickerel's [sic] leg is trolled along a stream, and your part of the profits would be the frog's. No, you must be a common man, or at least travel as one, and then nobody will know that you are there or have been there. I would not undertake a simple pedestrian excursion with one of these, because to enter a village, or a hotel, or a private house, with such a one, would be too great a circumstance, would create too great a stir. You could only go half as far with the same means, for the price of board and lodgings would rise everywhere; so much you have to pay for wearing that kind of coat. Not that the difference is in the coat at all, for the character of the scurf is determined by that of the true liber beneath. Innkeepers, stablers, conductors, clergymen, know a true wayfaring man at first sight and let him alone. It is of no use to shove your gaiter shoes a mile further than usual. Sometimes it is mere shiftlessness or want of originality— the clothes wear them; sometimes it is egotism, that cannot afford to be treated like a common man—they wear the clothes. They wish to be at least fully appreciated by every stage-driver and schoolboy. They would like well enough to see a new place, perhaps, but then they would like to be regarded as important public personages. They would consider it a misfortune if their names were left out of the published list of passengers because they came in the steerage—an obscurity from which they might never emerge.

June 12. . . . I have not found the white spruce yet.

July 12. . . . It would be worth the while, methinks, to make a map of the town with all the good springs on it, indicating whether they were cool, perennial, copious, pleasantly located, etc. The farmer is wont to celebrate the virtues of some one on his own farm above all others. Some cool rills in the meadows should be remembered also, for some such in deep, cold, grassy meadows are as cold as springs. I have sometimes drank warm or foul water, not knowing such cold streams were at hand. By many a spring I know where to look for the dipper or glass which some mower has left. When a spring has been allowed to fill up, to be muddied by cattle, or, being exposed to the sun by cutting down the trees and bushes, to dry up, it affects me sadly, like an institution going to decay. Sometimes I see, on one side the tub—the tub overhung with various wild plants and flowers, its edge almost completely concealed even from the searching eye—the white sand freshly cast up where the spring is bubbling in. Often I sit patiently by the spring I have cleaned out and deepened with my hands, and see the foul water rapidly dissipated like a curling vapor and giving place to the cool and clear. Sometimes I can look a yard or more into a crevice under a rock, toward the sources of a spring in a hillside, and see it come cool and copious with incessant murmuring down to the light. There are few more refreshing sights in hot weather.

Aug. 10. . . . I hear the neighbors complain sometimes about the peddlers selling their help *false* jewelry, as if they themselves wore *true* jewelry; but if their help pay as much for it as they did for theirs, then it is just as *true* jewelry as theirs, just as becoming to them and no more; for unfortunately it is the cost of the article and not the merits of the wearer that is considered. The money is just as well spent, and perhaps better earned. I don't care how much false jewelry the peddlers sell, nor how many of the eggs which you steal are rotten. What, pray, is *true* jewelry? The hardened tear of a diseased clam, murdered in its old age. Is that fair play? If not, it is no jewel. The mistress wears this in her ear, while her help has one made of paste which you cannot tell from it. False jewelry! Do you know of any shop where *true* jewelry can be bought? I always look askance at a jeweller and wonder what *church* he can belong to.

Sept. 2. . . . Measured the thorn at Yellow Birch Swamp. At one foot from ground it is a foot and ten inches in circumference. The first branch is at two feet seven inches. The tree spreads about eighteen feet. The height is about seventeen feet.

Sept. 26. . . . What blundering fellows these crickets are, both large and small! They were not only tumbling into the river all along shore, but into this sandy gully, to escape from which is a Sisyphus labor. I have not sat there many minutes watching two foraging crickets which have decided to climb up two tall and slender weeds almost bare of branches, as a man shins up a liberty-pole sometimes, when I find that one has climbed to the summit of my knee. They are incessantly running about on the sunny bank. Their still larger cousins, the mole crickets, are creaking loudly and incessantly all along the shore. Others have eaten themselves cavernous apartments, sitting room and pantry at once, in windfall apples.

Oct. 4. . . . While I lived in the woods I did various jobs about the town—some fence-building, painting, gardening, carpentering, etc., etc. One day a man came from the east edge of the town and said that he wanted to get me to brick up a fireplace, etc., etc., for him. I told him that I was not a mason, but he knew that I had built my own house entirely and would not take no for an answer. So I went.

It was three miles off, and I walked back and forth each day, arriving early and working as late as if I were living there. The man was gone away most of the time, but had left some sand dug up in his cow-yard for me to make mortar with. I bricked up a fireplace, papered a chamber, but my principal work was whitewashing ceilings. Some were so dirty that many coats would not conceal the dirt. In the kitchen I finally resorted to yellow-wash to cover the dirt. I took my meals there, sitting down with my employer (when he got home) and his hired men. I remember the awful condition of the sink, at which I washed one day, and when I came to look at what was called the towel I passed it by and wiped my hands on the air, and thereafter I resorted to the pump. I worked there hard three days, charging only a dollar a day.

About the same time I also contracted to build a wood-shed of no mean size, for, I think, exactly six dollars, and cleared about half of it by a close calculation and swift working. The tenant wanted me to throw in a gutter and latch, but I carried off the board that was left and gave him no latch but a button. It stands yet—behind the Kettle house. I broke up Johnny Kettle's old "trow," in which he kneaded his bread, for material. Going home with what nails were left in a flower [sic] bucket on my arm, in a rain, I was about getting into a hay-rigging, when my umbrella frightened the horse, and he kicked at me over the fills, smashed the bucket on my arm, and stretched me on my back; but while I lay on my back, his leg being caught over the shaft, I got up, to see him sprawling on the other side. This accident, the sudden bending of my body backwards, sprained my stomach so that I did not get quite strong there for several years, but had to give up some fence-building and other work which I had undertaken from time to time.

Oct. 7. . . . I do not know how to entertain one who can't take long walks. The first thing that suggests itself is to get a horse to draw them, and that brings us at once into contact with stablers and dirty harness, and I do not get over my ride for a long time. I give up my forenoon to them and get along pretty well, the very elasticity of the air and promise of the day abetting me, but they are as heavy as dumplings by mid-afternoon. If they can't walk, why won't they take an honest nap and let me go in the afternoon? But, come two o'clock, they alarm me by an evident disposition to sit. In the midst of the most glorious Indian-summer afternoon, there they sit, breaking your chairs and wearing out the house, with their backs to the light, taking no note of the lapse of time.

Oct. 9. . . . It has come to this—that the lover of art is one, and the lover of nature another, though true art is but the expression of our love of nature. It is monstrous when one cares but little about trees but much about Corinthian columns, and yet this is exceedingly common.

Oct. 12. . . . This was what those scamps did in California. The trees were so grand and venerable that they could not afford to let them grow a hair's breadth bigger, or live a moment longer to reproach themselves. They were so big that they resolved they should never be bigger. They were so venerable that they cut them right down. It was not for the sake of the wood; it was only because they were very grand and venerable.

Oct. 14. . . . Another, the tenth of these memorable days. We have had some fog the last two or three nights, and this forenoon it was slow to disperse, dog-day-like, but this afternoon it is warmer even than yesterday. I should like it better if it were not so warm. I am glad to reach the shade of Hubbard's Grove; the coolness is refreshing. It is indeed a golden autumn. These ten days are enough to make the reputation of any climate. A tradition of these days might be handed down to posterity. They deserve a notice in history, in the history of Concord. All kinds of crudities have a chance to get ripe this year. Was there ever such an autumn? And yet there was never such a panic and hard times in the commercial world. The merchants and banks are suspending and failing all the country over, but not the sandbanks, solid and warm, and streaked with bloody blackberry vines. You may run upon them as much as you please—even as the crickets do, and find their account in it. They are the stockholders in these banks, and I hear them creaking their content. You may see them on change any warmer hour. In these banks, too, and such as these, are my .funds deposited, a fund of health and enjoyment. Their (the crickets) prosperity and happiness and, I trust, mine do not depend on whether the New York banks suspend or no. We do not rely on such slender security as the thin paper of the Suffolk Bank. To put your trust in such a bank is to be swallowed up and undergo suffocation. Invest, I say, in these country banks. Let your capital be simplicity and contentment. . . .

I take all these walks to every point of the compass, and it is always harvest-time with me. I am always gathering my crop from these woods and fields and waters, and no man is in my way or interferes with me. My crop is not their crop. Today I see them gathering in their beans and corn, and they are a spectacle to me, but are soon out of my sight. I am not gathering beans and corn. . . .

Sat in the old pasture beyond the Corner Spring Woods to look at that pine wood now at the height of its change, pitch and white. Their change produces a very singular and pleasing effect. They are regularly parti-colored. The last year's leaves, about a foot beneath the extremities of the twigs on all sides, now changed and ready to fall, have their period of brightness as well as broader leaves. They are a clear yellow, contrasting with the fresh and liquid green of the terminal plumes, or this year's leaves. These two quite distinct colors are thus regularly and equally distributed over the whole tree. You have the warmth of the yellow and the coolness of the green. So it should be with our own maturity, not yellow to the very extremity of our shoots, but youthful and untried green ever putting forth afresh at the extremities, foretelling a maturity as yet unknown. The ripe leaves fall to the ground and become nutriment for the green ones, which still aspire to heaven. In the fall of the leaf, there is no fruit, there is no true maturity, neither in our science and wisdom.

Oct. 15. . . . Concord Bank has suspended [because of the Panic of 1857].

Oct. 20. . . . I had gone but little way on the old Carlisle road when I saw Brooks Clark, who is now about eighty and bent like a bow, hastening along the road, barefooted, as usual, with an axe in his hand; was in haste perhaps on account of the cold wind on his bare feet. It is he who took the *Centinel* so long. When he got up to me, I saw that besides the axe in one hand, he had his shoes in the other, filled with knurly apples and a dead robin. He stopped and talked with me a few moments; said that we had had a noble autumn and might now expect some cold weather. I asked if he had found the robin dead. No, he said, he found it with its wing broken and killed it. He also added that he had found some apples in the woods, and as he hadn't anything to carry them in, he put 'em in his shoes. They were queer-looking trays to carry fruit in. How many he got in along toward the toes, I don't know. I noticed, too, that his pockets were stuffed with them. His old tattered frock coat was hanging in strips about the skirts, as were his pantaloons about his naked feet. He appeared to have been out on a scout this gusty afternoon, to see what he could find, as the youngest boy might. It pleased me to see this cheery old man, with such a feeble hold on life, bent almost double, thus enjoying the evening of his days. . . .

Oct. 22. . . . What a perfect chest the chestnut is packed in! I now hold a green bur in my hand which, round, must have been two and a quarter inches in diameter, from which three plump nuts have been extracted. It has a straight, stout stem three sixteenths of an inch in diameter, set on strongly and abruptly. It had gaped in four segments or quarters, revealing the thickness of its walls, from five eighths to three quarters of an inch. With such wonderful care Nature has secluded and defended these nuts, as if they were her most precious fruits, while diamonds are left to take care of themselves. First it bristles all over with sharp green prickles, some nearly half an inch long, like a hedgehog rolled into a ball; these rest on a thick, stiff, bark-like rind, one sixteenth to one eighth of an inch thick, which, again, is most daintily lined with a kind of silvery fur or velvet plush one sixteenth of an inch thick, even rising in a ridge between the nuts, like the lining of a casket in which the most precious commodities are kept. I see the brown-spotted white cavities where the bases of the nuts have rested and sucked up nourishment from the stem. The little stars on the top of the nuts are but shorter and feebler spines which mingle with the rest. They stand up close together, three or more, erecting their tiny weapons, as an infant in the brawny arms of its nurse might put out its own tiny hands, to fend off the aggressor. There is no waste room. The chest is packed quite full; half-developed nuts are the waste paper used in the packing, to fill the vacancies. At last Frost comes to unlock this chest; it alone holds the true key. Its lids straightway gape open, and the October air rushes in, dries the ripe nuts, and then with a ruder gust shakes them all out in a rattling shower down upon the withered leaves.

Oct. 29. . . . . There are some things of which I cannot at once tell whether I have dreamed them or they are real; as if they were just, perchance, establishing, or else losing, a real basis in my world. This is especially the case in the early morning hours, when there is a gradual transition from dreams to waking thoughts, from illusions to actualities, as from darkness, or perchance moon and star light, to sunlight. Dreams are real, as is the light of the stars and moon, and theirs is said to be a *dreamy* light. Such early morning thoughts as I speak of occupy a debatable ground between dreams and waking thoughts. They are a sort of permanent dream in my mind. At least, until we have for some time changed our position from prostrate to erect, and commenced or faced some of the duties of the day, we cannot tell what we have dreamed from what we have actually experienced.

This morning, for instance, for the twentieth time at least, I thought of that mountain in the easterly part of our town (where no high hill actually is) which once or twice I had ascended, and often allowed my thoughts alone to climb. I now contemplate it in my mind as a familiar thought which I have surely had for many years from time to time, but whether anything could have reminded me of it in the middle of yesterday, whether I ever before remembered it in broad daylight, I doubt. I can now eke out the vision I had of it this morning with my old and yesterday forgotten dreams.

My way up used to lie through a dark and unfrequented wood at its base—I cannot now tell exactly, it was so long ago, under what circumstances I first ascended, only that I shuddered as I went along (I have an indistinct remembrance of having been out overnight alone) and then I steadily ascended along a rocky ridge half clad with stinted trees, where wild beasts haunted, till I lost myself quite in the upper air and clouds, seeming to pass an imaginary line which separates a hill, mere earth heaped up, from a mountain, into a super-terranean grandeur and sublimity. What distinguishes that summit above the earthy line, is that it is unhandselled, awful, grand. It can never become familiar; you are lost the moment you set foot there. You know no path, but wander, thrilled, over the bare and pathless rock, as if it were solidified air and cloud. That rocky, misty summit, secreted in the clouds, was far more thrillingly awful and sublime than the crater of a volcano spouting fire.

. . . I think that men generally are mistaken with regard to amusements. Everyone who deserves to be regarded as higher than the brute may be supposed to have an earnest purpose, to accomplish which is the object of his existence, and this is at once his work and his supremest pleasure; and for diversion and relaxation, for suggestion and education and strength, there is offered the never-failing amusement of getting a living—never-failing, I mean, when temperately indulged in. I know of no such amusement—so wholesome and in every sense profitable—for instance, as to spend an hour or two in a day picking some berries or other fruits which will be food for the winter, or collecting driftwood from the river for fuel, or cultivating the few beans or potatoes which I want. Theatres and operas, which intoxicate for a season, are as nothing compared to these pursuits. And so it is with all the true arts of life. Farming and building and manu-facturing and sailing are the greatest and wholesomest amusements that were ever invented (for God invented them), and I suppose that the farmers and mechanics know it, only I think they indulge to excess generally, and so what was meant for a joy becomes the sweat of the brow. Gambling, horse-racing, loafing, and rowdyism generally, after all tempt but few. The mass are tempted by those other amusements, of farming, etc. It is a great amusement, and more profitable than I could have invented, to go and spend an afternoon hour picking cranberries. By these various pursuits your experience becomes singularly complete and rounded. The novelty and significance of such pursuits are remarkable. Such is the path by which we climb to the heights of our being; and compare the poetry which such simple pursuits have inspired with the unreadable volumes which have been written about art.

Nov. 20. . . . In books, that which is most generally in-teresting is what comes home to the most cherished private experience of the greatest number. It is not the book of him who has travelled the farthest over the surface of the globe, but of him who has lived the deepest and been the most at home. If an equal emotion is excited by a familiar homely phenomenon as by the Pyramids, there is no advantage in seeing the Pyramids. It is on the whole better, as it is simpler, to use the common language. We require that the reporter be very permanently planted before the facts which he observes, not a mere passer-by; hence the facts cannot be too homely. A man is worth most to himself and to others, whether as an observer, or poet, or neighbor, or friend, where he is most himself, most contented and at home. There his life is the most intense and he loses the fewest moments. Familiar and surrounding objects are the best symbols and illustrations of his life. If a man who has had deep experiences should endeavor to describe them in a book of travels, it would be to use the language of a wandering tribe instead of a universal language. The poet has made the best roots in his native soil of any man, and is the hardest to transplant. The man who is often thinking that it is better to be somewhere else than where he is excommunicates himself. If a man is rich and strong anywhere, it must be on his native soil. Here I have been these forty years learning the language of these fields that I may the better express myself. If I should travel to the prairies, I should much less understand them, and my past life would serve me but ill to describe them. Many a weed here stands for more of life to me than the big trees of California would if I should go there. We only need travel enough to give our intellects an airing. In spite of Malthus and the rest, there will be plenty of room in this world, if every man will mind his own business. I have not heard of any planet running against another yet.

Nov. 25. . . . . This is November of the hardest kind—bare frozen ground covered with pale-brown or straw-colored herbage, a strong, cold, cutting northwest wind which makes me seek to cover my ears, a perfectly clear and cloudless sky. The cattle in the fields have a cold, shrunken, shaggy look, their hair standing out every way, as if with electricity, like the cat's. Ditches and pools are fast skimming over, and a few slate-colored snowbirds, with thick, shuffling twitter, and fine-chipping tree sparrows flit from bush to bush in the otherwise deserted pastures. This month taxes a walker's resources more than any. For my part, I should sooner think of going into quarters in November than in the winter. If you do feel any fire at this season out of doors, you may depend upon it, it is your own. It is but a short time, these afternoons, before the night cometh, in which no man can walk. If you delay to start till three o'clock, there will be hardly time left for a long and rich adventure—to get fairly out of town. November Eatheart—is that the name of it? Not only the fingers cease to do their office, but there is often a be-numbing of the faculties generally. You can hardly screw up your courage to take a walk when all is thus tightly locked or frozen up and so little is to be seen in field or wood. I am inclined to take to the swamps or woods as the warmest place, and the former are still the openest. Nature has her-self become like the few fruits which she still affords, a very thick-shelled nut with a shrunken meat within. If I find any-thing to excite or warm my thoughts abroad, it is an agree-able disappointment, for I am obliged to go abroad willfully and against my inclinations at first. The prospect looks so barren, so many springs are frozen up, not a flower per-chance and but few birds left, not a companion abroad in all these fields for me, I am slow to go forth. I seem to an-ticipate a fruitless walk. I think to myself hesitatingly. Shall I go there, or there, or there? and cannot make up my mind to any route, all seem so unpromising, mere surface walking and fronting the cold wind, so that I have to force myself to it often and at random. But then I am often unexpectedly compensated, and the thinnest yellow light of November is more warming and exhilarating than any wine they tell of; and then the mite which November contributes becomes equal in value to the bounty of July. I may meet with something which interests me, and immediately it is as warm as in July, as if it were the south instead of the northwest wind that blowed.

Nov. 29. . . . A week or so ago, as I learn, Miss Emeline Barnett told a little boy who boards with her, and who was playing with an open knife in his hand, that he must be careful not to fall down and cut himself with it, for once Mr. David Loring, when he was a little boy, fell down with a knife in his hand and cut his throat badly. It was soon re-ported, among the children at least, that little David Loring, the grandson of the former, had fallen down with a knife in his hand as he was going to school, and nearly cut his throat; next, that Mr. David Loring the grandfather (who lives in Framingham) had committed suicide, had cut his throat, was not dead, indeed, but was not expected to live; and in this form the story spread like wildfire over the town and county. Nobody expressed surprise. His oldest acquaintances and best friends, his legal adviser, all said, "Well, I can believe it." He was known by many to have been speculating in Western lands, which, owing to the hard times, was a failure, and he was depressed in consequence. Sally Cummings helped spread the news. Said there was no doubt of it, but there was Fay's wife (L.'s daughter) knew nothing of it yet, they were as merry as crickets over there. Others stated that Wetherbee, the expressman, had been over to Northboro, and learned that Mr. Loring had taken poison in Northboro. Mr. Rhodes was stated to have received a letter from Mr. Robbins of Framingham giving all the particulars. Mr. Wild, it was said, had also got a letter from his son Silas in Framingham, to whom he had written, which confirmed the report. As Wild went downtown, he met Meeks the carpenter and inquired in a significant way if he got anything new. Meeks simply answered, "Well, David Loring won't eat another Thanksgiving dinner." A child at school wrote to her parents at Northboro, telling the news. Mrs. Loring's sister lives there, and it chances that her husband committed suicide. They were therefore, slow to communicate the news to her, but at length could not contain themselves longer and told it. The sister was terribly affected; wrote to her son (L.'s nephew) in Worcester, who immediately took the cars and went to Framingham and when he arrived there met his uncle just putting his family into the cars. He shook his hand very heartily indeed, looking, however, hard at his throat, but said not a word about his errand. Already doubts had arisen, people were careful how they spoke of it, the expressmen were mum, Adams and Wetherbee never said Loring. The Framingham expressman used the same room with Adams in Boston. A. simply asked, "Any news from Framingham this morning? Seen Loring lately?" and learned that all was well.

Dec. 2. . . . Roads were once described as leading to a meetinghouse, but not so often nowadays.

Dec. 13. . . . In sickness and barrenness it is encouraging to believe that our life is dammed and is coming to a head, so that there seems to be no loss, for what is lost in time is gained in power. All at once, unaccountably, as we are walking in the woods or sitting in our chamber, after a worthless fortnight, we cease to feel mean and barren.

Dec. 27. . . . The commonest and cheapest sounds, as the barking of a dog, produce the same effect on fresh and healthy ears that the rarest music does. It depends on your appetite for sound.

1858

Thoreau crowded a good deal into this year. He visited Worcester, New York City, and Cape Ann, among other localities. He did some mountain climbing, making his way up Monadnock at one time and Mt. Washington at another. He surveyed extensively. He wrote with apparent vigor. The young Atlantic Monthly *printed two installments of a selection from the writing about the Maine woods entitled "Chesuncook." However, the editor James Russell Lowell, who had long disliked Thoreau, cut out a sentence in the second installment. It was the last sentence and in it Thoreau said that a pine tree was immortal. He wrote Lowell a scathing letter about censorship and submitted nothing further to the* Atlantic *till it had a new editor. The journal is admirable again and extraordinarily full.*

Jan. 28. [George] Minott has a sharp ear for the note of any migrating bird. Though confined to his dooryard by the rheumatism, he commonly hears them sooner than the widest rambler. Maybe he listens all day for them, or they come and sing over his house—report themselves to him and receive their season ticket. He is never at fault. If he says he heard such a bird, though sitting by his chimney-side, you may depend on it. He can swear through glass. He has not spoiled his ears by attending lectures and caucuses, etc. The other day the rumor went that a flock of geese had been seen flying north over Concord, midwinter as it was, by the almanac. I traced it to Minott, and yet I was compelled to doubt. I had it directly that he had heard them within a week. I saw him—I made haste to him. His reputation was at stake. He said that he stood in his shed—it was one of the late warm, muggy, April-like mornings—when he heard one short but distinct *honk* of a goose. He went into the house, he took his cane, he exerted himself, or that sound imparted strength to him. Lame as he was, he went up on to the hill—he had not done it for a year—that he might hear all around. He saw nothing, but he heard the note again. It came from over the brook. It was a wild goose, he was sure of it. And hence the rumor spread and grew. He thought that the back of the winter was broken—if it had any this year—but he feared such a winter would kill him too.

I was silent; I reflected; I drew into my mind all its members, like the tortoise; I abandoned myself to unseen guides. Suddenly the truth flashed on me, and I remembered that within a week I had heard of a box at the tavern, which had come by railroad express, containing three wild geese and directed to his neighbor over the brook. The April-like morning had excited one so that he honked; and Minott's reputation acquired new lustre.

March 2. . . . The last new journal [the *Atlantic Monthly*] thinks that it is very liberal, nay, bold, but it dares not publish a child's thought on important subjects, such as life and death and good books. It requires the sanction of the divines just as surely as the tamest journal does. If it had been published at the time of the famous dispute between Christ and the doctors, it would have published only the opinions of the doctors and suppressed Christ's. There is no need of a law to check the license of the press. It is law enough, and more than enough, to itself. Virtually, the community have come together and agreed what things shall be uttered, have agreed on a platform and to excommunicate him who departs from it, and not one in a thousand dares utter anything else. There are plenty of journals brave enough to say what they think about the government, this being a free one; but I know of none, widely circulated or well conducted, that dares say what it thinks about the Sunday or the Bible. They have been bribed to keep dark. They are in the service of hypocrisy.

March 5. . . . We read the English poets; we study botany and zoology and geology, lean and dry as they are; and it is rare that we get a new suggestion. It is ebb-tide with the scientific reports, Professor ——— in the chair. We would fain know something more about these animals and stones and trees around us. We are ready to skin the animals alive to come at them. Our scientific names convey a very partial information only; they suggest certain thoughts only. It does not occur to me that there are other names for most of these objects, given by a people who stood between me and them, who had better senses than our race. How little I know of that *arbor-vitae* when I have learned only what science can tell me! It is but a word. It is not a *tree of life*. But there are twenty words for the tree and its different parts which the Indian gave, which are not in our botanies, which imply a more practical and vital science. He used it every day. He was well acquainted with its wood, and its bark, and its leaves. No science does more than arrange what knowledge we have of any class of objects. But, generally speaking, how much more conversant was the Indian with any wild animal or plant than we are, and in his language is implied all that intimacy, as much as ours is expressed in our language. How many words in his language about a moose, or birch bark, and the like! The Indian stood nearer to wild nature than we. The wildest and noblest quadrupeds, even the largest fresh-water fishes, some of the wildest and noblest birds and the fairest flowers have actually receded as *we* advanced, and we have but the most distant knowledge of them. A rumor has come down to us that the skin of a lion was seen and his roar heard here by an early settler. But there was a race here that slept on his skin. It was a new light when my guide gave me Indian names for things for which I had only scientific ones before. In proportion as I understood the language, I saw them from a new point of view.

May 1. . . . When I am behind Cheney's this warm and still afternoon, I hear a voice calling to oxen three quarters of a mile distant, and I know it to be Elijah Wood's. It is wonderful how far the *individual* proclaims himself. Out of the thousand millions of human beings on this globe, I know that this sound was made by the lungs and larynx and lips of E. Wood, am as sure of it as if he nudged me with his elbow and shouted in my ear. He can impress himself on the very atmosphere, then, can launch himself a mile on the wind, through trees and rustling sedge and over rippling water, associating with a myriad sounds, and yet arrive distinct at my ear; and yet this creature that is felt so far, that was so noticeable, lives but a short time, quietly dies and makes no more noise that I know of. I can tell him, too, with my eyes by the very gait and motion of him half a mile distant. Far more wonderful his purely spiritual influence—that after the lapse of thousands of years you may still detect the individual in the turn of a sentence or the tone of a thought! ! E. Wood has a peculiar way of modulating the air, imparts to it peculiar vibrations, which several times when standing near him I have noticed, and now a vibration, spreading far and wide over the fields and up and down the river, reaches me and maybe hundreds of others, which we all know to have been produced by Mr. Wood's pipes. . . .

May 6. . . . The thinker, he who is serene and self-possessed, is the brave, not the desperate soldier. He who can deal with his thoughts as a material, building them into poems in which future generations will delight, he is the man of the greatest and rarest vigor, not sturdy diggers and lusty polygamists. He is the man of energy, in whom subtle and poetic thoughts are bred. Common men can enjoy partially; they can go a-fishing rainy days; they can *read* poems perchance, but they have not the vigor to beget poems. They can enjoy feebly, but they cannot create. Men talk of freedom! How many are free to think? free from fear, from perturbation, from prejudice? Nine hundred and ninety-nine in a thousand are perfect slaves. How many can exercise the highest human faculties? He is the man truly—courageous, wise, ingenious—who can use his thoughts and ecstacies as the material of fair and durable creations. One man shall derive from the fisherman's story more than the fisher has got who tells it. The mass of men do not know how to cultivate the fields they traverse. The mass glean only a scanty pittance where the thinker reaps an abundant harvest. What is all your building, if you do not build with thoughts? No exercise implies more real manhood and vigor than joining thought to thought. How few men can tell what they have thought! I hardly know half a dozen who are not too lazy for this. They cannot get over some difficulty, and therefore they are on the long way round. You conquer fate by thought. If you think the fatal thought of men and institutions, you need never pull the trigger. The consequences of thinking inevitably follow. There is no more Herculean task than to think a thought about this life and then get it expressed.

May 10. . . . I hear in several places the low dumping notes of awakened bullfrogs, what I call their *pebbly* notes, as if they were cracking pebbles in their mouths; not the plump *dont dont* or *ker dont,* but *kerdle dont dont.* As if they sat round mumbling pebbles. At length, near Ball's Hill, I hear the first regular bullfrog's trump. Some fainter ones far off are very like the looing [*sic*] of cows. This sound, heard low and far off over meadows when the warmer hours have come, grandly inaugurates the summer. I perspire with rowing in my thick coat and wish I had worn a thin one. This trumpeter, marching or leaping in the van of advancing summer, whom I now hear coming on over the green meadows, seems to say, *"Take off your coat, take off your coat, take off your coat!"* He says, "Here comes a gale that I can breathe. This is something like; this is what I call summer." I see three or four of them sitting silent in one warm meadow bay. Evidently their breeding season now begins. But they are soon silent as yet, and it is only an occasional and transient trump that you hear. That season which is bounded on the north, on the spring side at least, by the trump of the bullfrog. This note is like the first colored petals within the calyx of a flower. It conducts us toward the germ of the flower summer. He knows no winter. I hear in his tone the rumors of summer heats. By this note he reassures the season. Not till the air is of that quality that it can support this sound does he emit it. It requires a certain sonorousness. The van is led by the croaking wood frog and the little peeping hylodes, and at last comes this pursy trumpeter, the air growing more and more genial, and even sultry, as well as sonorous. As soon as Nature is ready for him to play his part, she awakens him with a warmer, perchance a sultry, breath and excites him to sound his trombone. It reminds me at once of tepid waters and of bathing. His trump is to the ear what the yellow lily or spatter-dock is to the eye. He swears by the powers of mud. It is enough for the day to have heard only the first half-trump of an early awakened one from far in some warm meadow bay. It is a certain revelation and anticipation of the livelong summer to come. It gives leave to the corn to grow and to the heavens to thunder and lighten. It gives leave to the invalid to take the air. Our climate is now as tropical as any. It says, Put out your fires and sit in the fire which the sun has kindled.

June 13. Louring all day.

Aug. 9. . . . It is surprising to what extent the world is ruled by cliques. They who constitute, or at least lead, New England or New York society, in the eyes of the world, are but a clique, a few "men of the age" and of the town, who work best in the harness provided for them. The institutions of almost all kinds are thus of a sectarian or party character. Newspapers, magazines, colleges, and all forms of government and religion express the superficial activity of a few, the mass either conforming or not attending. The newspapers have just got over that eating-fullness or dropsy which takes place with the annual commencements and addresses before the Philomathean or Alpha Beta Gamma societies. Neither they who make these addresses nor they who attend to them are representatives of the latest age. The boys think that these annual recurrences are part and parcel of the annual revolution of the system. There are also regattas and fireworks and "surprise parties" and horse-shows. So that I am glad when I see or hear of a man anywhere who does not know of these things nor recognize these particular fuglers. . . .

Aug. 18. . . . Last evening one of our neighbors, who has just completed a costly house and front yard, the most showy in the village, illuminated in honor of the Atlantic telegraph. I read in great letters before the house the sentence "Glory to God in the highest." But it seemed to me that that was not a sentiment to be illuminated, but to keep dark about. A simple and genuine sentiment of reverence would not emblazon these words as on a signboard in the streets. They were exploding countless crackers beneath it, and gay company, passing in and out, made it a kind of housewarming. I felt a kind of shame for [it], and was inclined to pass quickly by, the ideas of indecent exposure and cant being suggested. What is religion? That which is never spoken.

Aug. 22. P.M. I have spliced my old sail to a new one, and now go out to try it in a sail to Baker Farm. It is a "square sail," some five feet by six. I like it much. It pulls like an ox, and makes me think there's more wind abroad than there is. The yard goes about with a pleasant force, almost enough, I would fain imagine, to knock me overboard. How sturdily it pulls, shooting us along, catching more wind than I knew to be wandering in this river valley! It suggests a new power in the sail, like a Grecian god. I can even worship it, after a heathen fashion. And then, how it becomes my boat and the river—a simple homely square sail, all for use not show, so low and broad! *Ajacean.* The boat is like a plow drawn by a winged bull. If I had had this a dozen years ago, my voyages would have been performed more quickly and easily. But then probably I should have lived less in them. I land on a remote shore at an unexpectedly early hour, and have time for a long walk there. Before, my sail was so small that I was wont to raise the mast with the sail on it ready set, but now I have had to rig some tackling with which to haul up the sail.

Aug. 29. . . . I remember when boiled green corn was sold piping hot on a muster field in this town, and my father says that he remembers when it used to be carried about the streets of Boston in large baskets on the bare heads of Negro women, and gentlemen would stop, buy an ear, and eat it in the street.

Sept. 18. . . . Finding grapes, we [Thoreau and Ellery Channing] proceeded to pluck them, tempted more by their fragrance and color than their flavor, though some were very palatable. We gathered many without getting out of the boat, as we paddled back, and more on shore close to the water's edge, piling them up in the prow of the boat till they reached to the top of the boat—a long sloping heap of them and very handsome to behold, being of various colors and sizes, for we even added green ones for variety. Some, however, were mainly green when ripe. You cannot touch some vines without bringing down more single grapes in a shower around you than you pluck in bunches, and such as strike the water are lost, for they do not float. But it is a pity to break the handsome clusters.

Thus laden, the evening air wafting the fragrance of the cargo back to us, we paddled homeward. The cooler air is so clear that we see Venus plainly some time before sundown. The wind had all gone down, and the water was perfectly smooth. The sunset was uncommonly fair. Some long amber clouds in the horizon, all on fire with gold, were more glittering than any jewelry. An Orient city to adorn the plates of an annual could not be contrived or imagined more gorgeous. And when you looked with head inverted the effect was increased tenfold, till it seemed a world of enchantment. We only regretted that it had not a due moral effect on us scapegraces.

Nevertheless, when, turning my head, I looked at the willowy edge of Cyanean Meadow and onward to the sobercolored but fine-grained Clamshell Hills, about which there was no glitter. I was inclined to think that the truest beauty was that which surrounded us but which we failed to discern, that the forms and colors which adorn our daily life, not seen afar in the horizon, are our fairest jewelry. The beauty of Clamshell Hill, near at hand, with its sandy ravines, in which the cricket chirps. This is an Occidental city, not less glorious than that we dream of in the sunset sky.

Oct. 1. . . . . Let a full-grown but young cock stand near you. How full of life he is, from the tip of his bill through his trembling wattles and comb and his bright eye to the extremity of his clean toes! How alert and restless, listening to every sound and watching every motion! How various his notes, from the finest and shrillest alarum as a hawk sails over, surpassing the most accomplished violinist on the short strings, to a hoarse and terrene voice or cluck! He has a word for every occasion; for the dog that rushes past, and partlet cackling in the barn. And then how, elevating himself and flapping his wings, he gathers impetus and air and launches forth that world-renowned ear-piercing strain! not a vulgar note of defiance, but the mere effervescence of life, like the bursting of a bubble in a wine cup. Is any gem so bright as his eye?

Oct. 12. . . . . I have heard of judges, accidentally met at an evening party, discussing the efficacy of the laws and courts, and deciding that, with the aid of the jury system, "substantial justice was done." But taking those cases in which honest men refrain from going to law, together with those in which men, honest and dishonest, do go to law, I think that the law is really a "humbug," and a benefit principally to the lawyers. This town has made a law recently against cattle going at large, and assigned a penalty of five dollars. I am troubled by an Irish neighbor's cow and horse, and have threatened to have them put in the pound. But a lawyer tells me that these town laws are hard to put through, there are so many quibbles. He never knew the complainant to get his case if the defendant were a-mind to contend. However, the cattle were kept out several days, till a Sunday came, and then they were all in my grounds again, as I heard, but all my neighbors tell me that I cannot have them impounded on that day. Indeed, I observe that very many of my neighbors do *for this reason* regularly turn their cattle loose on Sundays. The judges may discuss the question of the courts and law over their nuts and raisins, and mumble forth the decision that "substantial justice is done," but I must believe they mean that they do really get paid a "substantial" salary.

Oct. 18. . . . Little did the fathers of the town anticipate this brilliant success when they caused to be imported from further in the country some straight poles with the tops cut off, which they called sugar maple trees—and a neighboring merchant's clerk, as I remember, by way of jest planted beans about them. Yet these which were then jestingly called bean-poles are these days far the most beautiful objects noticeable in our streets. They are worth all and more than they have cost—though one of the selectmen did take the cold which occasioned his death in setting them out—if only because they have filled the open eyes of children with their rich color so unstintedly so many autumns. We will not ask them to yield us sugar in the spring, while they yield us so fair a prospect in the autumn. Wealth may be the inheritance of few in the houses, but it is equally distributed on the Common. All children alike can revel in this golden harvest. These trees, throughout the street, are at least equal to an annual festival and holiday, or a week of such—not requiring any special police to keep the peace—and poor indeed must be that New England village's October which has not the maple in its streets. This October festival costs no powder nor ringing of bells, but every tree is a liberty-pole on which a thousand bright flags are run up. Hundreds of children's eyes are steadily drinking in this color, and by these teachers even the truants are caught and educated the moment they step abroad. It is as if some cheap and innocent gala-day were celebrated in our town every autumn —a week or two of such days.

. . . I know of one man at least, called an excellent and peculiarly successful farmer, who has thoroughly repaired his house and built a new barn with a barn cellar, such as every farmer seems fated to have, who has not a single tree or shrub of any kind about his house or within a considerable distance of it.

. . . A village needs these innocent stimulants of bright and cheery prospects to keep off melancholy and superstition. Show me two villages, one embowered in trees and blazing with all the glories of October, the other a merely trivial and treeless waste, and I shall be sure that in the latter will be found the most desperate and hardest drinkers. . . .

Oct. 27. . . . It is remarkable that the autumnal change of our woods has left no deeper impression on our literature yet. There is no record of it in English poetry, apparently because, according to all accounts, the trees acquire but few bright colors there. Neither do I know any adequate notice of it in our own youthful literature, nor in the traditions of the Indians. One would say it was the very phenomenon to have caught a savage eye, so devoted to bright colors. In our poetry and science there are many references to this phenomenon, but it has received no such particular attention as it deserves. High-colored as are most political speeches, I do not detect any reflection, even, from the autumnal tints in them. They are as colorless and lifeless as the herbage in November.

Nov. 1. . . . We are not wont to see our dooryard as a part of the earth's surface. The gardener does not perceive that some ridge or mound in his garden or lawn is related to yonder hill or the still more distant mountain in the horizon, is, perchance, a humble spur of the last. We are wont to look on the earth still as a sort of chaos, formless and lumpish. I notice from this height that the curving moraine forming the west side of Sleepy Hollow is one of several arms or fingers which stretch away from the hill range that runs down the north side of the Boston road, turning northward at the Court House; that this finger-like moraine is continued northward by itself almost to the river, and points plainly enough to Ponkawtasset Hill on the other side, even if the Poplar Hill range itself did not indicate this connection; and so the sloping cemetery lots on the west of Sleepy Hollow are related to the distant Ponkawtasset. The smooth-shaven knoll in the lawn, on which the children swing, is, perchance, only a spur of some mountains of the moon, which no traveller has ever reached, heaved up by the same impulse.

Nov. 3. . . . Nothing makes me so dejected as to have met my friends, for they make me doubt if it is possible to

have any friends. I feel what a fool I am. I cannot conceive
of persons more strange to me than they actually are; not
thinking, not believing, not doing as I do; interrupted by
me. My only distinction must be that I am the greatest
bore they ever had. Not in a single thought agreed; regularly
balking one another. But when I get far away, my thoughts
return to them. That is the way I *can* visit them. Perhaps it
is unaccountable to me why I care for them. Thus I am
taught that my friend is not an actual person. When I have
withdrawn and am alone, I forget the actual person and
remember only my ideal. Then I have a friend again. I
am not so ready to perceive the illusion that is in Nature.
I certainly come nearer, to say the least, to an actual and joyful intercourse with her. Every day I have more or less communion with her, *as I think*. At least, I do not feel as if
I must withdraw out of nature. I feel like a welcome guest.
Yet, strictly speaking, the same must be true of nature and
of man; our ideal is the only real. It is not the finite and
temporal that satisfies or concerns us in either case.

Nov. 4. . . . On the first, when I stood on Poplar Hill, I
saw a man, far off by the edge of the river, splitting
billets off a stump. Suspecting who it was, I took out my
glass, and beheld [John] Goodwin, the one-eyed Ajax,
in his short blue frock, short and square-bodied, as broad
as for his height he can afford to be, getting his winter's
wood; for this is one of the phenomena of the season. As
surely as the ants which he disturbs go into winter quarters
in the stump when the weather becomes cool, so does G.
revisit the stumpy shores with his axe. As usual his powder-
flask peeped out from a pocket on his breast, his gun was
slanted over a stump near by, and his boat lay a little further
along. He had been at work laying wall still further off, and
now, near the end of the day, betook himself to those pursuits which he loved better still. It would be no amusement
to me to see a gentleman buy his winter wood. It is to see
G. get his. I helped him tip over a stump or two. He said
that the owner of the land had given him leave to get them
out, but it seemed to me a condescension for him to ask
any man's leave to grub up these stumps. The stumps to
those who can use them, I say—to those who will split
them. He might as well ask leave of the farmer to shoot
the musquash and the meadow-hen, or I might as well ask
leave to look at the landscape. Near by were large hollows

in the ground, now grassed over, where he had got out white oak stumps in previous years. But, strange to say, the town does not like to have him get his fuel in this way. They would rather the stumps would rot in the ground, or be floated down-stream to the sea. They have almost without dissent agreed on a different mode of living, with their division of labor. They would have him stick to laying wall, and buy corded wood for his fuel, as they do. He has drawn up an old bridge sleeper and cut his name in it for security, and now he gets into his boat and pushes off in the twilight, saying he will go and see what Mr. Musquash is about.

Nov. 8. . . . I wandered over bare fields where the cattle, lately turned out, roamed restless and unsatisfied with the feed; I dived into a rustling young oak wood where not a green leaf was to be seen; I climbed to the geological axis of elevation and clambered over curly-pated rocks whose strata are on their edges, amid the rising woods; and again I thought, They are all gone surely, and left me alone. Not even a man Friday remains. What nutriment can I extract from these bare twigs? Starvation stares me in the face. *"Nay, nay!"* said a nut-hatch, making its way, head downward, about a bare hickory close by. "The nearer the bone the sweeter the meat. Only the superfluous has been swept away. Now we behold the naked truth. If at any time the weather is too bleak and cold for you, keep the sunny side of the trunk, for there is a wholesome and inspiring warmth such as the summer never afforded. There are the winter mornings, with the sun on the oak wood tops. While buds sleep, thoughts wake." ("Hear! hear!" screamed the jay from a neighboring copse, where I had heard a tittering for some time.) "Winter has a concentrated and nutty kernel if you know where to look for it." And then the speaker shifted to another tree, further off, and reiterated his assertions, and his mate at a distance confirmed them; and I heard a suppressed chuckle from a red squirrel that heard the last remark, but had kept silent and invisible all the while. Is that you? "Yes-sir-ee," said he. Then, running down a slanting bough, he called out rather impudently, "Look here! just get a snug-fitting fur coat and a pair of fur gloves like mine, and you may laugh at a northeast storm," and then he wound up with a slang phrase, in his own lingo, accompanied by a flourish of his tail, just as a newsboy twirls his fingers with his thumb on his nose and inquires, "Does your mother know you are out?"

Nov. 9. . . . It is of no use to plow deeper than the soil is, unless you mean to follow up that mode of cultivation persistently, manuring highly and carting on muck at each plowing—making a soil, in short. Yet many a man likes to tackle mighty themes, like immortality, but in his discourse he turns up nothing but yellow sand, under which what little fertile and available surface soil he may have is quite buried and lost. He should teach frugality rather—how to postpone the fatal hour—should plant a crop of beans. He might have raised enough of these to make a deacon of him, though never a preacher. Many a man runs his plow so deep in heavy or stony soil that it sticks fast in the furrow. It is a great art in the writer to improve from day to day just that soil and fertility which he has, to harvest that crop which his life yields, whatever it may be, not be straining as if to reach apples or oranges when he yields only ground-nuts. He should be digging, not soaring. Just as earnest as your life is, so deep is your soil. If strong and deep, you will sow wheat and raise bread of life in it.

Nov. 16. . . . Preaching? Lecturing? Who are ye that ask for these things? What do ye want to hear, ye puling infants? A trumpet-sound that would train you up to mankind, or a nurse's lullaby? The preachers and lecturers deal with men of straw, as they are men of straw themselves. Why, a free-spoken man, of sound lungs, cannot draw a long breath without causing your rotten institutions to come toppling down by the vacuum he makes. Your church is a baby-house made of blocks, and so of the state. It would be a relief to breathe one's self occasionally among men. If there were any magnanimity in us, any grandeur of soul, anything but sects and parties undertaking to patronize God and keep the mind within bounds, how often we might encourage and provoke one another by a free expression! I will not consent to walk with my mouth muzzled, not till I am rabid, until there is danger that I shall bite the unoffending and that my bite will produce hydrophobia.

Freedom of speech! It hath not entered into your hearts to conceive what these words mean. It is not leave given me by your sect to say this or that; it is when leave is given to your sect to withdraw. The church, the state, the school, the magazine, think they are liberal and free! It is the freedom of a prison-yard. I ask only that one fourth part of my honest thoughts be spoken aloud. What is it you tolerate, you church today? Not truth, but a lifelong hypocrisy. Let us have institutions framed not out of our rottenness, but out of our soundness. This factitious piety is like stale gingerbread. I would like to suggest what a pack of fools and cowards we mankind are. They want me to agree not to breathe too hard in the neighborhood of their paper castles. . . .

. . . There is nothing to redeem the bigotry and moral cowardice of New Englanders in my eyes. . . .

Nov. 20. . . . Who are bad neighbors? They who suffer their neighbors' cattle to go at large because they don't want their ill will—are afraid to anger them. They are abettors of the ill-doers.

Who are the religious? They who do not differ much from mankind generally, except that they are more conservative and timid and useless, but who in their conversation and correspondence talk about kindness of Heavenly Father. Instead of going bravely about their business, trusting God ever, they do like him who says "Good sir" to the one he fears, or whistles to the dog that is rushing at him. And because they take His name in vain so often they presume that they are better than you. Oh, their religion is a rotten squash.

Nov. 30. . . . I have seen a dark cloud as wide as the sky rolling up from the northwest and blasting all my hopes, at sight of which I have dismissed the sun for three weeks and resigned myself to my fate. But when, after being absorbed in other meditations, I have looked around for that cloud half an hour after, I have distinguished only an indistinct white film far in the southeast which only added to the glory of the day by reflecting its light.

. . . I cannot but see still in my mind's eye those little striped breams poised in Walden's glaucous water. They balance all the rest of the world in my estimation at present, for this is the bream that I have just found, and for the time I neglect all its brethren and am ready to kill the fatted calf on its account. For more than two centuries have men fished here and have not distinguished this permanent settler of the township. It is not like a new bird, a transient visitor that may not be seen again for years, but there it dwells and has dwelt permanently, who can tell how long? When my eyes first rested on Walden the striped bream was poised in it, though I did not see it, and when Tahatawan paddled his canoe there. How wild it makes the pond and the township to find new fish in it! America renews her youth here. But in my account of this bream I cannot go a hair's breadth beyond the mere statement that it exists —the miracle of its existence, my contemporary and neighbor, yet so different from me! I can only poise my thought there by its side and try to think like a bream for a moment. I can only think of precious jewels, of music, poetry, beauty, and the mystery of life. I only see the bream in its orbit, as I see a star, but I care not to measure its distance or weight. The bream, appreciated, floats in the pond as the centre of the system, another image of God. Its life no man can explain more than he can his own. I want you to perceive the mystery of the bream. I have a contemporary in Walden. It has fins where I have legs and arms. I have a friend among the fishes, at least a new acquaintance. Its character will interest me, I trust, not its clothes and anatomy. I do not want it to eat. Acquaintance with it is to make my life more rich and eventful. It is as if a poet or an anchorite had moved into the town, whom I can see from time to time and think of yet oftener. Perhaps there are a thousand of these striped bream which no one had thought of in that pond—not their mere impressions in stone, but in the full tide of the bream life.

Dec. 29. P.M. Skate to Israel Rice's.

I think more of skates than of the horse or locomotive as annihilators of distance, for while I am getting along with the speed of the horse, I have at the same time the satisfaction of the horse and his rider, and far more adventure and variety than if I were riding. We never cease to be surprised when we observe how swiftly the skater glides along.

1859

In February Thoreau's father died. Thoreau's feelings about him seem to have had a certain amount of ambivalence but he felt, on balance, no small affection for the unobtrusive man. Thoreau took over the family graphite business and in addition did extensive surveying, especially in the meadowland adjoining Concord's rivers. His health had its ups and downs. After John Brown's epochal raid on Harpers Ferry, he loomed enormously large in Thoreau's universe. He defended the raid ardently and gave two of his most fervent lectures, "A Plea for Captain John Brown" and "After the Death of John Brown." He did much of his preparatory writing of both in the journal.

Jan. 2. P.M. To Cliffs and Walden.

Going up the hill through Stow's young oak woodland, I listen to the sharp, dry rustle of the withered oak leaves. This is the voice of the wood now. It would be comparatively still and more dreary here in other respects, if it were not for these leaves that hold on. It sounds like the roar of the sea, and is enlivening and inspiriting like that, suggesting how all the land is seacoast to the aerial ocean. It is the sound of the surf, the rut of an unseen ocean, billows of air breaking on the forest like water on itself or on sand and rocks. It rises and falls, wells and dies away, with agreeable alternation as the sea surf does. Perhaps the landsman can foretell a storm by it. It is remarkable how universal these grand murmurs are, these backgrounds of sound—the surf, the wind in the forest, waterfalls, etc. —which yet to the ear and in their origin are essentially one voice, the earth-voice, the breathing or snoring of the creature. The earth is our ship, and this is the sound of the wind in her rigging as we sail. Just as the inhabitant of Cape Cod hears the surf ever breaking on its shores, so we countrymen hear this kindred surf on the leaves of the forest. Regarded as a voice—though it is not articulate—as our articulate sounds are divided into vowels (but this is nearer a consonant sound), labials, dentals, palatals, sibilants, mutes, aspirate, etc., so this may be called *folial* or *frondal*, produced by air driven against the leaves and comes nearest to our sibilants or aspirate.

Jan. 19. Wednesday. P.M. To Great Meadows via Sleepy Hollow.

It is a remarkably warm, still, and pleasant afternoon for winter, and the wind, as I discover by my handkerchief, southwesterly. I noticed last night, just after sunset, a sheet of mackerel sky far in the west horizon, very finely imbricated and reflecting a coppery glow, and again I saw still more of it in the east this morning at sunrise, and now, at 3:30 P.M., looking up, I perceive that almost the entire heavens are covered with a very beautiful mackerel sky. This indicates a peculiar state of the atmosphere. The sky is most wonderfully and beautifully mottled with evenly distributed cloudlets, of indescribable variety yet regularity in their form, suggesting fishes' scales, with perhaps small fish-bones thrown in here and there. It is white in the midst, or most prominent part, of the scales, passing into blue in the crannies. Something like this blue and white mottling, methinks, is seen on a mackerel, and has suggested the name. Is not the peculiar propriety of this term lost sight of by the meteorologists? It is a luxury for the eye to rest on it. What curtains, what tapestry to our halls! Directly overhead, of course, the scales or cloudlets appear large and coarse, while far on one side toward the horizon they appear very fine. It is as if we were marching to battle with a shield, a testudo, over our heads. I thus see a *flock* of small clouds, like sheep, some twenty miles in diameter, distributed with wonderful regularity. But they are being steadily driven to some new pasture, for when I look up an hour afterward not one is to be seen and [the] sky is beautifully clear. The form of these cloudlets is, by the way, like or akin to that of waves, of ripple-marks on sand, of small drifts, wave-like, on the surface of snow, and to the first small openings in the ice of the midstream.

Feb. 3. Five minutes before 3 P.M., Father died.
. . . I have touched a body which was flexible and warm, yet tenantless—warmed by what fire? When the spirit

that animated some matter has left it, who else, what else, can animate it?

How enduring are our bodies, after all! The forms of our brothers and sisters, our parents and children and wives, lie still in the hills and fields round about us, not to mention those of our remoter ancestors, and the matter which composed the body of our first human father still exists under another name.

March 3. . . . The lecturer who tries to read his essay without being abetted by a good hearing is in the predicament of a teamster who is engaged in the Sisyphean labor of rolling a molasses-hogshead up an inclined plane alone, while the freight-master and his men stand indifferent with their hands in their pockets. I have seen many such a hogshead which had rolled off the horse and gone to smash, with all its sweets wasted on the ground between the truckman and the freight house—and the freight-masters thought that the loss was not theirs.

March 11. . . . My mother says that she has been to the charitable society . . . One old jester of the town used to call it "the *chattable* society."

. . . There is always some accident in the best things, whether thoughts or expressions or deeds. The memorable thought, the happy expression, the admirable deed are only partly ours. The thought came to us because we were in a fit mood; also we were unconscious and did not know that we had said or done a good thing. We must walk consciously only part way toward our goal, and then leap in the dark to our success. What we do best or most perfectly is what we have most thoroughly learned by the longest practice, and at length it falls from us without our notice, as a leaf from a tree. It is the *last* time we shall do it—our unconscious leavings.

March 28. . . . It is now high time to look for arrowheads, etc. I spend many hours every spring gathering the crop which the melting snow and rain have washed bare. When, at length, some island in the meadow or some sandy field elsewhere has been plowed, perhaps for rye, in the fall, I take note of it, and do not fail to repair thither as soon as the earth begins to be dry in the spring. If the spot chances never to have been cultivated before, I am the first to gather a crop from it. The farmer little thinks that another reaps a harvest which is the fruit of his toil. As much ground is turned up in a day by the plow as Indian implements could not have turned over in a month, and my eyes rest on the evidences of an aboriginal life which passed here a thousand years ago perchance. Especially if the knolls in the meadows are washed by a freshet where they have been plowed the previous fall, the soil will be taken away lower down and the stones left—the arrowheads, etc., and soapstone pottery amid them—somewhat as gold is washed in a dish or tom. I landed on two spots this afternoon and picked up a dozen arrowheads. It is one of the regular pursuits of the spring. As much as sportsmen go in pursuit of ducks, and gunners of musquash, and scholars of rare books, and travellers of adventures, and poets of ideas, and all men of money, I go in search of arrowheads when the proper season comes round again. So I help myself to live worthily, and loving my life as I should. . . .

April 1. Some have planted peas and lettuce.

April 3 . . . . Men's minds run so much on work and money that the mass instantly associate all literary labor with a pecuniary reward. They are mainly curious to know how much money the lecturer or author gets for his work. They think that the naturalist takes so much pains to collect plants or animals because he is paid for it. An Irishman who saw me in the fields making a minute in my notebook took it for granted that I was casting up my wages and actually inquired what they came to, as if he had never dreamed of any other use for writing. I might have quoted to him that the wages of sin is death, as the most pertinent answer. "What do you get for lecturing now?" I am occasionally asked. It is the more amusing since I only lecture about once a year out of my native town, often not at all; so that I might as well, if my objects were merely pecuniary, give up the business. Once, when I was walking on Staten Island, looking about me as usual, a man who saw me would not believe me when I told him that I was indeed from New England but was not looking at that region with a pecuniary view—a view to speculation; and he offered me a handsome bonus if I would sell his farm for him.

April 8. . . . What a pitiful business is the fur trade,

which has been pursued now for so many ages, for so many years by famous companies which enjoy a profitable monopoly and control a large portion of the earth's surface, unweariedly pursuing and ferreting out small animals by the aid of the loafing class tempted by rum and money, that you may rob some little fellow-creature of its coat to adorn or thicken your own, that you may get a fashionable covering in which to hide your head, or a suitable robe in which to dispense justice to your fellow-men! Regarded from the philosopher's point of view, it is precisely on a level with rag and bone picking in the streets of the cities.

April 24. . . . There is a season for everything, and we do not notice a given phenomenon except at that season, if, indeed, it can be called the same phenomenon at any other season. There is a time to watch the ripples on Ripple Lake, to look for arrowheads, to study the rocks and lichens, a time to walk on sandy deserts; and the observer of nature must improve these seasons as much as the farmer his. So boys fly kites and play ball or hawkie at particular times all over the state. A wise man will know what game to play today, and play it. We must not be governed by rigid rules, as by the almanac, but let the season rule us. The moods and thoughts of man are revolving just as steadily and incessantly as nature's. Nothing must be postponed. Take time by the forelock. Now or never! You must live in the present, launch yourself on every wave, find your eternity in each moment. Fools stand on their island opportunities and look toward another land. There is no other land; there is no other life but this, or the like of this. Where the good husbandman is, there is the good soil. Take any other course, and life will be a succession of regrets. Let us see vessels sailing prosperously before the wind, and not simply stranded barks. There is no world for the penitent and regretful.

May 1. Hear the ruby-crowned wren.

We accuse savages of worshipping only the bad spirit, or devil, though they may distinguish both a good and a bad; but they regard only that one which they fear and worship the devil only. We too are savages in this, doing precisely the same thing. This occurred to me yesterday as I sat in the woods admiring the beauty of the blue butterfly. We are not chiefly interested in birds and insects, for example, as they are ornamental to the earth and cheering to man, but we spare the lives of the former only on condition that they eat more grubs than they do cherries, and the only account of the insects which the State encourages is of the "Insects *Injurious* to Vegetation." We too admit both a good and a bad spirit, but we worship chiefly the bad spirit, whom we fear. We do not think first of the good but of the harm things will do us.

The catechism says that the chief end of man is to glorify God and enjoy him forever, which of course is applicable mainly to God as seen in his works. Yet the only account of its beautiful insects—butterflies, etc.—which God has made and set before us which the State ever thinks of spending any money on is the account of those which are injurious to vegetation! This is the way we glorify God and enjoy him forever. Come out here and behold a thousand painted butterflies and other beautiful insects which people the air, then go to the libraries and see what kind of prayer and glorification of God is there recorded. Massachusetts has published her report on "Insects Injurious to Vegetation," and our neighbor the "Noxious Insects of New York." We have attended to the evil and said nothing about the good. This is looking a gift horse in the mouth with a vengeance. Children are attracted by the beauty of butterflies, but their parents and legislators deem it an idle pursuit. The parents remind me of the devil, but the children of God. Though God may have pronounced his work good, we ask, "Is it not poisonous?"

Science is inhuman. Things seen with a microscope begin to be insignificant. So described, they are as monstrous as if they should be magnified a thousand diameters. Suppose I should see and describe men and houses and trees and birds as if they were a thousand times larger than they are! With our prying instruments we disturb the balance and harmony of nature.

July 20. The little Holbrook boy showed me an egg which I unhesitatingly pronounced a peetweet's, given him by Joe Smith. The latter, to my surprise, declares it a meadow-hen's; saw the bird and young, and says the latter were quite black and had hen bills. Can it be so?

Aug. 12. When I came downstairs this morning, it raining hard and steadily, I found an Irishman sitting with his coat on his arm in the kitchen, waiting to see me. He wanted to

inquire what I thought the weather would be today! I sometimes ask my aunt, and she consults the almanac. So we shirk
the responsibility.

Aug. 26. . . . That first frost on the seventeenth
was the first stroke of winter aiming at the scalp of
summer. Like a stealthy and insidious aboriginal enemy, it
made its assault just before daylight in some deep and far-
away hollow and then silently withdrew. Few have seen the
drooping plants, but the news of this stroke circulates rapidly
through the village. Men communicate it with a tone of
warning. The foe is gone by sunrise, but some fearful neighbors who have visited their potato and cranberry patches
report this stroke. The implacable and irresistible foe to all
this tender greenness is not far off, nor can we be sure, any
month in the year, that some scout from his low camp may
not strike down the tenderest of the children of summer. The
earliest and latest frosts are not distinguishable. This foe will
go on steadily increasing in strength and boldness, till his
white camps will be pitched over all the fields, and we shall
be compelled to take refuge in our strongholds.

Aug. 27. . . . All our life, i.e. the living part of it, is a
persistent dreaming awake. The boy does not camp in his
father's yard. That would not be adventurous enough, there
are too many sights and sounds to disturb the illusion; so he
marches off twenty or thirty miles and there pitches his tent,
where stranger inhabitants are tamely sleeping in their beds
just like his father at home, and camps in *their* yard, perchance. But then he dreams uninterruptedly that he is anywhere but where he is.
    . . . There are various ways in which you can tell if a
watermelon is ripe. If you have had your eye on the patch
much from the first, and so know which formed first, you
may presume that these will ripen soonest; or else you may
incline to those which lie nearest the centre of the hill or
root, as the oldest. Next the dull dead color and want of
bloom are as good signs as any. Some look green and livid
and have a very fog or mildew of bloom on them, like a
fungus. These are as green as a leek through and through, and
you'll find yourself in a pickle if you open one. Others have
a dead dark greenness, the circulations being less rapid in
their cuticles and their blooming period passed, and these
you may safely bet on. If the vine is quite green and lively,

the death of the quirl at the root of the stem is almost a sure sign. For fear we should not discover it before, this is placed for a sign that there is redness and ripeness (if not mealiness) within. Of two otherwise similar, take that which yields the lowest tone when struck with your knuckles, i.e., which is hollowest. The old or ripe ones sing base; the young, tenor or falsetto. Some use the violent method of pressing to hear if they crack within, but this is not to be allowed. Above all no tapping on the vine is to be tolerated, suggestive of a greediness which defeats its own purpose. It is very childish. . . .

. . . I served my apprenticeship and have since done considerable journey-work in the huckleberry field, though I never paid for my schooling and clothing in that way. It was itself some of the best schooling I got, and paid for itself. Occasionally in still summer forenoons, when perhaps a mantua-maker was to be dined, and a huckleberry pudding had been decided on, I, a lad of ten, was dispatched to the huckleberry hills, all alone. My scholastic education could be thus far tampered with and an excuse might be found. No matter how few and scarce the berries on the near hills, the exact number necessary for a huckleberry pudding could surely be collected by 11 o'clock. My rule in such cases was never to eat one till my dish was full. At other times when I had companions, some used to bring such curiously shaped dishes that I was often curious to see how the berries disposed of themselves in them. Some brought a coffee-pot to the huckleberry field, and such a vessel possessed this advantage at least, that if a greedy boy had skimmed off a handful or two on his way home, he had only to close the lid and give his vessel a shake to have it full again. This was done all round when we got as far homeward as the Dutch house. This can probably be done with any vessel that has much side to it.

I once met with a whole family—father and mother and children—ravaging a huckleberry field in this wise: they cut up the bushes, and, as they went, beat them over the edge of a bushel basket, till they had it full of berries, ripe and green, leaves, sticks, etc., and so they passed along out of my sight like wild men.

Sept. 1. . . . Bought a pair of shoes the other day, and, observing that as usual they were only wooden-pegged at the toes, I required the seller to put in an extra row of iron pegs there while I waited for them. So he called to his boy to bring those zinc pegs, but I insisted on iron pegs and no zinc ones. He gave me considerable advice on the subject of shoes, but I suggested that even the wearer of shoes, of whom I was one, had an opportunity to learn some of their qualities. I have learned to respect my own opinion in this matter. As I do not use blacking and the seller often throws in a box of blacking when I buy a pair of shoes, they accumulate on my hands.

Sept. 16. . . . Again and again I am surprised to observe what an interval there is, in what is called civilized life, between the shell and the inhabitant of the shell—what a disproportion there is between the life of man and his conveniences and luxuries. The house is neatly painted, has many apartments. You are shown into the sitting room, where is a carpet and couch and mirror and splendidly bound Bible, daguerreotypes, ambrotypes, photographs of the whole family even, on the mantelpiece. One could live here more deliciously and improve his divine gifts better than in a cave surely. In the bright and costly saloon man will not be starving or freezing or contending with vermin surely, but he will be meditating a divine song or a heroic deed, or perfuming the atmosphere by the very breath of his natural and healthy existence. As the parlor is preferable to the cave, so will the life of its occupant be more god-like than that of the dweller in the cave. I called at such a house this afternoon, the house of one who in Europe would be called an operative. The woman was not in the third heavens, but in the third kitchen, as near the wood-shed or to outdoors and to the cave as she could instinctively get, for there she belonged— a coarse scullion or wench, not one whit superior, but in fact inferior, to the squaw in a wigwam—and the master of the house, where was he? He was drunk somewhere, on some mow or behind some stack, and I could not see him. He had been having a spree. If he had been as sober as he may be tomorrow, it would have been essentially the same; for refinement is not in him, it is only in his house—in the appliances which he did not invent. So is it in the Fifth Avenue and all over the civilized world. There is nothing but confusion in our New England life. The hogs are in the parlor. This man and his wife—and how many like them!— should have sucked their claws in some hole in a rock, or lurked like gypsies in the outbuildings of some diviner race.

They've got into the wrong boxes; they rained down into these houses by mistake, as it is said to rain toads sometimes. They wear these advantages helter-skelter and without appreciating them, or to satisfy a vulgar taste, just as savages wear the dress of civilized men, just as that Indian chief walked the streets of New Orleans clad in nothing but a gaudy military coat which his Great Father had given him. Some philanthropists trust that the houses will civilize the inhabitants at last. The mass of men, just like savages, strive always after the outside, the clothes and finery of civilized life, the blue beads and tinsel and centre tables. It is a wonder that any load ever gets moved, men are so prone to put the cart before the horse.

. . . I am invited to take some party of ladies or gentlemen on an excursion—to walk or sail, or the like—but by all kinds of evasions I omit it, and am thought to be rude and unaccommodating therefore. They do not consider that the wood-path and the boat are my studio, where I maintain a sacred solitude and cannot admit promiscuous company. I will see them occasionally in an evening or at the table, however. They do not think of taking a child away from its school to go a-huckleberrying with them. Why should not I, then, have my school and school hours to be respected? Ask me for a certain number of dollars if you will, but do not ask me for my afternoons.

Sept. 18. . . . Dr. Josiah Bartlett handed me a paper today, desiring me to subscribe for a statue to Horace Mann. I declined, and said that I thought a man ought not any more to take up room in the world after he was dead. . . .

Sept. 22. . . . It would be fit that the tobacco plant should spring up on the house-site, aye on the grave, of almost every householder of Concord. These vile weeds are sown by vile men. . . .

Sept. 24. . . . To my senses the dicksonia fern has the most wild and primitive fragrance, quite unalloyed and untamable, such as no human institutions give out—the early morning fragrance of the world, antediluvian, strength and hope imparting. They who scent it can never faint. It is ever a new and untried field where it grows, and only when we think original thoughts can we perceive it. . . .

Sept. 26. . . . Observed the spiders at work at the head of Willow Bay. Their fine lines are extended from one flag or bur-reed to another, even six or eight feet, perfectly parallel with the surface of the water and only a few inches above it. I see some—though it requires a very favorable light to detect them, they are so fine—blowing off perfectly straight horizontally over the water, only half a dozen inches above it, as much as seven feet, one end fastened to a reed, the other free. They look as stiff as spears, yet the free end waves back and forth horizontally in the air several feet. They work thus in calm and fine weather when the water is smooth. Yet they can run over the surface of the water readily.

Oct. 3. . . . How all poets have idealized the farmer's life! What graceful figures and unworldly characters they have assigned to them! Serene as the sky, emulating nature with their calm and peaceful lives. As I come by a farmer's today, the house of one who died some two years ago, I see the decrepit form of one whom he had engaged to "carry through," taking his property at a venture, feebly tying up a bundle of fagots with his knee on it, though time is fast loosening the bundle that he is. When I look down on that roof I am not reminded of the mortgage which the village bank has on that property—that that family long since sold itself to the devil and wrote the deed with their blood. I am not reminded that the old man I see in the yard is one who has lived beyond his calculated time, whom the young one is merely "carrying through" in fulfillment of his contract; that the man at the pump is watering the milk. I am not reminded of the idiot that sits by the kitchen fire.

Oct. 4. . . . All men sympathize by their lower natures; the few, only, by their higher. The appetites of the mistress are commonly the same as those of her servant, but her society is commonly more select. The help may have some of the tenderloin, but she must eat it in the kitchen.

Oct. 9. P.M. Boston.
Read a lecture to Theodore Parker's society.

Oct. 10. . . . Colder weather, and the cat's fur grows.

Oct. 14 . . . . I hear a man laughed at because he went to Europe twice in search of an imaginary wife who, he thought, was there, though he had never seen nor heard of her. But the majority have gone further while they stayed in America, have actually allied themselves to one whom they thought their wife and found out their mistake too late to mend it. It would be cruel to laugh at these.

Oct. 15. . . . Each town should have a park, or rather a primitive forest, of five hundred or a thousand acres, where a stick should never be cut for fuel, a common possession forever, for instruction and recreation. We hear of cow-commons and ministerial lots, but we want *men*-commons and lay lots, inalienable forever. Let us keep the New World *new,* preserve all the advantages of living in the country. There is meadow and pasture and wood-lot for the town's poor. Why not a forest and huckleberry field for the town's rich? All Walden Wood might have been preserved for our park forever, with Walden in its midst, and the Easterbrooks Country, an unoccupied area of some four square miles, might have been our huckleberry field. If any owners of these tracts are about to leave the world without natural heirs who need or deserve to be specially remembered, they will do wisely to abandon their possession to all, and not will them to some individual who perhaps has enough already. As some give to Harvard College or another institution, why might not another give a forest or huckleberry field to Concord? A town is an institution which deserves to be remembered. We boast of our system of education, but why stop at schoolmasters and schoolhouses? We are all schoolmasters, and our schoolhouse is the universe. To attend chiefly to the desk or schoolhouse while we neglect the scenery in which it is placed is absurd. If we do not look out we shall find our fine schoolhouse standing in a cow-yard at last.

Oct. 16. . . . Talk about learning our *letters* and being *literate!* Why, the roots of *letters* are *things.* Natural objects and phenomena are the original symbols or types which express our thoughts and feelings, and yet American scholars, having little or no root in the soil, commonly strive with all their might to confine themselves to the imported symbols alone. . . .

Oct. 18. . . . Why can we not oftener refresh one another with original thoughts? If the fragrance of the dicksonia fern is so grateful and suggestive to us, how much more refreshing and encouraging—re-creating—would be fresh and fragrant thoughts communicated to us fresh from a man's experience and life! I want none of his pity, nor sympathy, in the common sense, but that he should emit and communicate to me his essential fragrance, that he should not be forever repenting and going to church (when not otherwise sinning), but, as it were, going a-huckleberrying in the fields of thought, and enrich all the world with his visions and his joys.

Why do you flee so soon, sir, to the theatres, lecture rooms, and museums of the city? If you will stay here awhile I will promise you strange sights. You shall walk on water; all these brooks and rivers and ponds shall be your highway. You shall see the whole earth covered a foot or more deep with purest white crystals, in which you slump or over which you glide, and all the trees and stubble glittering in icy armor.

Oct. 19. . . . One comment I heard of by the postmaster of this village on the news of [John] Brown's death: "He died as the fool dieth." I should have answered this man, "He did not live as the fool liveth, and he died as he lived."

. . . Our foes are in our midst and all about us. Hardly a house but is divided against itself. For our foe is the all but universal woodenness (both of head and heart), the want of vitality, of man, the effect of vice—whence are begotten fear and superstition and bigotry and persecution and slavery of all kinds. Mere figureheads upon a hulk, with livers in the place of hearts. A church that can never have done with excommunicating Christ while it exists. Our plains were overrun the other day with a flock of adjutant-generals, as if a brood of cockerels had been let loose there, waiting to use their spurs in what sort of glorious cause, I ask. What more probable in the future, what more certain heretofore, than in grinding in the dust four hundred thousands of feeble and timid men, women, and children? The United States exclaims: "Here are four millions of human creatures which we have stolen. We have abolished among them the relations of father, mother, children, wife, and we mean to keep them in this condition. Will you, O Massachusetts, help us to do so?" And Massachusetts promptly answers, "Aye!"

Oct. 20. . . . As I approached the pond, I saw a hind in a potato field (digging potatoes), who stood stock-still for ten minutes to gaze at me in astonishment, till I had sunk into the woods amid the hills about the pond, and when I emerged again, there he was, motionless still, on the same spot, with his eye on me, resting on his idle hoe, as one might watch at the mouth of a fox's hole to see him come out. Perchance he may have thought *nihil humanum,* etc., or else he was transfixed with thought—which is worth a bushel or two of potatoes, whatever his employer may say —contrasting his condition with my own, and though he stood so still, civilization made some progress. But I must hasten away or he'll lose his day. I was as indifferent to his eyeshot as a tree walking, for I am used to such things. Perchance he will relate his adventure when he gets home at night, and what he has seen, though he did not have to light a candle this time. I am in a fair way to become a valuable citizen to him, as he is to me. He raises potatoes in the field for me; I raise curiosity in him. He stirs the earth; I stir him. What a power am I! I cause the potatoes to rot in the ground. I affect distant markets surely. But he shall not spoil my day; I will get in my harvest nevertheless. This will be nuts to him when the winter evenings come; he will tell his dream then. Talk of reaping machines! I did not go into that field at all. I did not meddle with the potatoes. He was the only crop I gathered at a glance. Perchance he thought, "I harvest potatoes; he harvests me!"

Oct. 22. . . . I foresee the time when the painter will paint that scene [of Harpers Ferry], the poet will sing it, the historian record it, and, with the Landing of the Pilgrims and the Declaration of Independence, it will be the ornament of some future national gallery, when the present form of slavery shall be no more. We shall then be at liberty to weep for John Brown. Then and not till then we will take our revenge.

Dec. 8. . . . Two hundred years ago is about as great an antiquity as we can comprehend or often have to deal with. It is nearly as good as two thousand to our imaginations. It carries us back to the days of aborigines and the Pilgrims; beyond the limits of oral testimony, to history which begins already to be enamelled with a gloss of fable, and we do not quite believe what we read; to a strange style of writing and spelling and of expression; to those ancestors whose names we do not know, and to whom we are related only as we are to the race generally. It is the age of our very oldest houses and cultivated trees. Nor is New England very peculiar in this. In England also, a house two hundred years old, especially if it be a wooden one, is pointed out as an interesting relic of the past.

Dec. 12. . . . There is a certain Irish woodchopper who, when I come across him at his work in the woods in the winter, never fails to ask me what time it is, as if he were in haste to take his dinner-pail and go home. This is not as it should be. Every man, and the woodchopper among the rest, should love his work as much as the poet does his. All good political arrangements proceed on this supposition. If labor mainly, or to any considerable degree, serves the purpose of a police, to keep men out of mischief, it indicates a rottenness at the foundation of our community.

Dec. 13. P.M. On river to Fair Haven Pond.
My first true winter walk is perhaps that which I take on the river, or where I cannot go in the summer. It is the walk peculiar to winter, and now first I take it. I see that the fox too has already taken the same walk before me, just along the edge of the button-bushes, where not even he can go in the summer. We both turn our steps hither at the same time.

Dec. 15. . . . Philosophy is a Greek word by good rights, and it stands almost for a Greek thing. Yet some rumor of it has reached the commonest mind. M. [Marshall] Miles, who came to collect his wood bill today, said, when I objected to the small size of his wood, that it was necessary to split wood fine in order to cure it well, that he had found that wood that was more than four inches in diameter would not dry, and moreover a good deal depended on the manner in which it was corded up in the woods. He piled his high and tightly. If this were not well done the stakes would spread and the wood lie loosely, and so the rain and snow find their way into it. And he added, "I have handled a good deal of wood, and I think that I understand the *philosophy* of it."

Dec. 25. . . . How different are men and women, e.g. in respect to the adornment of their heads! Do you ever see an old or jammed bonnet on the head of a woman at a public meeting? But look at any assembly of men with their hats on; how large a proportion of the hats will be old, weather-beaten, and indented, but I think so much the more picturesque and interesting! One farmer rides by my door in a hat which it does me good to see, there is so much character in it—so much independence to begin with, and then affection for his old friends, etc., etc. I should not wonder if there were lichens on it. Think of painting a hero in a bran-new hat! The chief recommendation of the Kossuth hat is that it looks old to start with, and almost as good as new to end with. Indeed, it is generally conceded that a man does not look the worse for a somewhat dilapidated hat. But go to a lyceum and look at the bonnets and various other headgear of the women and girls—who, by the way, keep their hats on, it being too dangerous and expensive to take them off!! Why, every one looks as fragile as a butterfly's wings, having just come out of a bandbox—as it will go into a bandbox again when the lyceum is over. Men wear their hats for use; women theirs for ornament. I have seen the greatest philosopher in the town with what the traders would call "a shocking bad hat" on, but the woman whose bonnet does not come up to the mark is at best a "bluestocking." The man is not particularly proud of his beaver and musquash, but the woman flaunts her ostrich and sable in your face.

Dec. 26. . . . I see a brute with a gun in his hand, standing motionless over a musquash-house which he has destroyed. I find that he has visited every one in the neighborhood of Fair Haven Pond, above and below, and broken them all down, laying open the interior to the water, and then stood watchful, close by, for the poor creature to show its head there for a breath of air. There lies the red carcass of one whose pelt he has taken on the spot, flat on the bloody ice. And for his afternoon's cruelty that fellow will be rewarded with a ninepence, perchance. When I consider what are the opportunities of the civilized man for getting ninepences and getting light, this seems to me more savage than savages are. Depend on it that whoever thus treats the musquash's house, his refuge when the water is frozen thick, he and his family will not come to a good end. . . .

Dec. 29. . . . The clouds were very remarkable this cold afternoon, about twenty minutes before sunset, consisting of very long and narrow white clouds converging in the horizon (melon-rind-wise) both in the west and east. They looked like the skeletons and backbones of celestial sloths, being pointed at each end, or even like porcupine quills or ivory darts sharp at each end. So long and slender, but pronounced, with a manifest backbone and marrow. It looked as if invisible giants were darting them from all parts of the sky at the setting sun. These were long darts indeed. Well underneath was an almost invisible rippled vapor whose grain was exactly at right angles with the former, all over the sky, yet it was so delicate that it did not prevent your seeing the former at all. Its filmy arrows all pointed athwart the others. I know that in fact those slender white cloud sloths were nearly parallel across the sky, but how much handsomer are the clouds because the sky is made to appear concave to us! How much more beautiful an arrangement of the clouds than parallel lines! At length those white arrows and bows, slender and sharp as they were, gathering toward a point in the west horizon, looked like flames even, forked and darting flames of ivory-white, and low in the west there was a piece of rainbow but little longer than it was broad.

Dec. 31. . . . A man may be old and infirm. What, then, are the thoughts he thinks? what the life he lives? They and it are, like himself, infirm. But a man may be young, athletic, active, beautiful. Then, too, his thoughts will be like his person. They will wander in a living and beautiful world. If you are well, then how brave you are! How you hope! You are conversant with joy! A man thinks as well through his legs and arms as his brain. We exaggerate the importance of exclusiveness of the headquarters. Do you suppose they were a race of consumptives and dyspeptics who invented Grecian mythology and poetry? The poet's words are, "You would almost say the body thought!" I quite say it. I trust we have a good body then.

1860

There was more on John Brown. Thoreau now published his lecture "A Plea for Captain John Brown" in an anthology, Echoes of Harper's Ferry. He also published an address entitled "The Succession of Forest Trees" in Horace Greeley's New York Tribune. This was the year that saw his interest in the wood-lots of Concord reach a peak. He was fascinated by the way the trees succeeded one another under varying conditions. He surveyed, lectured, and traveled, spending most of a summer week with Ellery Channing on Monadnock. Almost at the end of the year he became ill; he started by catching a cold while engaged in a count of tree rings. The journal reflects the variety of his activities during the year and, especially in its latter part, his concern with trees. This is the final year in which the journal is full. The writing keeps its fluency but an idea of Thoreau's altered stance can be gained through a look at the list of subjects for July that Bradford Torrey provided: "Sunlight on a Grain-Field— Young Marsh Hawks—The Swift Camilla—Temperature of the Springs—Temperature of the Brooks—Temperature of the River—Rose-breasted Grosbeaks—The Lights and Shadows of the Grass—Proserpine's Hair—The Checker-board Fields— Water-Lilies at Night—The Grasses and Sedges of the Landscape—The Cultivated Grasses—The Abundant Lily Pads— The Bull-Frog's Eye—The Lily Pads—Pollywogs—A Box Turtle—The House-Leek—The Beauty of the Crops—Lightning—The Under Sides of Leaves—A Golden-winged Warbler —The Little Auk—Petrels—Other Birds found at Wayland— Detecting Poor Shingles—Young Wild Ducks—Shad-Bush Berries—Potato Balls—Rain on the Water." The Transcendentalism is gone; the exact fact appears to reign in the pages of the journal. But not quite. Thoreau is still capable of drawing a cosmic generalization from the fact, still ready to ask, What does this mean?

Feb. 2. . . . The fox seems to get his living by industry and perseverance. He runs smelling for miles along the most favorable routes, especially the edge of rivers and ponds, until he smells the track of a mouse beneath the snow or the fresh track of a partridge, and then follows it till he comes upon his game. After exploring thus a great many quarters, after hours of fruitless search, he succeeds. There may be a dozen partridges resting in the snow within a square mile, and his work is simply to find them with the aid of his nose. Compared with the dog, he affects me as high-bred, unmixed. There is nothing of the mongrel in him. He belongs to a noble family which has seen its best days—a younger son. Now and then he starts, and turns and doubles on his track, as if he heard or scented danger. (I watch him through my glass.) He does not mind us at the distance of only sixty rods. I have myself seen one place where a mouse came to the surface today in the snow. Probably he has smelt out many such galleries. Perhaps he seizes them *through* the snow.

March 25. . . . To speak of the general phenomena of March: When March arrives, a tolerably calm, clear, sunny, spring-like day, the snow is so far gone that sleighing ends and our compassion is excited by the sight of horses laboriously dragging wheeled vehicles through mud and water and slosh. We shall no longer hear the jingling of sleigh-bells. The sleigh is housed, or, perchance, converted into a wheeled vehicle by the travelling peddler caught far from home. The wood-sled is perhaps abandoned by the roadside, where the snow ended, with two sticks put under its runners—there to rest, it may be, while the grass springs up green around it, till another winter comes round. It may be near where the wagon of the careless farmer was left last December on account of the drifted snow. As March approaches, at least, peddlers will do well to travel with wheels slung under their sleighs, ready to convert their sleighs into wheeled vehicles at an hour's warning. Even the boy's sled gets put away by degrees, or when it is found to be in the way, and his thoughts are directed gradually to more earthly games. There are now water privileges for him by every roadside.

The prudent farmer has teamed home, or to market, his last load of wood from the lot, nor left that which was corded a year ago to be consumed by the worms and the weather. He will not have to sell next winter oak wood rotted an inch deep all round, at a reduction in the price if he deals with knowing customers. He has hauled his last logs to mill. No more shall we see the sled-track shine or hear the sled squeak along it.

The boy's sled gets put away in the barn or shed or garret, and there lies dormant all summer, like a woodchuck in the winter. It goes into its burrow just before woodchucks come out, so that you may say a woodchuck never sees a sled, nor a sled a woodchuck—unless it were a prematurely risen woodchuck or a belated and unseasonable sled. Before the woodchuck comes out the sled goes in. They dwell at the antipodes of each other. Before sleds rise woodchucks have set. The ground squirrel too shares the privileges and misfortunes of the woodchuck. The sun now passes from the constellation of the sled into that of the woodchuck.

The snow-plow, too, has now nothing more to do but to dry-rot against another winter, like a thing whose use is forgotten, incredible to the beholder, its vocation gone.

March 26. . . . I had a suit once in which, methinks, I could glide across the fields unperceived half a mile in front of a farmer's windows. It was such a skillful mixture of browns, dark and light properly proportioned, with even some threads of green in it by chance. It was of loose texture and about the color of a pasture with patches of withered sweet-fern and lechea. I trusted a good deal to my invisibility in it when going across lots, and many a time I was aware that to it I owed the near approach of wild animals.

No doubt my dusty and tawny cowhides surprise the street walkers who wear patent-leather or Congress shoes, but they do not consider how absurd such shoes would be in my vocation, to thread the woods and swamps in. Why should I wear *Congress* who walk alone, and not where there is any congress of my kind?

April 15. . . . At this season of the year, we are continually expecting warmer weather than we have.

May 2. . . . A crowd of men seem to generate vermin even of the human kind. In great towns there is degradation undreamed of elsewhere—gamblers, dog-killers, rag-pickers. Some live by robbery or by luck. There was the Concord muster (of last September). I see still a well-dressed man carefully and methodically searching for money on the muster fields, far off across the river. I turn my glass upon him and notice how he proceeds. (I saw them searching there in the fall till the snow came.) He walks regularly and slowly back and forth over the ground where the soldiers had their tents—still marked by the straw—with his head prone, and poking in the straw with a stick, now and then turning back or aside to examine something more closely. He is dressed, methinks, better than an average man whom you meet in the streets. How can he pay for his board thus? He dreams of finding a few coppers, or perchance a half-dime, which have fallen from the soldiers' pockets, and no doubt he *will* find something of the kind, having dreamed of it—having knocked, this door will be opened to him.

May 17. . . . Standing in the meadow near the early aspen at the island, I hear the first fluttering of leaves—a peculiar sound, at first unaccountable to me. The breeze causes the now fully expanded aspen leaves there to rustle with a pattering sound, striking on one another. It is much like a gentle surge breaking on a shore, or the rippling of waves. This is the first softer music which the wind draws from the forest, the woods generally being comparatively bare and just bursting into leaf. It was delicious to behold that dark mass and hear that soft rippling sound.

June 10. . . . There is much handsome interrupted fern in the Painted-Cup Meadow, and near the top of one of the clumps we noticed something like a large cocoon, the color of the rusty cinnamon fern wool. It was a red bat, the New York bat, so called. It hung suspended, head directly downward, with its little sharp claws or hooks caught through one of the divisions at the base of one of the pinnae, above the fructification. It was a delicate rusty brown in color, very like the wool of the cinnamon fern, with the whiter bare spaces seen through it early in the season. I thought at first glance it was a broad brown cocoon, then that it was the plump body of a monstrous emperor moth. It was rusty or reddish brown, white or hoary within or beneath the tips, with a white apparently triangular spot beneath, about the insertion of the wings. Its wings were very compactly folded up, the principal bones (darker-reddish) lying flat along the under side of its body, and a hook on each meeting its opposite under the chin of the creature. It did not look like fur, but more like the plush of the ripe cat-tail head, though more loose—all trembling in the wind and with the pulsations of the animal. I broke off the top of the fern and let the bat lie on its back in my hand. I held it and turned it about for ten or fifteen minutes, but it did not awake. Once or twice it opened its eyes a little, and even it raised its head, opened its mouth, but soon drowsily dropped its head and fell asleep again. Its ears were rounded and nearly bare. It was more attentive to sounds than to motions. Finally, by shaking it, and especially by hissing or whistling, I thoroughly awakened it, and it fluttered off twenty or thirty rods to the woods. I cannot but think that its instinct taught it to cling to the interrupted fern, since it might readily be mistaken for a mass of its fruit. Raised its old-haggish head. Unless it showed its head wide awake, it looked like a tender infant.

June 23. . . . At 7 P.M. the river is fifteen and three fourths inches above summer level.

It rained hard on the twentieth and part of the following night—two and one eighth inches of rain in all, there being no drought—raising the river from some two or three inches above summer level to seven and a half inches above summer level at 7 A.M. of the twenty-first.

At 7 P.M. of the twenty-first, 11 1/2 inches above summer level.

6 A.M.	22d,	11 15/16
7 P.M.	22d,	15 1/8
7 A.M.	23d,	15
7 P.M.	23d.	15 3/4

Thus two and one eighth inches of rain at this season, falling in one day, with little or no wind, raises the river while it is falling some four inches; on the next day it rises four more; the next night it rises seven sixteenths inch more; the next day (second after the rain) it rises three and three sixteenths inches; the next night it falls one eighth of an inch; it rises again three fourths of an inch, or five eighths absolutely; i.e. it rises still the third day after the rain. That is, after a remarkably heavy rain of one day it does not rise as much in a night as it ordinarily falls in a day at this season.

July 12. . . . The best way to drink, especially at a shallow spring, or one so sunken below the surface as to be difficult to reach, is through a tube. You can commonly find growing near a spring a hollow reed or weed of some kind suitable for this purpose, such as rue or touch-me-not or water saxifrage, or you can carry one in your pocket.

July 15. . . . On Hill. No crops clothe the earth with richer hues and make a greater impression of luxuriousness than the cultivated grasses. Field after field, densely packed like the squares of a checkerboard, all through and about the villages, paint the earth with various shades of green and other colors. There is the rich glaucous green of young grain now, of various shades, depending on its age and kind; the flashing blades of corn which does not yet hide the bare ground; the yellowing tops of ripening grain; the dense uniform red of red-top, the most striking and high-colored of all (that is, culti-vated); the very similar purple of the fowl-meadow (the most deep-piled and cumulous-looking, like down) along the low river-banks; the very dark and dusky, as it were shadowy, green of herd's-grass at a distance, as if clouds were always passing over it—close at hand it is of a dark purplish or slaty purple, from the color of its anthers; the fresh light green where June grass has been cut, and the fresh dark green where clover has been cut; and the hard, dark green of pastures (red-top) generally—not to speak of the very light-colored wiry fescue there.

The solid square fields of red-top look singularly like bare ground at a distance, but when you know it to be red-top you see it to be too high-colored for that. Yet it thus sug-gests a harmony between itself and the ground. Look down on a field of red-top now in full bloom, a quarter of a mile west of this hill—a very dense and red field—at 2:30 P.M. of this very warm and slightly hazy but not dogdayish day, in a blazing sun. I am surprised to see a very distinct white vapor, like a low cloud in a mountainous country, or a smoke, drift-ing along close over the red-top. Is it not owing to the con-trast between this hot noontide air and the moist coolness of that dense grass-field?

Then there is the cheerful yellowish green of the meadows, where the sedges prevail, i.e. yellowest where wettest, with darker patches and veins of grass, etc., in the higher and drier parts. I can just distinguish with my naked eye—know-ing where to look—the darker green of pipes on the peat meadows two miles from the hill.

The potato-fields are a very dark green.

Aug. 1. . . . How much of beauty—of color, as well as form—on which our eyes daily rest goes unperceived by us! No one but a botanist is likely to distinguish nicely the different shades of green with which the open surface of the earth is clothed—not even a landscape-painter if he does not know the species of sedges and grasses which paint it. With respect to the color of grass, most of those even who attend peculiarly to the aspects of Nature only observe that it is more or less dark or light, green or brown, or velvety, fresh or parched, etc. But if you are studying grasses you look for another and different beauty, and you find it, in the wonderful variety of color, etc., presented by the various species. Take the bare, unwooded earth now, and consider the beautiful variety of shades (or tints?) of green that clothe it under a bright sun. The pastured hills of Conantum, now just imbrowned (probably by the few now stale flowering tops of the red-top which the cows have avoided as too wiry), present a hard and solid green or greenish brown, just touched here and there delicately with light patches of sheep's fescue (though it may be only its radical leaves left), as if a dew lay on it there—and this has some of the effect of a watered surface—and the whole is dotted with a thousand little shades of projecting rocks and shrubs. Then, looking lower at the meadow in Miles's field, that is seen as a bright-yellow and sunny stream (yet with a slight tinge of glaucous) between the dark-green potato fields, flowing onward with windings and expansions, and, as it were, with rips and waterfalls, to the river meadows.

Again, I sit on the brow of the orchard, and look northwest down the river valley (at mid-afternoon). There flows, or rests, the calm blue winding river, lake-like, with its smooth silver-plated sides, and wherever weeds extend across it, there too the silver plate bridges it, like a spirit's bridge across the Styx; but the rippled portions are blue as the sky. This river reposes in the midst of a broad brilliant yellow valley amid green fields and hills and woods, as if, like the Nanking or Yang-ho (or what-not), it flowed through an Oriental Chinese meadow where yellow is the imperial color. The immediate and raised edge of the river, with its willows and button-bushes and polygonums, is a light green, but the immediately adjacent low meadows, where the sedge prevails, is a brilliant and cheerful yellow, intensely, incredibly bright, such color as you never see in pictures; yellow of various tints, in the lowest and sedgiest parts deepening to so much color as if gamboge had been rubbed into the meadow there; the most cheering color in all the landscape; shaded with little darker isles of green in the midst of this yellow sea of sedge. Yet it is the bright and cheerful yellow, as of spring, and with nothing in the least autumnal in it. How this contrasts with the adjacent fields of red-top, now fast falling before the scythe!

Aug. 9. . . . There were a great many visitors to the summit [of Mt. Monadnock], both by the south and north, i.e. the Jaffrey and Dublin paths, but they did not turn off from the beaten track. One noon, when I was on the top, I counted forty men, women, and children around me, and more were constantly arriving while others were going. Certainly more than one hundred ascended in a day. When you got within thirty rods you saw them seated in a row along the gray parapets, like the inhabitants of a castle on a gala-day; and when you behold Monadnock's blue summit fifty miles off in the horizon, you may imagine it covered with men, women, and children in dresses of all colors, like an observatory on a muster-field. They appeared to be chiefly mechanics and farmers' boys and girls from the neighboring towns. The young men sat in rows with their legs dangling over the precipice, squinting through spy-glasses and shouting and hallooing to each new party that issued from the woods below. Some were playing cards; others were trying to see their house or their neighbor's. Children were running about and playing as usual. Indeed, this peak in pleasant weather is the most trivial place in New England. There are probably more arrivals daily than at any of the White Mountain houses. Several were busily engraving their names on the rocks with cold-chisels, whose incessant clink you heard, and they had but little leisure to look off. The mountain was not free of them from sunrise to sunset, though most of them left about 5 P.M. At almost any hour of the day they were seen wending their way single file in various garb up or down the shelving rocks of the peak. These figures on the summit, seen in relief against the sky (from our camp), looked taller than life. I saw some that camped there, by moonlight, one night. On Sunday, twenty or thirty, at least, in addition to the visitors to the peak, came up to pick blueberries, and we heard on all sides the rattling of dishes and their frequent calls to each other.

Aug. 15. . . . See a blue heron.

Aug. 22. . . . When I used to pick the berries for dinner on the East Quarter hills I did not eat one till I had done, for going a-berrying implies more things than eating the berries. They at home got only the pudding: I got the forenoon out of doors, and the appetite for the pudding.

It is true, as is said, that we have as good a right to make berries private property as to make grass and trees such; but what I chiefly regret is the, in effect, dog-in-the-manger result, for at the same time that we exclude mankind from gathering berries in our field, we exclude them from gathering health and happiness and inspiration and a hundred other far finer and nobler fruits than berries, which yet we shall not gather ourselves there, nor even carry to market. We strike only one more blow at a simple and wholesome relation to nature. As long as the berries are free to all comers they are beautiful, though they may be few and small, but tell me that is a blueberry swamp which somebody has hired, and I shall not want even to look at it. In laying claim for the first time to the spontaneous fruit of our pastures we are, accordingly, aware of a little meanness inevitably, and the gay berry party whom we turn away naturally look down on and despise us. If it were left to the berries to say who should have them, is it not likely that they would prefer to be gathered by the party of children in the hay-rigging, who have come to have a good time merely?

. . . The recent heavy rains have washed away the bank [Clamshell bank of the Concord River] here considerably, and it looks and smells more mouldy with human relics than ever. I therefore find myself inevitably exploring it. On the edge of the ravine whose beginning I witnessed, one foot beneath the surface and just over a layer some three inches thick of pure shells and ashes—a gray-white line on the face of the cliff—I find several pieces of Indian pottery with a rude ornament on it, not much more red than the earth itself. Looking farther, I find more fragments, which have been washed down the sandy slope in a stream, as far as ten feet. I find in all thirty-one pieces, averaging an inch in diameter and about a third of an inch thick. Several of them made part of the upper edge of the vessel, and have a rude ornament encircling them in three rows, as if pricked with a stick in the soft clay, and also another line on the narrow edge itself. At first I thought to match the pieces again, like a geographical puzzle, but I did not find that any I [got] belonged together. The vessel must have been quite large, and I have not got nearly all of it. It appears to have been an impure clay with much sand and gravel in it, and I think a little pounded shell. It is [of] very unequal thickness, some of the unadorned pieces (probably the bottom) being half an inch thick, while near the edge it is not more than a quarter of an inch thick. There was under this spot and under the layer of shells a manifest hollowness in the ground, not yet filled up. I find many small pieces of bone in the soil of this bank, probably of animals the Indians ate.

Oct. 7. . . . Remarking to old Mr. B—— the other day on the abundance of the apples, "Yes," says he, "and fair as dollars too." That's the kind of beauty they see in apples.

. . . Many people have a foolish way of talking about small things, and apologize for themselves or another having attended to a small thing, having neglected their ordinary business and amused or instructed themselves by attending to a small thing; when, if the truth were known, their ordinary business was the small thing, and almost their whole lives were misspent, but they were such fools as not to know it.

Oct. 10. . . . They are hopelessly cockneys everywhere who learn to swim with a machine. They take neither disease nor health, nay, nor life itself, the natural way. I see dumb-bells in the minister's study, and some of their dumbness gets into his sermons. Some travellers carry them round the world in their carpetbags. Can he be said to travel who requires still this exercise? A party of school-children had a picnic at the Easterbrooks Country the other [day], and they carried bags of beans from their gymnasium to exercise with there. I cannot be interested in these extremely artificial amusements. The traveller is no longer a wayfarer, with his staff and pack and dusty coat. He is not a pilgrim, but he travels in a saloon, and carries dumb-bells to exercise with in the intervals of his journey.

Oct. 11. . . . The season is as favorable for pears as for apples. R. W. E.'s garden is strewn with them. They are not so handsome as apples—are of more earthy and homely colors —yet they are of a wholesome color enough. Many, inclining to a rough russet or even ferruginous, both to touch (rusty) and eye, look as if they were proof against frost. After all, the few varieties of wild pears here have more color and are handsomer than the many celebrated varieties that are cultivated. The cultivated are commonly of so dull a color that it is hard to distinguish them from the leaves, and if there are but two or three left you do not see them revealing themselves distinctly at a distance amid the leaves, as apples do, but I see that the gatherer has overlooked half a dozen large ones on this small tree, which were concealed by their perfect resemblance to the leaves—a yellowish green, spotted with darker-green rust or fungi (?). Yet some have a fair cheek, and, generally, in their form they are true pendants, as if shaped expressly to hang from the trees.

They are a more aristocratic fruit. How much more attention they get from the proprietor! The hired man gathers the apples and barrels them. The proprietor plucks the pears at odd hours for a pastime, and his daughter wraps them each in its paper. They are, perchance, put up in the midst of a barrel of Baldwins as if something more precious than these. They are spread on the floor of the best room. They are a gift to the most distinguished guest. Judges and ex-judges and honorables are connoisseurs of pears, and discourse of them at length between sessions. I hold in my hand a Bonne Louise which is covered with minute brown specks or dots one twelfth to one sixteenth [of an inch] apart, largest and most developed on the sunny side, quite regular and handsome, as if they were the termination or operculum of pores which had burst in the very thin pellicle of the fruit, producing a slight roughness to the touch. Each of these little ruptures, so to call them, is in form a perfect star with five rays; so that, if the apple is higher-colored, reflecting the sun, on the duller surface of this pear the whole firmament with its stars shines forth. They whisper of the happy stars under whose influence they have grown and matured. It is not the case with all of them, but only the more perfect specimens.

Oct. 16. . . . I have come up here this afternoon to see ———'s dense white pine lot beyond the pond, that was cut off last winter, to know how the little oaks look in it. To my surprise and chagrin, I find that the fellow who calls himself its owner has burned it all over and sowed winter-rye here. He, no doubt, means to let it grow up again in a year or two, but he thought it would be clear gain if he could extract a little rye from it in the meanwhile. What a fool! Here nature had got everything ready for this emergency, and kept them ready for many years—oaks half a dozen years old or more, with fusiform roots full charged and tops already pointing skyward, only waiting to be touched off by the sun—and he thought he knew better, and would get a little rye out of it first, which he could feel at once between his fingers, and so he burned it, and dragged his harrow over it. . . .

Nov. 5. . . . I am struck by the fact that the more slowly trees grow at first, the sounder they are at the core, and I think that the same is true of human beings. We do not wish to see children precocious, making great strides in their early years like sprouts, producing a soft and perishable timber, but better if they expand slowly at first, as if contending with difficulties, and so are solidified and perfected. Such trees continue to expand with nearly equal rapidity to an extreme old age.

Nov. 13. . . . Yellow butterflies still.

Nov. 17. . . . How they do things in West Acton. As we were walking through West Acton the other afternoon, a few rods only west of the centre, on the main road, the Harvard turnpike, we saw a rock larger than a man could lift, lying in the road, exactly in the wheel-track, and were puzzled to tell how it came there, but supposed it had slipped off a drag—yet we noticed that it was peculiarly black. Returning the same way in the twilight, when we had got within four or five rods of this very spot, looking up, we saw a man in the field, three or four rods on one side of that spot, running off as fast as he could. By the time he had got out of sight over the hill it occurred to us that he was blasting rocks and had just touched one off; so, at the eleventh hour, we turned about and ran the other way, and when we had gone a few rods, off went two blasts, but fortunately none of the rocks struck us. Some time after we had passed we saw the men returning. They looked out for themselves, but for nobody else. This is the way they do things in West Acton. We now understood that the big stone was blackened by powder.

Nov. 21. . . . Another finger-cold evening, which I improve in pulling my turnips—the usual amusement of such weather

—before they shall be frozen in. It is worth the while to see how green and lusty they are yet, still adding to their stock of nutriment for another year; and between the green and also withering leaves it does me good to see their great crimson round or scalloped tops, sometimes quite above ground, they are so bold. They remind you of rosy cheeks in cool weather, and indeed there is a relationship. All kinds of harvestry, even pulling turnips when the first cold weather numbs your fingers, are interesting, if you have been the sower, and have not sown too many.

Nov. 24. . . . The first spitting of snow—a flurry or squall —from out a gray or slate-colored cloud that came up from the west. This consisted almost entirely of pellets an eighth of an inch or less in diameter. These drove along almost horizontally, or curving upward like the outline of a breaker, before the strong and chilling wind. The plowed fields were for a short time whitened with them. The green moss about the bases of trees was very prettily spotted white with them, and also the large beds of cladonia in the pastures. They come to contrast with the red cockspur lichens on the stumps, which you had not noticed before. Striking against the trunks of the trees on the west side they fell and accumulated in a white line at the base. Though a slight touch, this was the first wintry scene of the season. The air was so filled with these snow pellets that we could not see a hill half a mile off for an hour. The hands seek the warmth of the pockets, and fingers are so benumbed that you cannot open your jack-knife. . . .

Nov. 28. . . . The mass of men are very easily imposed on. They have their runways in which they always travel, and are sure to fall into any pit or box trap set therein. Whatever a great many grown-up boys are seriously engaged in is considered great and good, and, as such, is sure of the recognition of the churchman and statesman. What, for instance, are the blue juniper berries in the pasture, which the cowboy remembers so far as they are beautiful merely, to church or state? Mere trifles which deserve and get no protection. As an object of beauty, though significant to all who really live in the country, they do not receive the protection of any community. Anybody may grub up all that exist. But as an article of commerce they command the attention of the civilized world. I read that "several hundred tons of them are imported annually from the continent" into England to flavor gin with; "but even this quantity," says my author, "is quite insufficient to meet the enormous consumption of the fiery liquid, and the deficiency is made up by spirits of turpentine." Go to the English Government, which, of course, is representative of the people, and ask, What is the use of juniper berries? The answer is, To flavor gin with. This is the gross abuse of juniper berries, with which an enlightened Government—if ever there shall be one—will have nothing to do.

Nov. 29. . . . We hear a good deal said about moonshine by so-called practical people, and the next day, perchance, we hear of their failure, they having been dealing in fancy stocks; but there really never is any moonshine of this kind in the practice of poets and philosophers; there never are any hard times or failures with them, for they deal with permanent values.

Dec. 3. . . . Talking with [R. F.?] Walcott and [Sam] Staples today, they declared that John Brown did wrong. When I said that I thought he was right, they agreed in asserting that he did wrong because he threw his life away, and that no man had a right to undertake anything which he knew would cost him his life. I inquired if Christ did not foresee that he would be crucified if he preached such doctrines as he did, but they both, though as if it was their only escape, asserted that they did not believe that he did. Upon which a third party threw in, "You do not think that he had so much foresight as Brown." Of course, they as good as said that, if Christ *had* foreseen that he would be crucified, he would have "backed out." Such are the principles and the logic of the mass of men.

Dec. 4. . . . Talk about slavery! It is not the peculiar institution of the South. It exists wherever men are bought and sold, wherever a man allows himself to be made a mere thing or a tool, and surrenders his inalienable rights of reason and conscience. Indeed, this slavery is more complete than that which enslaves the body alone. It exists in the Northern States, and I am reminded by what I find in the newspapers that it exists in Canada. I never yet met with, or heard of, a judge who was not a slave of this kind, and so the finest and most unfailing weapon of injustice. He fetches a slightly higher price than the black man only because he is a more valuable slave.

1861

Thoreau's health grew worse. His cold became bronchitis and bronchitis turned into something more ominous. He rallied for periods and made a number of efforts to carry on with his normal occupations. He arrived at the conclusion that travel could help to restore his health. He decided to try the dry air of Minnesota and he made the trip there in May with Horace Mann's young son as his companion. They returned in July with Thoreau's health, however, far from improved. His cough became more persistent. The journal this year reflects a debilitated man. Though entries start by being substantial they no longer occur each day. The entries for February are shorter than those for January. By April they are almost laconic; the entry for April 10 is only two words: "Purple finch." By late summer they are largely omitted. In fall the entries, such as they are, concentrate on what Thoreau could observe either within his house or just outside it. The final entry appears on November 3.

Jan. 3. . . . What are the natural features which make a township handsome? A river, with its waterfalls and meadows, a lake, a hill, a cliff or individual rocks, a forest, and ancient trees standing singly. Such things are beautiful; they have a high use which dollars and cents never represent. If the inhabitants of a town were wise, they would seek to preserve these things, though at a considerable expense; for such things educate far more than any hired teachers or preachers, or any at present recognized system of school education. I do not think him fit to be the founder of a state or even of a town who does not foresee the use of these things, but legislates chiefly for oxen, as it were.

. . . As boys are sometimes required to show an excuse for being absent from school, so it seems to me that men should show some excuse for being here. Move along; you may come upon the town, sir.

Jan. 14. . . . It is the discovery of science that stupendous changes in the earth's surface, such as are referred to the Deluge, for instance, are the result of causes still in operation, which have been at work for an incalculable period. There has not been a sudden re-formation, or, as it were, new creation of the world, but a steady progress according to existing laws. The same is true in detail also. It is a vulgar prejudice that some plants are "spontaneously generated," but science knows that they come from seeds, i.e. are the result of causes still in operation, however slow and unobserved. It is a common saying that "little strokes fall great oaks," and it does not imply much wisdom in him who originated it. The sound of the axe invites our attention to such a catastrophe; we can easily count each stroke as it is given, and all the neighborhood is informed by a loud crash when the deed is consummated. But such, too, is the rise of the oak; little strokes of a different kind and often repeated raise great oaks, but scarcely a traveller hears these or turns aside to converse with Nature, who is dealing them the while.

March 18. . . . Ah, willow! willow! Would that I always possessed thy good spirits.

No wonder its wood was anciently in demand for bucklers, for, take the whole tree, it is not only soft and pliant but tough and resilient (as Pliny says?), not splitting at the first blow, but closing its wounds at once and refusing to transmit its hurts.

March 18. . . . How various are the habits of men! Mother says that her father-in-law, Captain Minott, not only used to roast and eat a long row of little wild apples, reaching in a semicircle from jamb to jamb under the andirons on the reddened hearth (I used to buy many a pound of Spanish brown at the stores for mother to redden the jambs and hearth with), but he had a quart of new milk regularly placed at the head of his bed, which he drank at many draughts in the course of the night. It was so the night he died, and my grandmother discovered that he was dying, by his not turning over to reach his milk. . . .

1861. . . . After a violent easterly storm in the night, which clears up at noon (November 3, 1861), I notice that the surface of the railroad causeway, composed of gravel, is singularly marked, as if stratified like some slate rocks, on their edges, so that I can tell within a small fraction of a degree from what quarter the rain came. These lines, as it were of stratification, are perfectly parallel, and straight as a ruler, diagonally across the flat surface of the causeway for its whole length. Behind each little pebble, as a protecting boulder, an eighth or a tenth of an inch in diameter, extends northwest a ridge of sand an inch or more, which it has protected from being washed away, while the heavy drops driven almost horizontally have washed out a furrow on each side, and on all sides are these ridges, half an inch apart and perfectly parallel.

All this is perfectly distinct to an observant eye, and yet could easily pass unnoticed by most. Thus each wind is self-registering.

1862

Thoreau took to his bed, which was put in the parlor. He was able to receive some visitors and to do some work. He dictated a few letters to his sister Sophia; with her help he revised several essays for publication in the Atlantic Monthly, which was now blessed with a new editor. He died on May 6. The next month the first of the new essays for the Atlantic, "Walking," appeared and then two more. Before the year ended, the Week and Walden came out in new editions. Thoreau's writing was on its way to general acceptance.

The Thoreau Country

Today, despite the efforts of local politicians who hope to turn Walden Pond into a huge swimming pool and local subdividers who look greedily at the outskirts of Concord, some of the loveliest of the Thoreau country still survives. Mary Fenn, a devoted follower of Thoreau, has reported on the matter in the *Thoreau Society Bulletin* for Spring 1966. She notes that within Second Division the beautiful spring that Thoreau mentions is still flowing. The old Marlboro Road and the old Powder Mill Road still pass through remarkably attractive woodside. Some of the meadows remain unspoiled. Here and there in the Thoreau country we may still see the wild azalea, the gentian, and the birdsfoot violet, among other flowers. On the way from Concord to Carlisle an inviting wilderness that Thoreau roamed still exists; it has been saved by being accessible only by foot. Fairhaven Cliffs continue to afford a handsome view though changed in several respects since Thoreau's time. A very interesting piece of wild-flower country is located around the edge of the Ministerial Swamp. Beyond Walden Pond itself, and still safe from intruders, lies Heywood's Meadow where, as Mary Fenn remarks, Thoreau went to pick cranberries. It is a boggy, spring-fed area, as it was when he traveled through it. Some of the countryside remains wild and beautiful; it rewards the loving inspection of Thoreau's followers.

The map of the Thoreau country on the next pages first appeared in the Walden Edition of Thoreau's *Writings* in 1906. The work of Herbert W. Gleason, it locates, except for an occasional slip, many places and persons associated with the Concord that Thoreau knew.

327

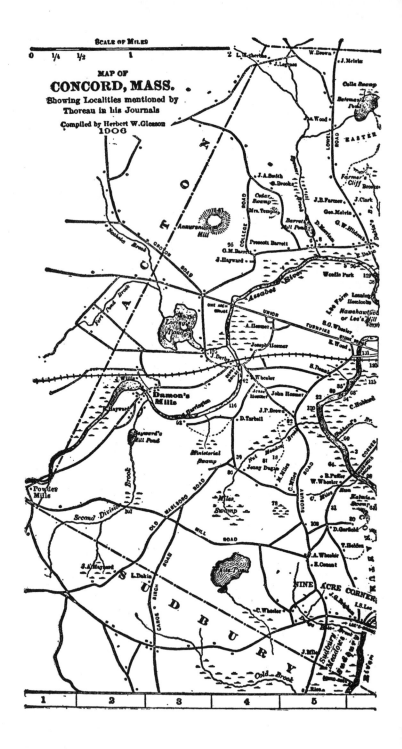

SCALE OF MILES

0   1/4   1/2   1   2

MAP OF
CONCORD, MASS.
Showing Localities mentioned by
Thoreau in his Journals

Compiled by Herbert W.Gleason
1906

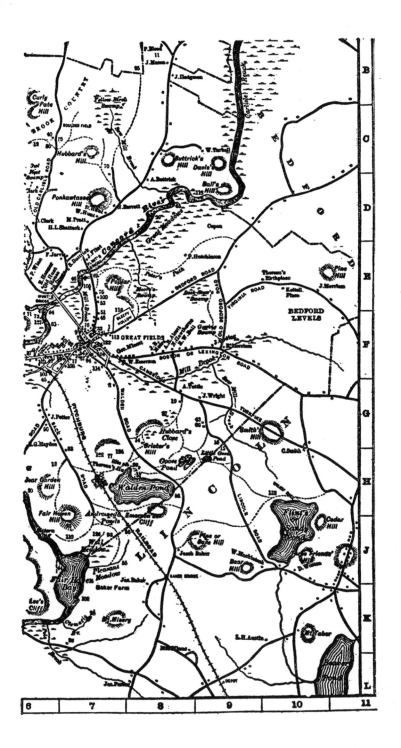

INDEX TO MAP OF CONCORD

[1] This name is spelled "Heywood" by Thoreau.

[2] This name was also given to a bay on the river in Sudbury.

[3] This is the "Saw Mill Brook" most frequently mentioned by Thoreau.

SELECTED BIBLIOGRAPHY

Thoreau's Writings

The Writings of Henry David Thoreau, Bradford Torrey with Francis Allen, eds., Walden Edition, 20 vols., 1906. Journal, vols. 7–20 of the Walden Edition, reprinted separately, 1949.

Collected Poems of Henry Thoreau, Carl Bode, ed., 1943; revised and enlarged edition issued in 1964.

The Making of Walden, James Lyndon Shanley, 1957. (The text of the initial version of *Walden* along with an explanation of the way it was determined.)

Consciousness in Concord, Perry Miller, ed., 1958. (The text of the so-called lost journal for parts of 1840–1841.)

The Portable Thoreau, Carl Bode, ed., 1947; revised edition issued in 1964. (A one-volume selection from Thoreau's writing.)

The Correspondence of Henry David Thoreau, Walter Harding and Carl Bode, eds., 1957. (Includes the letters to Thoreau as well as those from him.)

Biography

Canby, H. S., *Thoreau,* 1939. (A perceptive interpretation.)

Harding, Walter, *The Days of Henry Thoreau,* 1965. (The definitive factual biography.)

Krutch, J. W., *Henry David Thoreau,* 1948. (A biography and an analysis of Thoreau's ideas.)

Criticism

Christie, J. A., *Thoreau as World Traveler,* 1965.

Matthiessen, F. O., *American Renaissance*, 1941. (Partly devoted to Thoreau's ideas as connected with those of other Transcendental writers.)

Paul, Sherman, *The Shores of America: Thoreau's Inward Exploration*, 1958.

Van Doren, Mark, *Henry David Thoreau*, 1916. (Early study of Thoreau's ideas by an important critic.)

Guides

Harding, Walter, *The Thoreau Handbook*, 1959.

Leary, Lewis, "Thoreau," in *Eight American Authors: A Review of Research and Criticism*, Floyd Stovall, ed., 1956.

Bibliographies

A Bibliography of Henry David Thoreau, compiled by Francis Allen, 1908. (Listing of items by and about Thoreau from the beginning till 1908.)

A Henry David Thoreau Bibliography, 1908–1937, compiled by William White, 1939. (Continues Allen.)

"Contribution to a Bibliography of Thoreau, 1938–1945," compiled by Philip Burnham and Carvel Collins, in *Bulletin of Bibliography*, XIX (1946–1947), 16–18, 37–39. (Continues White.)

Thoreau Society Bulletin, Walter Harding, ed. 1941– . (Current bibliography in each number of this quarterly.)